WORDS TO LIVE BY

WORDS TO LIVE BY

DONALD R. TAYLOR

XULON PRESS

Xulon Press
2301 Lucien Way #415
Maitland, FL 32751
407.339.4217
www.xulonpress.com

© 2018 by Donald R. Taylor

All rights reserved solely by the author. The author guarantees all contents are original and do not infringe upon the legal rights of any other person or work. No part of this book may be reproduced in any form without the permission of the author. The views expressed in this book are not necessarily those of the publisher.

Unless otherwise indicated, Scripture quotations taken from the New American Standard Bible (NASB). Copyright © 1960, 1962, 1963, 1968, 1971, 1972, 1973, 1975, 1977, 1995 by The Lockman Foundation. Used by permission. All rights reserved.

Printed in the United States of America.

ISBN-13: 9781545627600

FOREWORD

WORDS TO LIVE BY IS A REFRESHING COMPILAtion of articles dealing with a variety of Biblical topics. The book opens with a series on the life of Christ, beginning with His birth and progressing to His death on the cross. The author weaves stories about significant events in Christ's earthly life, ending the book with Peter's summation of the spiritual importance of Christ's life and ministry.

Don Taylor has done a masterful job with his excellent writing skills to make this book so compelling that one does not want to put it down. He tells stories of his own earthly father, of his mission work in Europe, about his experience in leading Freed-Hardeman University students in study abroad, and of experiences encountered through many years of preaching the Gospel.

Don incorporates current events, songs, scriptures, and his personal experiences to show how they all fit a pattern in God's holy plan. Using the Bible, he points to references that shed insight on historical and current events. He helps the reader discover the kingdom of Heaven as a "hidden treasure" and as a "pearl of great price" that one must become active to find. He shows the value of searching the scriptures and how this active study can become so very important in the life of a Christian.

I highly recommend this book, *Words to Live By*, for a down-to-earth approach to becoming more spiritually aware of God's great plan through the ages, leading sinners to salvation. It will enhance your faith in God, give you insights to important life matters, and it is brief enough in its presentation that one will not tire of the stories

Words To Live By

Don tells. Knowing Don's sincere and dedicated heart helps one to appreciate even more the value of his writings.

Milton R. Sewell Ed.D. University of Alabama 1969
Chancellor, Freed-Hardeman University
President of Freed-Hardeman University 1990-2008
President of Mars Hill Bible School, Florence, Alabama 1983-1990

THE JOURNEY TO THE MANGER AND TO THE CROSS

MARY WAS PROBABLY A TEENAGER WHEN SHE conceived her first child. She was a virgin (Luke 1:30-34). When the angel Gabriel explained to her that the child would be the Savior, the Son of God, Mary humbly said, "Behold, the bondslave of the Lord; may it be done to me according to your word" (Luke 1:38).

We don't know how far along Mary's pregnancy was when she and Joseph made their journey south to Bethlehem to register for the census, but she probably would not have been in the final month, since Luke records that "while they were" in Bethlehem, "the days were completed for her to give birth" (Luke 2:6).

The distance from Nazareth to Bethlehem would have been shorter if they had taken the direct route through Samaria, but Jews usually took a longer route down the valley of the Jordan, on the eastern side of the river. They would have left Nazareth, crossing the mountains, going down toward the south shore of the Sea of Galilee, then crossing the river into what is now the kingdom of Jordan. The road would have been somewhat crowded with people who were also going home to register. Because of robbers, it was safer to travel in groups. We do not know if Mary and Joseph had a donkey, although they probably did, to carry what they needed for the journey and their likely extended stay in Bethlehem. The young expectant mother was probably strong and able to walk.

Words To Live By

There were no "hotels" like ours, and "inns" were very different from what we think today, so since the weather would have been mild whatever the season, they probably spent their nights under the stars, in a camp of some kind. The journey of at least eighty miles would have taken them about a week.

Arriving at Bethlehem, Mary and Joseph would have gone directly to the home of some near kinsmen, where, given the well-known reputation for hospitality of the citizens, they would have been graciously received. Luke's statement that "there was no room for them in the *inn*" (Luke 2:7) has been misunderstood, in my opinion. They had already been in Bethlehem for some period of time before she gave birth (Luke 2:6), but the mention that "there was no room" in the "inn" comes *after* the birth. The fact is that Luke here uses a word (*katalumati*) which, while it can designate an "inn," can also designate an "eating room," a "dining room," or a "guest chamber" (Thayer, Greek Lexicon). This word is different from another word (*pandocheion*) used by Luke in the parable of the "good Samaritan," where an "inn" or "a public house for the reception of strangers" (Thayer, Greek Lexicon) is obviously meant. My point is that when the time came for the baby to be born, there would have been no private room for the birth in the humble, crowded dwelling where they were lodged. Therefore, when the birth occurred, they took the child into the "manger," likely a cave adjoining the dwelling, where the animals were kept at night. This would have been a warm place, more private, and it was there that the shepherds found the mother and child in the early morning (Luke 2:15-16).

The Bible gives no indication of the time of year when Jesus was born, but we do know the exact time when Jesus died. He was "born to die." When Jesus was only forty days old (Luke 2:22), He was taken to the temple to be "presented to the Lord," on the occasion of Mary's "purification" ceremony, required by the Law of Moses. While they were in the temple, a "righteous and devout" man named Simeon, who had been "looking for the consolation of Israel," approached them. "Filled with the Spirit," this elderly man prophesied, "Behold, this Child is appointed for the fall and rise of many in Israel, and for a sign to be opposed – and a sword will pierce your own soul" (Luke 2:34-35). "A sword will pierce your own soul!" he said to Mary. Old Simeon had no idea what his words of prophecy really meant, but the reference was perhaps to the moment of her Child's torture on the cross for the salvation of mankind. Mary would be there, standing, watching, as her Son slowly died. She would hear her Son say to her, "Woman, behold, your son!" indicating the disciple John, who would, in a sense, take His place in her life (John 19:26-27). What pain must then have pierced that mother's heart!

There was no celebration of the *birthday* of Jesus until hundreds of years later. But His *death* has been celebrated every week, beginning on the first Pentecost following his death. Every Lord's day, when Christians eat the Lord's supper (1 Corinthians 11:26), we remember His death and proclaim His ultimate return for His people. It is certainly not wrong to celebrate His birth, but it is His death and resurrection that we celebrate when we meet on Sunday as a congregation. But without His birth, the other events could not have happened. I am happy that people think about the birth of our Lord, whatever be the occasion. I could only wish they thought about Him throughout the entire year.

Words To Live By

THE MURDER OF THE INNOCENTS

THE SMALL CONNECTICUT TOWN WAS GOING ABOUT its usual business. Shops and stores were opening; people were going to their jobs; mothers were busy cleaning house or planning for the noon meal; the children who were old enough were already at their desks at school, listening to their teachers.

Suddenly, without warning, death struck at the most vulnerable, the most innocent – the children. Within a matter of minutes, twenty of them died violent deaths. Along with the children, six of their teachers, including the principal, were murdered. The principal, with arms upraised, had rushed toward the murderer, trying to shield the teachers who were with her; a teacher standing at her desk in her classroom was shot, after having hidden her children safely in a closet. Another special education teacher, Robin Walker, "huddled kids in a corner and read stories to them while the shooting was going on. She kept them safe and together and calm until the police came." (*The Christian Chronicle*). This tragedy in New Town, Connecticut, is still fresh on our minds.

About 2,000 years ago, another similar tragedy occurred in a sleepy little mountain village called Bethlehem, the "house of bread." Life in that tiny village of farmers was proceeding about as described above when chaos suddenly erupted. Soldiers brandishing swords and spears descended upon the village, entering into every house, brutally slaying every little boy they found, two years old and under. Horrified mothers held to their breasts the bloody remains of their beloved children, as anxious fathers, hearing the screaming and wailing of their women folk, rushed back to their homes from their fields or shops, with no idea of what had happened. Matthew, remembering Jeremiah's sorrowful dirge (Jeremiah 31:15; Matthew 2:18), described the aftermath in these words:

> A voice was heard in Ramah,
> Weeping and great mourning,
> Rachel, weeping for her children;
> And she refused to be comforted,
> Because they were no more.

According to Alfred Edersheim, there would have been about twenty boys, two years and under, in Bethlehem at that time (*Life and Times of Jesus the Messiah*, II, 214).

In both New Town and Bethlehem, *innocents* died. These sinless children had done nothing which would have merited death. In the New Town massacre, the killer himself was but a youth, in all likelihood mentally disturbed. The Bethlehem murders, however, were ordered by an evil monarch who, routinely and viciously, squashed every hint of threat to his reign. King Herod, who had not hesitated to murder his own children to maintain his crown, did not hesitate for an instant before issuing the order to murder the innocent children of people he did not know.

The motive behind the senseless New Town massacre may never be understood. This massacre caused pain and anguish, but achieved no goal, worthy or unworthy. However, in King Herod's twisted, evil mind, the Bethlehem children died *to* preserve his crown. Additionally, we may say that the death of the Bethlehem innocents did allow another innocent Child, a boy named Jesus, to grow up in safety, unsuspected and undetected, as the supposed son of Joseph, a carpenter in an obscure Galilean village called Nazareth.

Ironically, the Innocent Child in whose place the innocents of Bethlehem died was destined Himself to die for others. At thirty-three years of age, during the dark of night, contrary to Roman law, He was judged and condemned as a blasphemer by select members of the Jewish high court, the Sanhedrin (Matthew 26), and delivered to a Roman Governor in the early morning hours. Then, after being cruelly scourged by Roman soldiers, He was nailed to a cross on a hill called Golgotha, opposite the city of Jerusalem (Matthew 27). As He agonized on that torture stake, He begged the Father to forgive those who, ignorant of Who He was, had done this terrible deed. And as He breathed His last, He whispered, "It is finished." His reason for being born was now fulfilled; He had completed His divine mission. His death had profound significance and eternal consequences.

This Child's safety had been purchased at the horrendous price of the massacre of some twenty other young Innocents on a distant morning in Bethlehem. In His turn, He, like them, died to save from eternal death countless millions of sinners. Like those children, He also was Innocent, a Just man; they died, Innocents for an Innocent! However, unlike them, He died for the guilty, the Just for the Unjust.

WHEN HEAVEN CAME DOWN

I WAS DEPRESSED. MY WIFE HAD BEEN VERY SICK FOR eighteen days in the hospital in Verviers, Belgium, and when she came home, she was confined for a while to the bed. My sister, who was at the time in Germany, came to help out, but she suddenly developed mysterious blisters of some sort on her entire body, including the inside of her mouth. The doctors visited our house nearly every day, but could not determine the cause of the blisters. On top of that, there were two small boys who required attention. I began to fall apart at the seams, weeping at the least thing, or for no reason. There were few people upon whom we could call, but God remembered us and restored health to Virginia, to my sister, and to me.

What about *you*? Many who will read this know from personal experience what my family and I were going through. You have perhaps lost through death the love of your life, a soulmate of many years. Perhaps your children have disappointed you in some sad way. Maybe you have contracted a dread disease or you have lost your job, and you wonder how you can possibly survive. All seems to be darkness around you. Don't forget about God!

I *know* that there is a God in heaven who cares for you and me. Peter tells us to "cast all our anxiety on Him, because He cares for you" (1 Peter 5:7). A wonderful hymn by Ruth Caye Jones urges us to remember Jesus:

> In times like these you need a Savior,
> In times like these you need an anchor.
> Be very sure, be very sure,
> Your anchor holds and grips the Solid Rock.

Indeed, we do need this "anchor of the soul" (Hebrews 6:19) to hold us to the Solid Rock, to keep us from drifting away during times of trouble and pain. Without this "hope both sure and steadfast and one which enters within the veil," one might conclude that there is no God in heaven, that there is no one who cares.

Sometimes, even Christians can collapse under the heavy weight of depression, so we should be careful not to judge those who do. I can name five people, all Christians, all acquaintances of ours, all of them relatively young, who took their lives because they could not bear to live. How tragic! What an utterly tragic waste! I suppose they just saw no other way out.

As we "run our race," we need to keep our eyes fixed and focused on Him who stands by the "finish line," waiting for us, and encouraging us to keep running (Hebrews 12:2). He "endured the cross" for us. He knows our troubles and problems. He is now sitting on the throne of God, looking down upon us, encouraging us not to quit, not to stop, "not to grow weary and lose heart" (Hebrews 12:3). Jesus came down from heaven, having divested Himself of all the powers and perks of deity (Philippians 2:6-7), becoming a human being like all of us, suffering the humility of temptations, enduring the pain and trouble that all of us go through from time to time, and for what? In part, it was to enable Him to serve as an example for us when we are troubled and depressed. Because He "suffered in the flesh," we also must "arm ourselves with the same purpose" (1 Peter 4:1). Jesus "gives help" to those who are troubled (Hebrews 2:16). He is "able to come to the aid" of those who are going through various kinds of trials and troubles (Hebrews 2:18).

As John Peterson's hymn reads,

> Oh what a wonderful, wonderful day, Day I will never forget;
> After I'd wandered in darkness away, Jesus my Savior I met.
> Oh what a tender compassionate friend,
> He met the need of my heart;
> Shadows dispelling, with joy I am telling,
> He made all the darkness depart!
> Heaven came down and glory filled my soul,
> When at the cross the Savior made me whole.

Indeed, Heaven did come down in the person of Jesus, our Lord. He dispelled the darkness of *my* personal depression, and He can scatter the shadows that creep into *your* heart if you will rely upon Him and call upon Him in time of need (Romans 8:26).

In such times, we remember the precious words of David:
I love You, O LORD, my strength.
The LORD is my rock and my fortress and my deliverer,
My God, my rock, in whom I take refuge;
My shield and the horn of my salvation, my stronghold.
I call upon the LORD, who is worthy to be praised,
And I am saved from my enemies.
(Psalm 18:1-3)

JESUS AND SINNERS

I HAVE, FROM TIME TO TIME, MENTIONED MY DAD IN some of my writings. His abuse of alcohol sapped the joy from many family gathering, for most of his life. Please don't misunderstand and think that I did not love my dad, or that my dad did not love his family. The fact was that he had become addicted to alcohol before he married, and alcohol addiction is extremely hard to overcome. Strokes and heart attacks eventually separated Dad from alcohol, and he realized he needed something else. Dad came to Christ about ten years before he died at age seventy-four. I mention him here, not to defame him, but because he was a large part of my youthful personal experience.

When I delivered the eulogy at my dad's funeral, I faced the dilemma of what to say about him. If I praised him overmuch, I ran the risk of misrepresenting him before people who knew him well. Therefore, I spoke of him as of a good man who made many mistakes, a "lost sheep" who came home before it was too late. I spoke of him as of one whom the Lord Jesus loved, and as one for whom He died. I am convinced that my dad was saved by the ineffable, indescribable grace of God, in the same way that God, through His kindness, has also saved me.

An indelible memory of mine was of a late Saturday night when we were looking for Daddy. We knew we would find him in a bar somewhere. There we were, just kids, looking for him, going into places where we would never have gone, and I am reminded of one of the Lord's most powerful parables, that of the lost sheep (Luke 15:4-7).

The religious elite often observed Jesus in the presence of "sinners" (Luke 15:2), and they criticized Him for it. "This man receives sinners and eats with them," they said. His enemies falsely implied that Jesus was agreeing with the lifestyle of these "sinners." Of course, tax collectors (KJV, "publicans") were known to be a dishonest lot, and undeniably sinful, and Jesus often associated with them. But when He was criticized for spending time with them, He simply said, "It is not those who are healthy who need a physician, but those who are sick" (Matthew 9:12). That was His divine mission. That is why he associated with such people. I think that Jesus was walking right beside us kids as we entered the bars and beer joints looking for my dad.

According to the Lord's parable, a shepherd was bedding down his large flock for the night. There was no enclosed sheepfold on the mountain slopes, but there were no doubt other flocks there, guarded by other shepherds, referred to in the parable as "friends and neighbors" (Luke 15:6). The shepherd counted his sheep, "...97, 98, 99." There were supposed to be 100! One of his sheep was missing! Without hesitation, the shepherd left the "ninety-nine" with his friends, certain of their safety, and rapidly retraced his steps over the past hours, where he had been pasturing his flock. Across hills and valleys and through thickets and briars he raced, anxiously searching, calling for the lost sheep. Eventually, he found the animal, armed it up and brought it down to the flock, where everyone rejoiced with him.

On one of our semesters in Europe with a group of university students, we were in the Bavarian village of Schwangau, where "mad" King Ludwig III grew up. When he became king, Ludwig nearly ruined his kingdom by building extravagant castles, notably the "Cinderella" castle called "Neuschwanstein," high above Schwangau. I had led the students to the top of the mountain and toured the castle with them, reminding them to get back to the bus stop by a certain hour for the last bus back to the train station. Eventually, all of the students arrived on time for the bus, except for one girl. I became more and more anxious as time passed and as it was becoming dark, I left the group at the bus stop and literally ran up the steep mountain path, stopping at every turn to call her name. I went all the way to the top, alarmed to think she might have fallen into a ravine, but I did not find her. I went back down the mountain, calling her name. When I arrived at the bus stop, she was there. What a relief! I felt a little like the Lord must feel when one lost soul returns home safely.

The Lord Jesus loved everyone, but He concentrated on the "lost sheep," while not neglecting those who were safe. He did not love

Words To Live By

the lost more than He loved the saved, but the lost seemed to need Him most.

There is no shame in being lost. We have all been "lost" at one time or another. The shame is in remaining lost, when so much has been done to find you and me.

In 1868, Elizabeth C. Clephane penned the poem which became the wonderful song, "The Ninety and Nine."

> There were ninety and nine that safely lay
> In the shelter of the fold,
> But one was out on the hills away,
> Far off from the gates of gold,
> Away on the mountains wild and bare,
> Away from the tender Shepherd's care.
>
> "Lord, Thou hast here Thy ninety and nine;
> Are they not enough for Thee?"
> But the Shepherd made answer:
> "This of mine has wandered away from Me.
> And although the road be rough and steep,
> I go to the desert to find My sheep."
>
> But all through the mountains, thunderriv'n,
> And up from the rocky steep,
> There arose a glad cry to the gate of heav'n,
> "Rejoice! I have found my sheep!"
> And the angels echoed around the throne,
> "Rejoice for the Lord brings back His own."

WHO CAN FORGIVE SINS?

Following His rejection at Nazareth, His native village (Luke 4:22-30), Jesus moved to Capernaum. Located on the northwest shore of the Sea of Galilee, Capernaum was one of the principal cities of Galilee. It was a bustling city, with an ample docking area for the fishermen who made their home there. The extensive ruins of the city measure nearly a half mile in length and a quarter mile in width, revealing colonnaded streets, and a large synagogue dating from the first century.

Where Jesus lived in the city is not known, but visitors can explore the octagonal building called "Peter's House," which may well have been the home of the apostle, being later modified to serve as a meeting place for a church. The large ruins of the first century synagogue are a short stroll up the street from "Peter's House." It was in Capernaum that Jesus called Matthew to be an apostle, and many miracles and healings were performed in this city by the sea.

Mark recorded that near the end of the first year of Christ's ministry, He returned to His home in Capernaum (Mark 2:1). When people there learned of His return, they flocked to His house, filling it so that there "was no longer room, not even near the door" (Mark 2:2), and Jesus taught them there. While He was inside speaking to the crowd, four men arrived, carrying a paralytic on a pallet. Unable to get into the crowded house through the door, the men carried the paralytic up the outside stairs to the roof of the building. In those days, an ordinary house had a flat roof of planks covered with mats or branches with a layer of clay on top. On this occasion, the four men decided to make an entry through the roof. Tearing open the covering and moving the planks, they began to lower the paralytic into the room below.

When Jesus saw what was happening, He recognized immediately that these men surely had great faith in His ability to heal their friend, so He said to the paralytic, "Son, your sins are forgiven" (Mark 2:5).

Words To Live By

Immediately, some of the scribes who were sitting there found fault with Jesus. That was probably the very reason they were there, to find some fault with Him. They didn't believe Jesus was the Messiah and were eager to disparage by any means what He was saying. "Why does this man speak that way?" they were thinking. "He is blaspheming; who can forgive sins but God alone?" (Mark 2:6-7). Part of what they were saying was true; only God can forgive sins. Unless Jesus was "God" it would, therefore, follow logically that He was blaspheming. And in the mind of these scribes, Jesus was only a man, a Nazarene, and could not possibly have the power to forgive sins.

Jesus, however, was immediately aware (Mark 2:8) of what these scribes were thinking, and said to them: "Why are you reasoning about these things in your hearts? Which is easier, to say to the paralytic, 'Your sins are forgiven': or to say, 'Get up, and pick up your pallet and walk'? But so that you may know that the Son of Man has authority on earth to forgive sin" – He said to the paralytic, "I say to you, get up, pick up your pallet and go home" (Mark 2:11). And immediately, the paralytic got up, picked up his pallet "in the sight of everyone," and went out (Mark 2:12).

"Who can forgive sins?" Jesus proved two things on that day in Capernaum. The first was that He could heal with just a word. While it may be true that the paralytic had "faith," there is no mention of it. Jesus saw the "faith" of the four men who had brought the paralytic and who were determined to get their friend into the presence of Jesus. Jesus healed many people who did not have faith, who did not even know who Jesus was, and who were not expecting to be healed. Jesus could heal people who were sick or crippled. He could even bring people back from the dead. That was the first thing he proved that day. The second thing that He proved was that He was God, not just a human being! Only God can forgive sins. Jesus could forgive sins, so the logical conclusion was that He was God. Which is easier, to forgive sins or to heal the paralytic? Only the power of God can perform these actions. Jesus did them so that the people in that house could "know that the Son of Man has authority on earth to forgive sins" (Mark 2:10).

Who Can Forgive Sins?

We, today, so far removed from the time of that great deed in the humble Galilean hometown of the Son of God, can still come to Him for forgiveness. Consider the words of F. R. Havergal's hymn:

> I bring my sins to Thee, the sins I cannot count,
> That all may cleansed be in Thy once opened fount!
> I bring them, Savior, all to Thee; the burden is too great for me.
> I bring my grief to Thee, the grief I cannot tell;
> No word shall needed be, Thou knowest all so well:
> I bring the sorrow laid on me, O suffering Savior, all to Thee
> My life I bring to Thee; I would not be my own;
> O Savior, let me be Thine ever, Thine alone:
> My heart, my life, my all I bring to Thee, my Savior and my King.

Words To Live By

WHEN JESUS WAS THRILLED!

I DON'T REMEMBER ANYWHERE IN SCRIPTURE WHERE it is written that Jesus *laughed*, although it is recorded at least three times that He *wept*. The first mention of Jesus' weeping is when He and His disciples met Mary and other village friends on the outskirts of Bethany. Mary and her friends were "weeping" and Jesus, being "deeply moved in spirit" and "troubled," also began to "weep" (John 11:33-35). The two words used by John for "weep" are different, however. In the case of Mary and her companions, John used the word *klaio* which indicates a "loud expression of grief," "to wail," but when he said "Jesus wept," he used the word *dakruo,* indicating a silent "shedding" of tears. Whereas Mary and the other mourners might appear to be out of control, as is sometimes seen at funerals, the Lord, though sad, was calm and in control.

The second occasion when Jesus wept was on the Sunday morning of His "triumphal entry" into Jerusalem. As He approached the summit of the Mount of Olives, He saw Jerusalem spread out in all her beauty across the Kiddron Valley, and He was deeply moved. Luke wrote, "When He approached Jerusalem, He saw the city and wept over it" (Luke 19:41). Luke used the word *klaio,* meaning that Jesus "wailed" loudly. We certainly can understand His deep feelings for the city, remembering its past glory as the guardian of God's temple, knowing that the city and temple would be utterly destroyed during the lifetime of his disciples. In agony, with deep emotion, Jesus cried out, "If you had known in this day, even you, the things which make for peace! But now they have been hidden from your eyes. For the days will come upon you when your enemies will throw up a barricade against you, and surround you and hem you in on every side, and they will level you to the ground and your children within you, and they will not leave in you one stone upon another, because you did not recognize the time of your visitation." (Luke 19:42-44).

The third time that Jesus wept is recorded, not in the gospels, but in the epistle to the Hebrews: "In the days of His flesh, He offered up both prayers and supplications with loud crying and tears to the One able to save Him from death, and He was heard because of His piety" (Hebrews 5:7). The words "loud crying" communicate to us the anguish felt by our Lord as He contemplated the terrible ordeal through which He was soon to pass, but the word *dakruo ("tears")*, as used earlier of His weeping at the tomb of Lazarus, indicates that Jesus was totally in control even as He faced the horrors of crucifixion.

The Lord was pictured by Isaiah, the prophet, as "a man of sorrows and acquainted with grief" (Isaiah 53:3), and this is how we often think of Him. But did Jesus ever *laugh*?

A quick word search shows that the words "laugh" or "laughter" are almost exclusively used in the Bible of "scorn" or "derision." Yet we know that since the beginning people have celebrated weddings and births and other joyful occasions, where they must have laughed. They were no different from us in that respect. It is noteworthy that Jesus, Himself, was invited to a wedding (John 2:1-2), where in accordance with the customs of the times there was certainly lots of cheering and laughter. Many of the Lord's parables refer to weddings and other feasts, and He spoke often of "happiness" and "rejoicing" (Matthew 5:3-12). We would certainly be in error to think that Jesus was somber, dour, or withdrawn. He was "made like His brethren in all things" (Hebrews 2:17).

Well into His ministry, Jesus sent out the Twelve, in pairs, on an extended "mission trip" which was also a part of their training as future apostles. When they returned at the end of their mission, they were filled with "joy" (Luke 10:17), reporting, "Lord, even the demons are subject to us in Your name!" Jesus also participated in their joy, saying, "I was watching Satan fall from heaven like lightning" (Luke 10:18). Jesus had been keeping up with their progress during their mission, perhaps getting reports from this or that city, and He was literally *thrilled* to see their joy. Luke records it this way: "At that very time [hour] He *rejoiced greatly* in the Holy Spirit," and began to pray, praising God for His wonderful work. Then He turned to the Twelve and said, "Blessed are the eyes which see

Words To Live By

the things that you see" (Luke 10:21-23). Instead of "Blessed" we could write "Happy," since the word *makarios* used by Luke literally means "happy."

But Jesus was more than just *happy* at what He had witnessed during the mission trip of His disciples. He was *super-happy, overjoyed*! Luke wrote that "He rejoiced greatly" (Luke 10:21). The verb *agalliao* used by Luke literally means to "exult" or to "rejoice exceedingly" (Thayer, Greek Lexicon). Mounce's *Dictionary of New Testament Words* defines *agalliao* as "to rejoice greatly, exult, be overjoyed." To say that the Lord was "thrilled" seems, therefore, to be an understatement.

Jesus was indeed thrilled to hear of the success of His disciples' labor for God, and we should also be thrilled to learn of the success of those who leave the comforts of home and country to work for God in often dangerous areas of the world. And we should be thrilled as we participate in spiritual worship on the Lord's Day.

> O Lord my God! When I in awesome wonder
> Consider all the worlds Thy hands have made.
> I see the stars, I hear the rolling thunder,
> Thy pow'r throughout the universe displayed.
>
> Then sings my soul, my Saviour God to Thee;
> How great Thou art, how great Thou art!
>
> (Stuart K. Hine)

"WHAT IS THE KINGDOM OF GOD LIKE?"

Suppose for a moment that someone approached you on the street and asked you, "What is the kingdom of God like?" What would you say? How would you answer that question?

Jesus was teaching in the synagogue on a Sabbath day when He noticed a woman nearby, who for eighteen years had been bent double by some sickness (Luke 13:10-11). He called her over and healed her with a word, "Woman, you are freed from your sickness." An indignant synagogue official immediately reprimanded Jesus for having healed the woman on the Sabbath. In this context the Lord felt it necessary to explain some concepts concerning the "kingdom of God." Obviously, the synagogue official did not understand the nature of God's kingdom; else he would have had a more caring attitude toward the afflicted woman. Jesus asked him and others who were listening, "What is the kingdom of God like?" (Luke 13:18).

Our quick response to the Lord's question might be, "The kingdom of God is the church." And it is certainly true that Jesus used the word "kingdom" in connection with the "church" that He was planning to build (Matthew 16:18-19). Paul wrote that God "rescued us from the *dominion* [kingdom] of darkness, and transferred us to the kingdom of His beloved Son" (Colossians 1:13). Peter called God's people "a royal priesthood, a holy nation" (1 Peter 2:9), and John wrote that Jesus "made us to be a kingdom, priests to His God and Father" (Revelation 1:6). These are all ways of describing those who comprise the worldwide *ekklesia* – the church, the congregation, the assembly – of God's people today.

I think, however, that when Christ asked the synagogue official what the kingdom of God is "like" (Luke 13:18), He was not thinking particularly about the *church*, but rather about *the rule or reign of God* over a person's heart and life. When He compared God's kingdom to a "mustard seed" (Luke 13:19), He was illustrating how God's power

Words To Live By

over a person may start out small, eventually taking over his entire being. When He likened the kingdom of God to "leaven" in a lump of dough (Luke 13:21), Jesus was illustrating the *rapid and thorough spread* of God's influence on a person's life and conduct.

In a parallel passage, Matthew wrote the "kingdom of heaven," instead of the "Kingdom of God," saying that it is "like a hidden treasure" (Matthew 13:44) that a man discovers and for which he is willing to sell all of his possessions. And again, the kingdom of heaven is "like a merchant seeking fine pearls," who when he discovers one pearl of great value is willing to sell all that he has to possess it (Matthew 13:45-46). The difference between these two illustrations is that while one man apparently discovers *accidently* the "hidden treasure," the other, a pearl merchant, is actively *"seeking"* valuable pearls. Some people do occasionally *stumble onto the truth* of God's word, while others search for it. In both instances, they find it and are willing to sell everything in order to possess it.

What is the kingdom of God like? My personal conduct or manner of life as a citizen of God's kingdom should serve to show what God's kingdom is like. God's kingdom is not defined by physical boundaries, and cannot be found on a map. It is a spiritual concept. In this way, my conduct as a Christian should demonstrate what the kingdom of heaven is like. The question then becomes "Will *my manner of life* adequately and correctly describe God's kingdom?

How has my contact with God affected me? How have I been transformed or changed by the gospel of Christ? Although we all might be called *"sons of God"* (Galatians 3:26), *"Christians"* (1 Peter 4:16), or *"saints"* (Philippians 1:1), we are all different. Each of us has reached some level of personal piety and godliness, and perhaps none of us is at the same level as another. But each one has progressed in the gospel to the degree that we have heard and heeded God's word. The Holy Spirit of God works in our hearts through God's word, "which performs its work in you who believe" (1 Thessalonians 2:13).

What is the kingdom of God like? If the story of the cross has affected me; if God's word has meant anything to me; if the "Light of the knowledge of the glory of God in the face of Christ" has transformed me "into the same image from glory to glory, just as from the Lord, the Spirit" (2 Corinthians 3:18; 4:6), then I ought to have a story to tell. I might not be able to tell someone in *words* what the kingdom of God is like, but I certainly ought to be able to illustrate in my life and conduct the meaning of God's reign. "For the kingdom of God does not consist in words but in power" (1 Corinthians 4:20).

> Have Thine own way, Lord! Have Thine own way!
> Thou art the Potter; I am the clay.
> Mold me and make me after Thy will,
> While I am waiting, Yielded and still.
> Have Thine own way, Lord! Have Thine own way!
> Hold o'er my being absolute sway!
> Fill with Thy spirit 'Till all shall see
> Christ only, always, living in me!
> (Pollard)

Words To Live By

"HELP MY UNBELIEF!"

THE LORD JESUS HAD INVITED THREE OF HIS DISCIples to go up with Him on a "high mountain" (Mark 9:2). While it is obvious that Peter, James, and John did not know why they had been invited, they may have reflected that they were being honored above the other nine disciples who were left at the foot of the hill. In view of the rather constant bickering that had been going on among the twelve over which one of them would be the "greatest" or the most important in the kingdom of heaven (Mark 9:30-37), it is possible that Jesus was intending to teach all of them and especially these three, an important lesson. Indeed, James and John, in particular, seemed most consumed by this idea of "greatness" (Cf. Matthew 20:20-24), and only a little earlier, the Lord had promised to Simon Peter that he would receive the "keys of the kingdom of heaven" (Matthew 16:18-19). Surely, one of *them* would be the "greatest" in the Messiah's coming kingdom.

As the four arrived at the summit of the mountain, Jesus was suddenly "transfigured," *changed*, before their very eyes! The disciples watched, amazed as they heard Moses and Elijah "talking with Jesus" about "His departure which He was about to accomplish at Jerusalem" (Luke 9:31). As he often did, Peter spoke before he thought, suggesting that they construct on the spot three "tabernacles" or "tents" for Moses, Elijah, and Jesus (Mark 9:5-6). What was he thinking? Opinions differ concerning Peter's reasoning here. Did he want simply to *provide shade* for these important persons? Was he thinking about the approaching *Feast of Booths*, where people camped out in makeshift booths or tents for a week? Or was he intending *to honor* Moses, Elijah, and Jesus, by erecting some sort of memorial to the occasion? Whatever might have been going through Peter's terrified mind at that moment, Jesus taught him a necessary lesson. The words had hardly left Peter's mouth when a dark cloud covered Moses, Elijah, and Jesus, so that the disciples could not see them. A voice spoke from the cloud, saying, "*This* is *"help My Unbelief!"*

My beloved Son, listen to *Him*" (Mark 9:7). At the same moment, the cloud lifted, and *only Jesus* was present. *Jesus* was the One to be heard and heeded. Here was someone greater than Moses or Elijah. These three disciples who had been so engrossed in thoughts of personal honor were being taught the all-important lesson that they were to listen to *Jesus*, who was their Master.

As the Lord led the way back down the mountain to where the other nine had been left only a few hours before, they discovered a confused situation (Mark 9:14). The nine were in the midst of a large crowd arguing with some scribes, and the disciples were obviously getting the worst of it. A distraught dad had brought his demon-possessed son to Jesus for healing, but not finding Jesus, the dad had asked the nine disciples to heal his son, but "they could not do it" (Mark 9:18). *They could not heal the boy!* They who for some time had already been casting out demons (Matthew 10:1-15) *could not cast this evil spirit out* of this small boy. How could this be?

Jesus said to the child's father, "Bring him to *me!*" (Mark 9:19). Bringing his son to Jesus, he said, "If you can do anything, take pity on us and help us!" (Mark 9:22). "If you can!" Jesus exclaimed. "All things are possible to him who believes." Immediately "the boy's father cried out and said, "I do believe; help my unbelief!" (Mark 9:24). This dad thought that Jesus was talking about *his* "unbelief," but it is quite possible that Jesus was addressing the "unbelief" of the *nine disciples*. Indeed, later, when Jesus and the disciples were alone, they asked Him "privately" why they could not "drive it out" (Mark 9:28), to which Jesus responded, "This kind cannot come out by anything but prayer" (Mark 9:29). The disciples had apparently come to think that the power to cast our demons was inherently *theirs*, but Jesus was teaching them that *the power was not in them, but in God*. Jesus was not saying that some demons are more difficult to drive out than are others. He was, however, saying that belief and trust in God give us power over Satan.

The pitiful, urgent cry of the afflicted boy's heartbroken dad should provoke in each of us the desire for a purer, more sincere faith in God. "I believe," said he, "Help my unbelief!" We also believe, but far too often we begin to think that the power is in us. When we encounter difficulties or situations that we cannot solve, we have a

Words To Live By

tendency to give up in despair. Some even become suicidal, believing there can be no outcome with which they can live. We think there is no way out, so we throw up our hands in unbelief.

The dad's statement sounds contradictory. On the one hand he said, "I *believe.*" Then he said. "Help my *unbelief.*" Which was it, belief or unbelief? Or was it both at the same time? For myself, I think it was both. *Perfect faith* rarely if ever dwells in a frail human being. Much later in life, the apostle John would write about "perfect love" that "casts out fear" (1 John 4:18). Since all of us occasionally experience "fears" of some kind, it follows that none of us has "perfect love." It is the same with faith. All of us have faith, but it is surely obvious that we must be growing in faith every day for the rest of our lives. Only God is perfect. There can be no perfection for us while in the flesh, except that "perfection" that God accomplishes for us through Jesus our Lord, as Paul wrote to the Philippians: "So that I may gain Christ, and may be found in Him, not having a righteousness of my own derived from the Law, but that which is through faith in Christ, the righteousness which comes from God on the basis of faith …. Not that I have already obtained it or have already become perfect, but I press on so that I may lay hold of that for which also I was laid hold of by Christ Jesus." (Philippians 3:9-12).

Peter, James, and John learned on the mountain's summit that Christ Jesus is the one to be heard and heeded. The other nine learned at the foot of the mountain that it is *prayer* which unleashes God's spiritual power that makes all of us able to "cast out" the evil one.

Yes, Lord, I believe! Help my unbelief.

"SHE HAS DONE WHAT SHE COULD"

I**T WAS TUESDAY AFTERNOON, TWO DAYS BEFORE THE** first day of Unleavened Bread, which, for faithful Jews, would actually begin on Thursday evening with the Passover meal.

The village of Bethany, just two miles south of Jerusalem, was humming with excitement. Many relatives of Bethany families who lived farther away, and pilgrims from distant parts, would have swelled the population of Bethany on this occasion. It is likely that every home was crowded with guests. It was certainly so with the home of Mary, Martha, and their brother Lazarus, where not only Jesus, but the twelve disciples also, were very likely lodged. Since we know that Mary and Martha must have been well off financially, this house was probably much more commodious than the usual house in the village.

Jesus and his disciples had arrived in Bethany four days earlier, on the previous Friday, "six days before the Passover" (John 12:1). On that particular Tuesday afternoon, John recounted, "They made Him a supper there, and Martha was serving" (John 12:2). His friend Lazarus, whom He had weeks earlier raised from the dead (John 11:39-46), was reclining at the table with the other guests. Both Matthew (26:6) and Mark (14:3) inform us that this formal evening meal took place, not in the home of Mary and Martha, but surprisingly "at the home of Simon the leper." Obviously, Simon "the Leper" was no longer a leper, since it would not have been lawful for him to receive guests. The nickname "the leper" was still used by the villagers to identify him. Simon was perhaps a friend of Martha's, since she felt free to serve her guests in his home.

At some point during the meal, Mary, the sister of Martha and Lazarus, silently approached Jesus as He reclined at the table. In those days, tables were low to the floor and people "reclined" on cushions, with their feet away from the table, so the Lord may not have noticed Mary as she drew near Him. Kneeling at His feet, she broke the long neck of a small "alabaster vial" which contained a "pound" (John 12:3) of "very costly perfume of pure nard," emptying the rich scented perfume on His feet (Mark 14:3). John adds that Mary then "wiped His feet with her hair" (John 12:2-3), obliging her to unbind her hair, which "a respectable woman" would not normally do in public (NASB *NOTES*). I think that Mary must have been overcome with sadness as she reflected that the life of her dear gentle friend, Jesus, was in danger. Jesus had certainly not withheld from his friends in Bethany that He was in mortal danger, for He had been telling the Twelve for some time that He would be killed in Jerusalem by the Jews (Mark 10:33-34). So, in humble abandon, without regard for what the other guests might think, Mary went to her knees like a servant, at the feet of Jesus.

Immediately, however, other guests began to criticize her for, of all things, wasting such costly perfume. "Some were indignantly remarking to one another" that the perfume could have been sold for over three hundred denarii, and the money given to the poor (Mark 14:5), and they were "scolding" Mary. Among those who were scolding her was Judas Iscariot, one of the Twelve.

Jesus told the guests, "Let her alone, so that she may keep it for the day of My burial. For you always have the poor with you, but you do not always have Me" (John 12:7-8). The Lord continued to say, "She has done what she could; she has anointed My body beforehand for the burial" (Mark 14:8).

"She has done what she could!" Mary could not protect her Lord from death. She would not be able to shield Him from the blows of those who would beat Him, and whether or not she realized what would happen within just a few short days, she seized the moment and did "what she could."

God requires of us only what we can do. God has often required men to do things they did not *want* to do, but never has He told them to do the impossible. He told the prophet Jonah to go to Nineveh and preach repentance to a warlike people. Jonah did not want to do this, but eventually he did, and was surprisingly successful. Elisha, by God's instruction, told the Syrian commander, Naaman, to dip seven times in the Jordan River to be cured of his leprosy (2 Kings 5). Naaman thought this was a rather stupid thing to require of someone who had leprosy, so he initially refused to do it. When he finally did what the prophet said, he was instantly cured. To dip in the Jordan to be cured of leprosy made no sense whatever. God's commands may not make sense to us, but they are never impossible to implement. He only requires of us "what we can do."

Jesus said that Mary's impulsive, but humble act would be talked about "wherever the gospel is preached" (Mark 14:9). Her example should inspire all of us to action, doing what we can do, not worrying about what we cannot do.

PALM SUNDAY

Jesus had arrived in Bethany on Friday afternoon to lodge in the home of his dear friends, Mary, Martha, and Lazarus (John 12:1). What a wonderful reunion that must have been! The Lord no doubt wanted to enjoy the company of His friends before beginning the most arduous week of his life. Only a few weeks at the most had passed since His friend Lazarus had succumbed to an illness and died. Jesus, who had been residing across the Jordan in Perea, out of harm's way, had returned briefly to Judea to raise him from the dead (John 11:1-46). Not long after that, the time having come for the fulfillment of His great work, Jesus returned to the quiet village for the last time. We know nothing of what transpired on that Friday evening, but we can suppose that on the following day, the Sabbath, Jesus and the Twelve rested according to the Law.

On the next day, Sunday, perhaps in the afternoon, Jesus and His disciples walked the two miles from Bethany to Jerusalem. As they approached the hill village of Bethphage, on the slopes of the Mount of Olives (Matthew 21:1), Jesus sent two of the disciples on ahead to procure a donkey for Himself. Jesus was planning to fulfill the prophecy of Zechariah 9:9, "Say to the daughter of Zion, 'Behold your King is coming to you, gentle, and mounted on a donkey, even on a colt, the foal of a beast of burden'" (Matthew 21:4-5). They proceeded on their way, the Lord Jesus riding the donkey, and His disciples following with Him, no doubt in amazement at what was happening in their very presence. As they walked along, the news of His arrival went before them, and people began to crowd the sides of the roadway. Men were taking their coats off and spreading them on the road, so that Jesus could ride over them (Luke 21:36) and others were cutting branches from the palm trees and spreading them in the road. As the crowds grew in size, so the noise increased in volume as people ran ahead of Him, shouting, "Hosanna to the

Palm Sunday

Son of David; Blessed is He who comes in the name of the Lord; Hosanna in the highest!" (Matthew 21:8-9).

As this joyous crowd walked with Him, singing and shouting praises to God, they arrived at the crest of the Mount of Olives and stopped. Looking down upon the holy city, Jerusalem, Jesus was overcome with sorrow for it and wept (Luke 19:41). The prophet Jeremiah had also shed many tears for this great city: "My sorrow is beyond healing," he had said, "my heart is faint within me! .... For the brokenness of the daughter of my people I am broken; I mourn, dismay has taken hold of me.... Oh that my head were waters and my eyes a fountain of tears, that I might weep day and night for the slain of the daughter of my people!" (Jeremiah 8:18 – 9:1). Our Lord, also, with death in His heart, said as He wept, "If you had known in this day, even you, the things which make for peace! But now they have been hidden from your eyes. For the days will come upon you when your enemies will throw up a barricade against you, and surround you and hem you in on every side, and they will level you to the ground and your children within you, and they will not leave in you one stone upon another, because you did not recognize the time of your visitation" (Luke 19:42-44). His prophecy would be fulfilled at the hands of the Roman legions in A.D. 66-70. Jesus does not seem to have stayed long in Jerusalem that Sunday. Mark says, "Jesus entered Jerusalem and came into the temple; and after looking around at everything, He left for Bethany with the twelve, since it was already late" (Mark 11:11).

The Lord returned, however, on Monday morning, to drive the thieving moneychangers from the temple (Mark 11:15-19). Having thus "cleansed" the temple, Jesus apparently continued to publicly teach until evening in the temple area known as the "Court of the Gentiles," effectively barring the way so that no one could "carry merchandise through the temple" (Mark 11:16).

Tuesday found Jesus in the temple area the entire day, teaching and proclaiming God's message to the multitudes who hung on His every word (Matthew 21:46; Luke 19:47-48). It was a day of controversy, confronted by the chief priests and the scribes (Luke 19:47), the Sadducees (Luke 20:27), and the Pharisees (Matthew 22:15). It was likely on Tuesday evening that Simon the Leper (Mark 14:3-9), a prominent citizen of Bethany, hosted a sumptuous meal for Jesus and the twelve (John 12:2). A pall of sadness must have hung over that meal and the conversation of the dinner guests. They were all painfully aware that suffering and death were standing at the door, and that the Lord Jesus, so loved by everyone there, was going to die. Jesus had spoken of it often in those last days, but it was so hard to imagine. During the meal, or perhaps just following, Mary, who had found such joy sitting at the Master's feet listening to Him speak of spiritual things, was filled with foreboding for her Friend. Not able to contain herself, she went to her room and got a "pound of pure nard," a very costly perfume, and anointed the feet of Jesus, wiping His feet with her long hair (John 12:3). When Judas Iscariot criticized her for such a "waste," Jesus said, "Let her alone, so that she may keep it for the day of My burial" (John 12:7).

On Wednesday, the Lord seems to have remained in Bethany, perhaps for a much-needed day of rest, but on Thursday He returned to Jerusalem for the Passover. He was arrested in Gethsemane during the midnight hours by the officers sent by the High Priest, unlawfully tried during the night, shamelessly mistreated, and crucified on Friday morning, thus fulfilling the Law and the Prophets.

That week, known by Christians as "Holy Week," was a successful conclusion for God's plan, bringing to fulfillment so many prophecies, achieving for sinful mankind what men could not do for themselves. So, we also shout, "Hosanna to the Son of David! Blessed is He who comes in the name of the Lord!"

"ELOI, ELOI, LAMA SABACHTHANI"

JESUS HAD ENDURED AN ALL-NIGHT ILLEGAL TRIAL before the entire Sanhedrin, chaired by the high priest, Caiaphas (Matthew 26:57-75). At daybreak, on Friday morning, accompanied by a throng of angry Jews, He was delivered bound to Pontius Pilate, the Roman governor (Matthew 27:1-2). Pilate was no doubt aware of what had been taking place and seems to have been waiting for them to arrive (John 18:28-29). The governor would certainly have been informed in advance of the Lord's arrest, since this involved a man who claimed to be the long-anticipated Messiah. In fact, the group that arrested Jesus in the garden of Gethsemane included a "chiliarch," a high-ranking commander in the Roman army (John 18:12).

Delivered to Pilate shortly after 6 A.M., Jesus was subjected to another round of interrogation (John 18:33-40), after which He was "scourged" (John 19:1). Bruised and covered with blood, with a "crown of thorns" crushed onto His head, our Lord was then subjected to public spectacle, where He had to hear a rowdy horde of people crying out, "Away with Him, Crucify Him" (John 19:15). After Pilate symbolically washed his hands of what he knew was a miscarriage of justice, he authorized the crucifixion of the Son of God (Luke 23:23-25).

At about nine A.M. (Mark 15:25 – the "third hour"), the large iron nails were driven through the hands and feet of our Lord. His anguish on the cross would last six horrible hours. At 12 noon (the "sixth hour"), a mysterious "darkness" covered the land until 3 P.M. (the "ninth hour"). Suddenly, when the darkness was ended, the Lord's anguished voice cried, "Eloi, Eloi, Lama Sabachthani?" Mark translated this for his Gentile readers, *"My God, My God, why have You forsaken Me?"* Shortly after this terrifying cry to God, Jesus again "uttered a loud cry" and died (Mark 15:34-35).

This outcry from our dying Savior was not accidental. Jesus was quoting during His final minutes a verse of Scripture written nearly nine hundred years earlier by King David, the prophet-poet and author of many of the *Psalms* (Psalm 22:1). When David penned these words, he had no idea that he was foretelling the death of the Messiah. He was no doubt voicing a very personal and heartfelt prayer to Yahweh, asking the Almighty why He had forsaken him, David. The "groaning" which David wrote about were, to his mind, his own. In his mind, he was speaking *of himself* when he wrote, "I am a worm and not a man" (Psalm 22:6). The "enemies" that surrounded David were *his own* (Psalm 22: 12). Thinking that his own death might be eminent, David cried out to God, saying "O Lord, be not far off; O You my help, hasten to my assistance" (Psalm 22:19).

The fact that Jesus purposely repeated David's obvious prophecy of His crucifixion does not diminish His suffering. We should remember that our Lord Jesus suffered as a *man*. He was yet in the flesh and His suffering was real. In view of the fact that the man Jesus had a profound knowledge of the Holy Scriptures, it is completely natural that His final words would be a citation from Scripture, and it is obvious why He cited *this particular psalm*. Unlike David, who did not know that his words were prophetic, Jesus was well aware that He was the Messiah, and that David's words concerned Him. Therefore, even as He cried out to God in His dying moments, Jesus was testifying to all who heard Him that He was indeed the promised Messiah, fulfilling David's prophecy.

This question – "Why have You forsaken Me" – should not be understood to mean that God had actually "forsaken" His divine Son. God had not forsaken King David, although David may have thought it so. I think that God realizes that because humans have never *seen* Him, they may sometimes waver in their faith. To us who cannot see God, it may indeed seem that in times of peril or suffering He is "far" from us. In those times of severe suffering, one might wonder if God really does care what happens to us. For example, David continued saying, "O my God, I cry by day, but You do not answer; and by night, but I have no rest" (Psalm 22:2). Unbelievers may taunt us, saying, "Commit yourself to the Lord; let Him deliver [you]! Let Him rescue [you] because He delights in [you]!" (Psalm 22:8). We commit ourselves to God and we beg Him to rescue us, but He is *"eloi, Eloi, Lama Sabachthani"*

silent. Because we do not receive what we ask for, we may begin to doubt that there is even a God, or at least that He cares.

Then we remember Jesus, who prayed to the Father in the darkness of the night, asking Him for deliverance, knowing the dreadful suffering He was about to endure the next day, and we observe that God did not deliver Him from that suffering. We remember that just as David did not deny God, neither did Jesus, and neither should we. The writer of *Hebrews* tells us to "run with endurance the race that is set before us, fixing our eyes on Jesus, the author and perfecter of faith, who for the joy set before Him endured the cross." Then he urges us not to "grow weary and lose heart." (Hebrews 12:2-3).

When we are tempted to accuse God of having "forsaken" us in our moment of suffering, let us remember that He is by our side, and that whatever happens, we will have the final victory through Jesus Christ.

Words To Live By

HE NAILED IT TO THE CROSS!

NO ONE HAS EVER TAKEN ME TO COURT FOR having failed to pay a debt. No one has ever forced me to move because of a failure to pay the rent. No one has ever come to my house to seize my car because I was behind on the payment.

Only once did a kindly person come forward to pay a debt for me, but He has also done the same for countless others. His name is Jesus, the humble carpenter of Nazareth. When He left His place beside the Father, becoming human, He also left behind all the prerogatives of Godhood (Philippians 2:6-7). He intended to live on earth as a laborer, working hard just like every other man of His village. He intended to face every temptation and trial that other humans faced (Hebrews 2:18; 4:15), so that He would be able to help them and comfort them in their time of need. And He intended to allow His enemies to torture and beat Him, then to kill Him by a cruel, slow death on a Roman cross – for me and for you. He must have thought often about this, for we read that, the evening before His arrest, He passed several hours "in agony" (Luke 22:44), when "His sweat became like drops of blood, falling down upon the ground." Mark recorded that earlier that last evening, Jesus was "very distressed and troubled" (Mark 14:33), and that He "fell to the ground and began to pray that if it were possible, the hour might pass Him by" (Mark 14:35). But Jesus knew that He could not escape His future. He had come to earth for the very purpose of dying, and He had to see it through to the bitter end.

This Man of many words and great deeds said but little while on the cross, but what He did say was significant. The "loud cry" that Mark mentioned (Mark 15:37) was no doubt His cry, "It is finished" (John 19:30), as "He bowed His head and gave up His spirit."

"It is finished!" He shouted. His great mission was accomplished. He had done what He came to do and we praise God for that, because

He Nailed It To The Cross!

He came to save *me*, and *you*, and whoever else will accept Him. He came to pay my debt and yours.

It may be that you do not realize that you have a huge debt that needs to be paid – your sins that have accumulated over the years – a mountain of wrongdoing. It has become fashionable to call sins "shortcomings," and everyone has them. We have come to think of "shortcomings" as not really all that bad, so we might not talk much about "sin," except when we are thinking of other people. Other people *sin*; I have *"shortcomings."* But God tells us that "all have sinned and fall short of the glory of God (Romans 3:23), and that the "wages of sin is death" (Romans 6:23). This mountain of "sin" that has built up became a debt that we could not pay, so God sent His Son into the world to save sinners.

Paul wrote to the Colossians that when Jesus died on the cross, He "canceled out the certificate of debt" that was "against us," and "nailed it to the cross" (Colossians 2:14). Paul was saying, in effect, that the Old Testament Law, with its hundreds of rules and regulations that no man could possibly keep perfectly, was "taken out of the way" at the cross. He was saying that God, through Christ, and by His suffering, has paid my debt and yours. This is only true, however, if we are "made alive together with Him" (Colossians 2:13). This includes accepting Christ as our Savior and King and being "buried with Him in baptism" (Colossians 2:10-12). He died on the cross; we must "die to sin." He arose again from the dead; we must also "walk in newness of life," in the "likeness of His resurrection" (Romans 6:1-5).

> There was one who was willing to die in my stead,
> That a soul so unworthy might live;
> And the path to the cross He was willing to tread,
> All the sins of my life to forgive.
> He is tender and loving and patient with me,
> While He cleanses my heart of its dross.
> But "there's no condemnation" – I know I am free,
> For my sins are all nailed to the cross.
> They are nailed to the cross! They are nailed to the cross!
> O how much He was willing to bear!
> With what anguish and loss, Jesus went to the cross!
> But He carried my sins with Him there.
> (Mrs. Frank Breck)

ONE SUNDAY MORNING

MARY OF MAGDALA ARRIVED AT THE TOMB VERY early that Sunday morning (John 20:1). This was the woman from whom Jesus had cast out "seven demons" (Mark 16:9), and she had become a faithful follower. Only three days earlier she had stood near the cross, along with His mother and aunt (John 19:25), watching Him die. Now, as she arrived, perhaps alone, at the Lord's garden tomb, it was "still dark." Even in the darkness she could see that the great round stone had been rolled away from the door of the tomb, and that there were no guards. She may have stayed there alone at a distance from the tomb, waiting for three other women, including Jesus' mother, who were bringing spices to anoint the body (Mark 16:1-2). Although it was still quite early, the sun had already risen when they got there. Conspicuously absent that morning were the Twelve.

As the four women approached the tomb, they were greatly surprised to see sitting by the entrance a young man "wearing a white robe" (Mark 16:5). He said to them, "Do not be amazed; you are looking for Jesus the Nazarene, who has been crucified. He has risen; He is not here; behold, here is the place where they laid Him" (Mark 15:6). Matthew called the young man an "angel of the Lord" (Matthew 28:2). The angel told the women to go to the apostles and inform them that Jesus had risen from the dead (Matthew 28:7; Mark 16:7). Mary Magdalene hurried off and found Peter and John, telling them what she had seen (John 20:2). Peter and John immediately ran to the tomb, finding it as the women had said. When they entered they noticed that the Lord's burial clothes had been neatly folded and laid aside (John 20:7-8). After the two men left the garden, Mary Magdalene, who had returned to the tomb with them, stayed for a little while alone, standing outside the tomb, wailing loudly. "As she wept, she stooped and looked into the tomb," perhaps for one final glance, but to her great amazement she saw "two angels in white sitting, one at the head and one at the feet, where the body of Jesus had been lying" (John 20:11-12). They asked her why she was weeping, and she responded, "Because they have taken away my Lord, and I do not know where they have laid Him" (John 20:13). Although the "young man" Mary had seen earlier had told her that Jesus had risen, she had not fully grasped his meaning. But as she turned to leave the tomb, she "saw Jesus standing there," but in the semi-darkness, she did not recognize Him. He said to her, "Woman, why are you weeping? Whom are you seeking?" (John 20:15). Thinking Him to be the gardener, she exclaimed, "Sir, if you have carried Him away, tell me where you have laid Him, and I will take Him away." Then Jesus gently spoke her name: "Mary!" And she recognized Him, calling Him "Rabboni," an Aramaic term of profound respect.

Later in the afternoon of that same day, two of the Lord's disciples were walking the dusty seven miles from Jerusalem to Emmaus. As they walked, they were discussing the things that had occurred that day, when, suddenly, "Jesus Himself approached and began traveling with them" (Luke 24:13-14). They were prevented from recognizing Him, so when He asked what they were talking about, they explained to Him that some women had amazed them, saying that Jesus, whom they had hoped was the Messiah, had been raised from the dead (Luke 24:22).

If the disciples of Jesus found it difficult to believe that He was resurrected, why should we be surprised today that many do not believe? Yet, the resurrection of Jesus from the dead was chosen by God to be the very foundation upon which Christianity was built. Paul wrote that Jesus was "declared the Son of God with power by the resurrection from the dead" (Romans 1:4). And, indeed, the resurrection of Christ is the single best attested event recorded in the gospel accounts. Many witnesses would have been able to testify publicly that they knew Jesus before He died and that they saw Him after He was raised from the dead (1 Corinthians 15:1-9). Although the Bible records many miracles done by Him during His ministry, it is to the *resurrection* that we appeal to prove that He is the Christ.

When Paul stood before King Herod Agrippa II and the Roman Governor Festus (Acts 25-26) to defend himself, he told them that he had personally encountered and spoken with the resurrected

Jesus of Nazareth. Four or five years earlier, while at Ephesus during the early spring of 55 A.D., Paul had addressed the question of the resurrection of the dead, declaring that Christ had appeared to him (1 Corinthians 15:8). When one considers all that the persecutor, Saul of Tarsus, gave up to become a Christian, one is forced to admit the honesty and sincerity of his faith. Saul did not profit materially from his conversion, nor did he achieve greater social rank or honor. In fact, in the eyes of the world, he lost everything of value when he left his prominent position in Judaism (Philippians 3:4-11) to serve a man whom most Jews regarded as a blasphemer and impostor. Instead of adulation and praise, he was hated, often beaten, and maligned (2 Corinthians 6:4-11).

Because Christ was raised from the dead, we too enjoy the expectation of a personal resurrection of the body, so that whether we are alive or dead when Jesus comes, we "will be caught up together" with all the saints of God to meet the Lord in the air, and so we shall "always be with the Lord" (1 Thessalonians 4:14-17). This precious hope must be nurtured and encouraged, if we are to maintain it. The four women who came to the tomb of Jesus early that Sunday morning would hardly forget what they saw and experienced. But we, at a distance of nearly two thousand years, without having seen angels at the empty tomb, are prone to forgetfulness.

Many people think about the Lord's resurrection only on "Easter Sunday," and I rejoice that they at least remember Him on that day. But when Christians *regularly* come together on the Lord's Day, *communing every week* with others of "like precious faith" (2 Peter 1:1) at the Lord's Supper (1 Corinthians 11:20), they are more likely to "hold fast the confession" of their hope "without wavering" (Hebrews 10:23). We cannot afford to forget.

WORSHIP, SYNAGOGUE, CHURCH

THE WORDS *WORSHIP, SYNAGOGUE,* AND *CHURCH* are often misunderstood, misused, and abused, but are nevertheless interwoven into the fabric of Judaism and Christianity, and for just cause.

"Worship" is primary among these words, for without *worship* there would be no "synagogue" or "church." The English word *worship* derives from the idea of *"worth"* or *"worthiness,"* for we worship what or whom we reverence or consider to be of great *worth*. The British still use the expression "Your Worship" when addressing certain persons of rank and dignity.

Worship has always been conceived in both *ceremonial* and *spiritual* terms. For example, Cain, a farmer, and Abel, a shepherd, brought physical products as offerings to God (Genesis 4:2-5). We are told that God accepted Abel's offering – a lamb – but rejected the vegetables or fruit offered by Cain. We have supposed, perhaps rightly, that God had previously given instructions to men concerning the "ceremonial" worship that they were to bring to Him, but the Bible does not state this. In fact, the Law of Moses, coming much later, while specifying certain animal sacrifices for special events (Leviticus 1; 6:8-13), also allowed offerings of *grain* and other *vegetables* along with animal sacrifices as acceptable offerings (Leviticus 2; 6:14-23). The writer of *Hebrews* says that Abel's offering was "a better sacrifice" than that of Cain (Hebrews 11:4) because he offered it "by faith" while Cain did not. If Cain's offering was rejected because it was not an animal, we are not told so in the Bible. The fact is that Abel offered to God a worship which was both "ceremonial" and "spiritual," but Cain only offered a ceremonial worship. The prophet Malachi railed against the people for offering to God animals which were *lame, sick,* or otherwise *"blemished"* (Malachi 1:13-14), showing that they did not *honor* or *revere* God. They were in effect saying that they "despised" the table of the Lord (Malachi 1:7). By the careless attention they gave to their offerings, they demonstrated that, as far as

Words To Live By

they were concerned, worship could be dispensed with. They said, "My, how tiresome it is!" (Malachi 1:13). Like Cain, their worship lacked "faith," and was only *ceremonial*. Jesus would later tell the Gentile woman at Jacob's well, "God is spirit, and those who worship Him must worship in spirit and truth" (John 4:24).

The second word "synagogue" does not appear in the Old Testament. Its origin is from the times of the exile, after the destruction of Jerusalem and the temple in 586 B.C., but several centuries before Christ. The word itself is from two Greek words meaning "to assemble" or "to congregate." Jews were apparently permitted to build altars and offer sacrifices in other places (Judges 6:25-26; 1 Samuel 6:9-10), but *national ceremonial worship* was authorized only on the altar which stood before the tabernacle or the temple in Jerusalem (cf. John 4:20). But for more than a hundred years following 586 B.C., there was no temple. During that time, faithful Jews could not go up to Jerusalem for the annual feasts (Leviticus 23) or receive the benefits of the *Yom Kippur*, the annual "day of atonement" (Leviticus 23:26-44). In exile in Babylon, without priests or the ability to offer the ceremonial worship required by the Law of Moses, an alternate plan developed to preserve Jewish beliefs and faith in God. Men of faith became teachers – "rabbis" – and meetings began to take place here and there, *assemblies* which came to be called "synagogues." When houses were built especially for these assemblies, the houses themselves were also called "synagogues." These synagogues became the centers of worship and education for faithful Jews. The Lord Jesus, Himself, regularly attended the worship assemblies at the local synagogue in Nazareth, where He also was often asked to read the Holy Scriptures (Luke 4:16-19).

The third word "church" is commonly used to translate the Greek noun *ekklesia*, which for the Greeks of the first century only meant an *assembly*, paralleling the word *synagogue*, and is used in Acts 19:39 of "a lawful assembly," convened for political purposes. Christ used the word *ekklesia* in Matthew 16:18 when speaking of his own "assembly" that he would build, which would never be "overpowered" by the forces of evil. Paul called this "assembly" the "body" of Christ" (Ephesians 1:22-23). When Paul addressed the divisive manner in which some of the Christians at Corinth were conducting themselves *during the weekly gathering of the church*, he wrote,

"But in giving this instruction, I do not praise you, because you *come together* not for the better but for the worse. For, in the first place, *when you come together as a church* [literally, "in the assembly" or "in church"], I hear that divisions exist among you" (1 Corinthians 11:17-18). He continued to say that in *such a divisive atmosphere* (1 Corinthians 11:20) "it is not *really* to eat the Lord's Supper" (*New Revised Standard Version*) or "it is not the Lord's Supper you eat" (*New International Version*). Indeed, Paul's meaning is that their unspiritual attitude rendered it impossible to worship God acceptably. Their intent in coming together "in church" was indeed to do that very thing – to eat the Lord's Supper, but their attitudes made it impossible. Paul wrote, "What! Do you not have houses in which to eat and drink?" Their problem was not in eating and drinking, but rather in the refusal of the "haves" to share with the "have nots" (1 Corinthians 11:21-22). To suppose that the *unacceptable worship* was because these people were mixing their normal meals with the Lord's Supper, is to miss the point. In those early times, congregations often met in homes, bringing their food with them, so they would have been eating and drinking at some point. But Paul's point was that some poor people had *no food to bring*, while the wealthier members had *food to spare*, but refused to share it with their poor brothers in Christ (1 Corinthians 11:22). In such a circumstance, *spiritual worship* was impossible and the *ceremonial* worship was unacceptable.

We today are not different from God's people of ages past. It is possible, if not usual, for us as well to consider "ceremonial" worship to be of more value than "spiritual" worship, or vice versa. While some consider that "going to church" and "going through the motions" is sufficient, others apparently think that they don't need to "go to church" on a regular basis; they can stay at home and worship during commercials, or worship on the lake while waiting for the fish to bite. Reasoning that God is everywhere, they see no great value in being in the assembly. But there is great value in meeting regularly in the assembly of God's church. In the first place, God's people are the "body of Christ," and the body must be joined together (1 Corinthians 12). Secondly, the Lord has placed the "Lord's Supper" in the weekly assembly (Acts 2:42; 20:7; 1 Corinthians 11:17-34). Finally, but not least, in the assembly we find good teaching, edification, and encouragement to love and help one another. As it is written, "Let us hold fast the confession of our hope without wavering; for He who promised is faithful, and let us consider how to stimulate one another to love and good deeds, not forsaking our own assembling together, as is the habit of some, but encouraging one another" (Hebrews 10:23-25).

BRING ME ANOTHER JAR!

LIFE WAS HARD IN THE NORTHERN KINGDOM OF Israel in those days. Ruling from Samaria, Israel's capital city, King Jehoram had continued on the course pursued by his evil parents, Ahab and Jezebel. "He clung to the sins of Jeroboam the son of Nebat, which he made Israel sin; he did not depart from them" (2 Kings 3:3). A war with Moab had resulted in "great wrath against Israel" (2 Kings 3:27), bringing hardship and famine to many.

Among those thus affected was "a certain woman of the wives of the sons of the prophets" (2 Kings 4:1). This good woman's husband had died, perhaps because of the war, and a "creditor" had come to take her two children to be his slaves. Desperate, she called upon the prophet Elisha for help. Elisha asked her, "What do you have in your house?" She had nothing in the house except a jar of oil (2 Kings 4:2). Elisha instructed her, "Go borrow vessels at large for yourself from all your neighbors, even empty vessels; do not get a few." Then he told her to go into her house with her children and shut the door behind her. Then she was to begin pouring her oil into these vessels. She continued pouring until all the vessels were full. When she ran out of vessels, the oil stopped flowing. Elisha then told her to sell the oil, pay her debts, and live on the remaining money.

The prophet had told her not to "get a few" vessels. I wonder what passed through her mind when all of her vessels were filled and the oil stopped flowing. Did she think, "Why didn't I get some more vessels?" When she made the decision to stop gathering vessels, she limited herself, and the oil stopped flowing. In a similar way, we often limit the blessings that God would like to give us. We seem to be saying to God, "I have enough vessels, Lord. Don't keep on pouring! I have enough."

God has placed before us a number of "vessels" which can be filled with blessings from Him. The first of these is prayer. Jesus teaches us that we "ought to pray at all times and not to lose heart" (Luke 18:1).

Words To Live By

The Lord said, "Will not God bring about justice for His elect who cry to Him day and night?" Our great problem, however, is "faith." When prayers are not answered swiftly, we grow discouraged and cease to pray. Jesus asks the question, "When the son of Man comes, will He find faith on the earth?" (Luke 18:8). Therefore, we should "pray without ceasing" (1 Thessalonians 5:17). To cease praying is to cease gathering "vessels."

A second "vessel" is the practice of reading and studying the word of God. Paul tells us that "Scripture" is "profitable for teaching, for reproof, for correction, for training in righteousness," and that God's word can make us "adequate, equipped for every good work" (2 Timothy 3:16-17). The word of God is spiritual food that helps us grow. Like babies need milk, adult Christians need "solid food" (Hebrews 5:12). The Christian who stops reading stops growing and becomes "dull of hearing" (Hebrews 5:11).

A third "vessel" is faithful attendance at worship on the Lord's Day. Many professed Christians rarely darken the doors where the saints meet on Sunday. There are good reasons why some do not come, and God sees and understands. But some just do not see the need for regular attendance. This is not just a modern phenomenon. It was happening within a few years of the birth of the church. The *Hebrews* writer warned against "forsaking our own assembling together, as is the habit of some" (Hebrews 10:25). What does one miss by not being a part of the assembly? In the same passage, the writer suggests that we are strengthened in our faith, so that we can "hold fast the confession of our hope without wavering," and that through our assembling together we "stimulate one another to love and good deeds" and are "encouraged" (Hebrews 10:23-25). Someone may say, "I don't get anything out of it," but could it be that he or she doesn't bring any "vessels." No vessels, no oil from God!

A fourth "vessel" is good works. We are taught to "be careful to engage in good deeds," an activity that is "good and profitable" (Titus 3:8). James, the Lord's brother, wrote that "faith, if it has no works, is dead, being by itself" (James 2:17). In fact, according to James, good works also perfect the faith of the one doing the work (James 2:22). Doing good deeds helps the doer perhaps even more than the one for whom the deeds are done. We are blessed when we serve others, when we encourage the disheartened, when we "show mercy," when we "contribute to the needs of the saints," and when we "weep with those who weep" (Romans 12:7-15).

If you don't feel as "blessed" as you want to feel, maybe it's because you have not brought enough "vessels." God does not limit us. Let's not limit ourselves! Don't bring just "a few" vessels.

Words To Live By

MY FATHER, THE ARTIST

FROM THE VERY TOP OF THE ARCH OF TRIUMPH IN Paris, we had a fabulous view of the great city. We could see for miles around in every direction. To the north, on a high hill, I pointed out to students the shining white Church of the Sacred Heart. Later, we walked past that church and around the corner on narrow cobblestone streets, to a square called Place du Tertre, where scores of artists were marketing their work. As we strolled through and around the square, we occasionally stopped to watch some artist doing a portrait of an excited tourist.

One particular artist had attracted a small crowd as he skillfully transferred to his sketchpad the features of the pretty young woman sitting before him. She, of course, could not see his work in progress, but it was visible to everyone who stood behind him watching. We were amazed to see her likeness come to life on the artist's sketchpad, here a line, there a line, detail by detail. When the artist finished his work and signed it, the crowd clapped and cheered. The young woman was pleased to see the finished portrait. Sometimes, however, a person may not be pleased with the artist's work, and may refuse to accept it. Perhaps the particular artist is not one of the best, but it may be that the displeased subject's opinion of himself is different from what the artist sees from his vantage point.

And I thought about *my* Father, the One in heaven, who is also an artist of renown. His work is not found in the art museums around the world, and, unfortunately, many people do not even credit Him for it. My Father, the artist, has created magnificent pastoral scenes, admired by millions. Who, for example, has driven through the Great Smoky Mountains in the autumn, and has not marveled at His workmanship? And who has ever sat in the dead of night, in total darkness, and contemplated the stars and the moon, without wondering at the power and wisdom of my Father? King David, who had spent countless nights in the Judean hills, watching his flocks, also looked with amazement at my Father's art, and wrote:

My Father, The Artist

> O Lord, Our Lord,
> How majestic is Your name in all the earth!
> Who have displayed Your splendor above the heavens!
> .... When I consider Your heavens, the work of Your fingers,
> The moon and the stars, which You have ordained;
> What is man that You take thought of him,
> And the son of man that you care for him?
> (Psalm 8:1-4)
>
> But the LORD made the heavens.
> Splendor and beauty are in His sanctuary.
> (Psalm 96:5-6)
>
> O Lord, how many are Your works!
> In wisdom You have made them all;
> The earth is full of Your possessions.
> There is the sea, great and broad,
> In which are swarms without number,
> Animals both small and great.
> (Psalm 104:24-25)

But my Father, the artist, does not limit Himself to landscapes. He also excels in "miniatures," like the Dutch masters who sometimes used a single horse hair to paint the tiniest details. My Father's miniatures can only be seen by powerful microscopes, so they often go unnoticed. Medical doctors, using tiny cameras, can now voyage through the bowels, arteries and veins, peering even into the human heart, a feat undreamed of by the psalmist David, who wrote:

> For You formed my inward parts;
> You wove me in my mother's womb.
> I will give thanks to You, for I am
> Fearfully and wonderfully made;
> Wonderful are Your works,
> And my soul knows it very well.
> My frame was not hidden from You,
> When I was made in secret,
> And skillfully wrought in the depths of the earth.
> (Psalm 139:13-15)

Neither is my Father limited to the human *body* as He tirelessly works His art. The apostle Paul described His *spiritual* artistry, as He labors to fashion and reshape the degenerate human spirit. Paul wrote that God gives us "a spirit of wisdom and of revelation in the knowledge of Him." He wrote of "the surpassing greatness of His power toward us who believe," according to "the working of the strength of His might, which He brought about in Christ" (Ephesians 1:17-20). Paul spoke of God's bringing spiritually "dead" people back to life through Christ (Ephesians 2:1-6). "For," wrote Paul, "we are His *workmanship*, created in Christ Jesus" (Ephesians 2:10).

Moses, in the Old Testament, delivered to the people a Law "engraved on tablets of *stone*," but my Father is working today "on tablets of *human hearts*" (2 Corinthians 3:3). He is not interested in how we look on the outside; it is the condition of the soul that interests Him. He wants to achieve a "new creature" (2 Corinthians 5:17), to "transform" my heart and yours into the image of the Lord Jesus (2 Corinthians 3:18). He effects this transformation "by the renewing" of our mind (Romans 12:2), by the effective working of "the word of God, which also performs its work in you who believe" (1 Thessalonians 2:13).

Just for a moment, picture yourself sitting before my Father, the artist, as He transfers to His sketchpad *your* spiritual features. When He allows you to see His finished work, will you be pleased with what you see? Artists are often unable to produce the work they desire, and are disappointed in the finished product. Much depends upon the subject, and in the spiritual sense, God cannot successfully work with an *unwilling* subject. For myself, when my Father finishes my "portrait," I hope that those watching will applaud and cheer.

I WISH I HAD KNOWN MY FATHER BETTER!

THIS IS A CONFESSION OF SORTS, I SUPPOSE. THE fact is, I wish I had known my dad better. I try to remember, but many of the memories are gone. Childhood, you know, is a funny thing, in that the baby quickly evolves into a toddler, the toddler rapidly becomes a child, the child suddenly steps forth as an adolescent, then a teen, and disappears in adulthood. Parents may think they "know" their child, but the child is there for so short a time that it seems quite impossible, in retrospect, to really "know" him or her. Most parents really *do* love their children and would do anything possible for them, even to the point of giving their lives to protect them. But really getting to *know* them?

The problem is that almost from the very beginning, the child is planning his escape. The baby you loved to hold no longer wants to be held. This seems to be emblematic of the teens who no longer want to eat with the family, or do the family things that you cherished when they were younger, preferring to be with their friends, or secluding themselves in their room, with plugs in their ears feeding them non-stop music. You say something to them, but they don't react, because they don't hear you. You yank the plugs from their ears, and they don't understand why.

Then, POOF! They're gone! They do come back, however, but those times become more and more infrequent. Mind you, I do not blame the child for this. It is a natural thing, and the caring parent will accept it, since now their children are beginning to experience the same feelings as they watch their children quickly disappear before their very eyes. The girl children do send cards, however, on significant dates; the boys usually don't. We are thankful for daughters-in-law!

I remember with some regret, my last visits home, before my father passed away. Dad could no longer walk well, so he sat in his chair, watching the commotion as all of the kids and grandkids invaded his small home. I spent most of those hours with my brother, outside the house, and very little time with my Dad, and for that I am now very sorry. It's too late now, but I would like to ask him things and really *listen* to him, because I think I did not *know* him as well as I thought.

And I want to get to know my Father better! Not my *earthly* dad, but my *"heavenly"* Father. My *earthly* father is gone, but my Father who is in heaven is there and time is short. I need to pay more attention to the things He says to me; I need to seek His advice; I need to talk to Him more, in private, just Him and me. I need to be around Him more, so that I can feel more at ease in His presence.

I think about my "older Brother," not the one who lives in Mississippi, but Jesus, the One who really spent quality time with our Father in heaven. Jesus was so *close* to our Father, not physically, but spiritually. He really *knew* our Father; the two of them were what you might call "bonded." So much so, that Jesus could say they were "one" (John 7:29; 17:21). Jesus was always with Him, often talking with Him in private, just the two of them (Mark 6:46; John 17:1-26). He was careful always to "honor" the Father (John 8:49) and to do what our Father asked Him to do (John 17:4). He always made Him look good, so that the Father never had to be ashamed of my older Brother (John 17:4-6).

I realize that, as a son to my Father in heaven, I have in no sense been the good son that Jesus was, and I know that my heavenly Father has sometimes had occasion to be ashamed of me, for which I am very sorry. I need to rethink my attitudes toward Him, like the young man we call "the prodigal" in the story told by Jesus (Luke 15:11-24). That boy had an older brother who had always remained faithful to his dad, at least on the surface (Luke 15:25-32). That older brother also needed an attitude adjustment, but there is no evidence that he would ever change.

Our Father in heaven wants to be *close* to us, so we ought to take advantage of every opportunity to be in His presence, when the "family" gathers to worship Him. We also need to schedule more time for personal "chats" with the Father, listening to Him (as we read the Bible), talking with Him (as we pray), even as our older Brother, Jesus, did. As children of God and "brothers and sisters" (Hebrews 2:17) of Jesus, we ought to cultivate a closer relationship with Him, so that like Jesus, we too can *"feel"* the love, and *experience* the care that God our Father wants for us. Maybe we can even come to really *love* the One we call *"ABBA"* (Romans 8:15), an Aramaic word similar in meaning to "Dad."

WHO DO YOU KNOW?

IT IS NOT *WHAT* YOU KNOW THAT COUNTS, BUT *WHO* you know. Indeed, this statement does have a ring of truth in the *business world*, and even more so in *political* circles. It seems that politicians can pretty much do anything they want and get away with it, whereas the ordinary person would be thrown into jail for even a lesser offense.

Who do you know? Have you ever met a movie star or a president of the United States? I remember that back in the 1970s, while running in a Montreal gym, I met a star baseball player with the Montreal Expos, and although a little embarrassed to ask for his autograph, I did anyway. And in 2007, I got my Little Bigger League baseball autographed by none other than Ozzie Smith, the Cardinals' great shortstop. And I can't forget swallowing my pride and shaking hands with a certain former governor of Mississippi, even though I detested his politics. And even greater was my delight to have dessert with the personal A*ide de Camp* of Belgium's King Albert in the royal palace in Brussels.

But the most important person I ever met who has made the greatest difference in my life is Jesus, the Son of God. No, my first meeting with Jesus did not compare with Paul's experience on the road to Damascus, when Paul (Saul) fell from his horse, struck blind for three days. I was but a child when I came to Jesus, but the event is still meaningful to me, continuing to grow in significance with each passing year. Getting to know Jesus ought to be for each of us the greatest single event of our lives. Paul wrote, "I count all things to be loss in view of the surpassing value of knowing Christ Jesus my Lord!" (Philippians 3:8). To know Jesus Christ is to know "the power of His resurrection and the fellowship of His sufferings" (Philippians 3:10). It is a transformational event which brings life and hope to the sinner. When Jesus meets a person with a willing heart, He lays "hold" of that person and changes him for good. Paul wrote, "Not that I have already obtained it or have already become perfect, but

I press on so that I may lay hold of that for which also I was laid hold of by Christ Jesus" (Philippians 3:12).

It's not necessarily who *we* know, but Who knows *us*! Paul reminded the Galatians of this fact, when some of them were losing their initial enthusiasm for Christ. He wrote them in his letter, "But now that you have come to know God, or rather *to be known by God*, how is that you turn back again to the weak and worthless" things of the world? (Galatians 4:9).

Do *you* know Jesus my Lord? Does He know *you*? He wants to know you and is calling you to Him through His word. "Come to Me," he is saying, "Come to me, all who are weary and heavy-laden, and I will give you rest. Take My yoke upon you and learn from Me, for I am gentle and humble in heart, and you will find rest for your souls. For My yoke is easy and My burden is light" (Matthew 11:28-30).

Lakey and Ellis expressed this question in their popular song, "Do You Know My Jesus?"
Have you a heart that's weary, tending a load of care?
Are you a soul that's seeking rest from the burden you bear?
Where is your heart, oh, pilgrim, what does your light reveal?
Who hears your call for comfort when naught but sorrow you feel?
Who knows your disappointments, who hears each time you cry?
Who understands your heartaches, who dries the
tears from your eyes?
Do you know my Jesus? Do you know my friend?
Have you heard He loves you? And that He will abide till the end?

In God's own good time, He will send His Son to bring His children home. When will this be? We cannot know the day or the hour, but we know that we must be ready when He comes for His own. The heartfelt cry of the early church was "Maranatha!" – "O our Lord come!" (1 Corinthians 16:22).

BULLS-EYE!

THE WORD "BULLS-EYE" CAME INTO USE IN 1825, but no indication is given concerning its derivation. Whatever its derivation might have been, the word has come to be used of the center of a target, or something "central or crucial." Marksmen, using a bow and arrow or a firearm, have always aimed at the bulls-eye, and it is rare that one is able consistently to hit it.

Although the word "bulls-eye" does not occur in the Bible, Christians have been taught to take aim for the bulls-eye. Jesus taught, "Therefore, you are to be perfect, as your heavenly Father is perfect" (Matthew 5:48). "Perfection" thus becomes the "bulls-eye" for the Christian, the goal for which every one of us should strive. But it should be obvious to all that Christ was not saying that every disciple would have to be "perfect" in every aspect of life, since that would contradict many other teachings of the Bible. Nevertheless, the field of history is littered with the carcasses of "saints" who have attempted heroic exploits in their pursuit of perfection, only to find failure. When our Lord set up His spiritual "target," He was only teaching that His disciples should "aim" at *perfection*; He would never have suggested that we aim at *imperfection*. Had He suggested anything less than perfection, we would all achieve that goal, without even trying.

"All have *sinned* and fall short of the glory of God," wrote Paul (Romans 3:23). Although we might get things right sometimes, not one of us has hit the "bulls-eye" every time. The Greek word *hamartano* that Paul uses for "sin" means to *miss the mark*, or to *fall short* of a goal. Paul's readers would have thought of an archer practicing his skill with the bow, aiming at the distant bulls-eye, sometimes hitting it, but missing it most of the time.

Once, in Hattiesburg, Mississippi, I discussed this point with a very sincere man who affirmed that he was living a sinless life. It didn't take very long to demonstrate to this man that he was in error on that point. He had taken the words of Christ literally, and had thought that it is indeed possible to live a perfect, sinless, life. The apostle John wrote, "If we say that we *have no sin*, we are deceiving ourselves" (1 John 1:8). He further wrote that "If we say that we *have not sinned*, we make [God] a liar and His word is not in us" (1 John 1:10). John said we have not only sinned in the past, but we continue to sin in the present.

John's treatise was specifically written to counter the errors of Gnostic teachers who were infiltrating the churches of his day. Those false teachers denied the very *existence* of sin, claiming that *any action of the fleshly body was normal*, thus acceptable (cf. 2 Peter 2:1-3; Jude 1:4,8). Notice that John does not say that sin is acceptable. He *does* argue that "if we confess our sins, [Christ] is faithful and righteous to forgive us our sins and to cleanse us from all unrighteousness" (1 John 1:9).

In his letter to the Philippians, Paul discussed his own striving for "perfection." He had "counted as loss" everything he had previously held dear in order to "gain Christ" (Philippians 3:7-8). He recognized that he possessed no "righteousness of [his] own" but "that which is through faith in Christ, the righteousness which comes from God on the basis of faith" (Philippians 3:9). Paul wanted desperately to "know" Christ and to "lay hold of that for which also [he] was laid hold of by Christ Jesus" (Philippians 3:10-12). But, in spite of all Paul had done in his quest for perfection, he could not boast that he had "already obtained it" or that he had "already become perfect." He did, however, say that he was pressing on, actively pursuing the goal that Christ had set before him. "I press on," he wrote, "toward the goal for the prize of the upward call of God in Christ Jesus" (Philippians 3:14).

Paul clearly said he had not personally "attained perfection," and neither can we claim it. As did Paul, we must "press on toward the goal" (Philippians 3:14). If we have "this attitude," striving daily to be Christ-like in our words and actions, God will count us as His children, and will "credit" us with a "righteousness" earned for us by Christ (Romans 4:2-5).

Nowhere in Scripture is it hinted that imperfection is "okay." Nowhere does Christ suggest that *lukewarmness* is acceptable. Nowhere does our Lord say it is okay to "miss the bulls-eye." Soldiers in Caesar's armies were required to be excellent marksmen in order to win battles for Caesar. As Christian "soldiers" we also must "practice" our skills, so that as we fight Satan on the spiritual battlefields that are common to us all, we might be able to say with Paul, "I have fought the good fight, I have finished the course, I have kept the faith," and at the end of the battle, God will "award" to us "the crown of righteousness" (2 Timothy 4:7-8). So, fight the *good* fight, and always aim for the bulls-eye!

LESSONS FROM THE JORDAN VALLEY

FROM ITS SOURCE TO THE POINT WHERE IT EMPTIES into the "Salt Sea" (Joshua 3:16), now called the Dead Sea, the Jordan River traverses nearly 200 winding miles. It begins with hundreds of tiny rivulets from the crest of Mount Herman, in northern Galilee, dropping 900 feet in only ten miles as it flows into the marshy basin called the "Waters of Merom," at the base of the mountain. From Merom, its official beginning point, the Jordan becomes an ever-growing stream which eventually flows into the Sea of Galilee.

A tourist to Israel who wants to visit a possible site of the "Sermon on the Mount" will have to ride a bus around the northern shore of the Sea of Galilee, crossing a small bridge where the Jordon empties its waters into the lake. This beautiful sea is constantly receiving fresh water from Merom and numerous other smaller creeks and springs on every side. A living body of water, it teems with fish, not only providing food for thousands of people, but also the livelihood of the fishermen who have plied their trade there for thousands of years.

Some fourteen miles to the south, flowing out of the Sea of Galilee, the Jordan continues its journey to the Dead Sea. As it continues southward, it grows larger, receiving additional water from several smaller tributaries such as the Yarmuk, the Arnon (the Mojib) and the Jabbok (the Zerka), all flowing down from the mountains east of the Jordan, and at least three smaller streams entering on the western side. The Jordan is at times a swiftly flowing stream, dropping nearly a thousand feet from Merom to the Dead Sea.

Only a few miles south of the city of Jericho, which lies in its fruitful, green valley, the Jordan flows into the Dead Sea, a body of water never mentioned in the New Testament, but known in the Old Testament as the Sea of Salt. Any fish life from the Jordan quickly dies as it enters the Dead Sea. Since there is no outlet for water from this sea, except for evaporation, the sea retains everything that comes into it. A huge number of noxious chemicals are found in its water, so that no fish or other animal life can survive there. Although tourists enjoy "swimming" in the lake, they are strongly advised not to get water in their eyes or mouth. The water becomes so "heavy" that it is impossible for a swimmer to sink.

What a difference between the Sea of Galilee and the Dead Sea! It is no wonder that these two opposite bodies of water, so close geographically, have been used to illustrate some valuable life lessons that Christians need to remember.

Consider the wonderful song by Lula Klingman Zahn, "There is a Sea."

> There is a sea which day by day receives the rippling rills,
> And streams that spring from wells of God, or fall from cedared hills;
> But what it thus receives it gives, with glad unsparing hand;
> A stream more wide, with deeper tide, flows on to lower land.
>
> There is a sea which day by day receives a fuller tide;
> But all its store it keeps, nor gives, to shore nor sea beside.
> It's Jordan stream, now turned to brine, lies heavy as molten lead;
> Its dreadful name doth e'er proclaim that sea is waste and dead.
>
> Which shall it be for you and me, who God's good gifts obtain?
> Shall we accept for self alone, or take to give again?
> For He who once was rich indeed laid all His glory down,
> That by His grace our ransomed race should share
> His wealth and crown.

How true it is that Christ, the Son of God, willingly gave up His position in heaven (Philippians 2:6-9) to enrich us! "For you know the grace of our Lord Jesus Christ, that though He was rich, yet for your sake He became poor, so that you through His poverty might become rich" (2 Corinthians 8:9). When we imitate Christ as *liberal givers*, "zealous for good deeds" (Titus 2:14), we resemble the Sea of Galilee. We receive God's rich blessings, and we share them with others. This kind of giving often creates a virtual river of giving, which grows larger as it progresses.

However, if we receive God's liberal blessings but refuse to share them, we resemble the Dead Sea that receives but keeps everything for itself. Like the Dead Sea, the life that is in us dies. Like the Dead Sea, we stagnate. How tragic! As the song asks, "Which shall it be for you and me, who God's good gifts obtain? Shall we accept for self alone, or take to give again?

Words To Live By

ONWARD, CHRISTIAN SOLDIERS!

From the Swiss city of Montreux, we took the bus southward around scenic Lake Geneva, getting off at the Chillon stop. The massive walls of the turreted castle of Chillon rose high above us. Sitting several meters out from the shore, the castle was completely surrounded by water. Paying the entrance fee, we crossed the foot bridge and entered the castle through massive wooden gates. At some point, as we explored the castle, we entered the dark dungeon, some of which was below the level of the water. Small openings allowed a sparse light to penetrate the darkness; there was no air movement within the damp rooms which had been crudely carved out of solid rock.

As I studied that dreary space, I thought about the unhappy souls who had been imprisoned there. Escape would have been impossible. I already knew the name of Francois de Bonnivard who spent six miserable years there, chained by his feet to iron pins which still can be seen on the massive stone walls. A leader in the Swiss reformation movement, Bonnivard was finally rescued in 1536. Lord Byron, the English Romantic poet, wrote:

> Chillon! Thy prison is a holy place,
> And thy sad floor an altar – for 'twas trod,
> Until his very steps have left a trace
> Worn, as if thy cold pavement were a sod,
> By Bonnivard! – May none those marks efface!
> For they appeal from tyranny to God.
> (Sonnet on Chillon)

Nearly eighteen hundred years before Byron etched his name on a pillar of Chillon's dungeons, our Lord Jesus walked the holy ground of the Jerusalem temple, shouting words of warning to the scribes and Pharisees, "Jerusalem, Jerusalem, who kills the prophets and stones those who are sent to her! How often I wanted to gather your children together, the way a hen gathers her chicks under her wings, and you were unwilling. Behold, your house is being left to you desolate! For I say to you, from now on you will not see Me until you say, 'Blessed is He who comes in the name of the LORD!'" (Matthew 23:37-39).

The writer of *Hebrews* also wrote eloquently of those holy men and women of faith who had willingly given their lives for truth and righteousness: "(They) experienced mockings and scourgings, yes, also chains and imprisonment. They were stoned, they were sawn in two, they were tempted, they were put to death with the sword; they went about in sheepskins, in goatskins, being destitute, afflicted, ill-treated (men of whom the world was not worthy), wandering in deserts and mountains and caves and holes in the ground." (Hebrews 11:35-38).

May it please God that such sufferings never befall us! May peace and tranquility forever be the heritage of our children and grandchildren, so that their lives might be blessed by the sweet gospel of Jesus Christ. But if that happens not to be the case, and if persecution does afflict us and them, may we have the assurance and the faith that those before us had.

The apostle Paul encourages us to "be strong in the Lord and in the strength of his might," in order to "stand firm against" the devil (Ephesians 6:10). He reminds us that "our struggle" is against the "world forces of this darkness," against "the spiritual forces of wickedness," and he instructs us to arm ourselves with "the full armor of God" (Ephesians 6:12-13). We are Christian soldiers! We are spiritual combatants! We must train ourselves and strengthen what is weak, so as to be able to stand firm in the great battle being waged against us by the adversary. And we need to keep our eyes upon our Leader, Jesus Christ, "with all prayer and petition" (Ephesians 6:18), because He is the "Captain" (*King James Version*: Hebrews 2:10) of our salvation. Sabine Baring-Gould's great hymn encourages us:

> Onward, Christian soldiers, marching as to war,
> With the cross of Jesus going on before!
> Christ, the royal Master, Leads against the foe;
> Forward into battle, See His banners go!

Paul wrote that the word of God is the "sword of the Spirit." Will we be capable wielders of that "sword" when the time comes? We need to be able to "handle" the word of God "accurately" (2 Timothy 2:15), but unless we "practice" the use of this mighty "sword," it may prove not to be powerful in *our hands*. What about you and me? Are we studying daily how to use God's word? Are we practicing daily to be the "Christian soldiers" that we will need to be, that we *ought* to be? Peter urges us to *"grow* in the grace and knowledge of our Lord and Savior Jesus Christ" (2 Peter 3:18). He urges us to grow in faith, in moral excellence, in knowledge, in self-control, in our ability to keep on going, in godliness, in brotherly kindness and in love (2 Peter 1:5-7). We are told that if we "practice these things" we will never stumble. And our precious Lord will not be ashamed to own us as true soldiers of the cross.

THE MEDAL OF HONOR

Everett Knight, my mother's first cousin, was in his mid-twenties when, in the thick of battle and pinned down by Nazi machine gun fire from a nearby concrete bunker, he decided that his only hope for survival was to go on the offensive. Many of his soldier buddies lay dead or wounded and these would also die unless he could save them. So, he suddenly rose up and charged the bunker, firing as he ran, pausing only to toss grenades ahead of him. When eventually the smoke cleared, he had by himself destroyed the bunker, saved many of his comrades, and captured a host of German soldiers. For his valor and bravery under fire, Everett, known as "Son" by friends and family, received many medals for distinguished service.

The Congressional Medal of Honor is the highest medal awarded by the U.S. government, so comparatively only a few receive it. it is not something a person can seek. No one goes into battle planning to earn it. It cannot be bought or sold, and is awarded only to those who merit it because of truly heroic service.

I don't know if Son Knight received that medal, but I do know that his dreams were often haunted by the memories of what he considered to be terrible deeds done by him in the heat of battle. He found it almost impossible to forgive himself or to believe that God could forgive him for killing so many other human beings.

I think also of another "medal" of honor which is obtained by people who by their great faith and spiritual service receive it from the King of Kings and Lord of Lords. Paul wrote about it as he lay in a Roman prison for the third time, waiting for the imperial judgment (2 Timothy 4:6-8): "For I am already being poured out as a drink offering, and the time of my departure has come. I have fought the good fight, I have finished the course, I have kept the faith; in the future there is laid up for me the crown of righteousness, which the Lord, the righteous Judge, will award to me on that day; and not only

Words To Live By

to me, but also to all who have loved His appearing." A "*crown*," Paul said, will be "awarded" to him! This "crown," or "medal of honor," could not be bought, sold, or earned. It is "awarded" to those who "have loved" the Lord and have loved His "appearing." It is awarded to those who fight "the good fight," who finish "the course," and who keep "the faith." Paul reminisced to the Thessalonians about his struggles as he brought the gospel to them. He wrote, "For we wanted to come to you – I, Paul, more than once – and yet Satan hindered us. For who is our hope or joy or crown of exultation? Is it not even you, in the presence of our Lord Jesus at His coming? For you are our glory and joy." (1 Thessalonians 2:18-20).

I think of the first century church in the city of Smyrna, a "poor" church, yet spiritually "rich" (Revelation 2:9). Several years later, one of their elders, Polycarp, would die in flames, bound to a stake, because he would refuse to deny Christ. To this church, Jesus promised, "Be faithful until death, and I will give you the crown of life" (Revelation 2:10).

Unlike the Congressional Medal of Honor, which is awarded to only a few of the bravest of the brave, the "crown of life," or the "crown of righteousness," as Paul referred to it, will be awarded to "all who have loved His appearing." It is awarded by Christ to every faithful soldier of the cross, not just to those who, in our eyes, appear to be the most deserving. This is because we are saved by "grace" through "faith," and not by "works" (Ephesians 2:8). The soldiers who fight heroically on the front lines could not do so without those who faithfully labor, unseen and unknown, many miles from the fight, to keep them supplied. And the armies abroad could not survive without the continual service of those at home who work in the factories, or who struggle to keep the "home fires" burning.

The apostle Paul wrote to the Philippian church from Rome, during his two-year imprisonment there, addressing them as "my beloved brethren whom I long to see, my joy and crown" (Philippians 4:1). He urged them to "stand firm in the Lord." Paul was suffering on the "front lines" of the war, and he called these people back home his "crown." In a real sense, they "had his back." They were "concerned" about him and had more than once sent supplies to him while he was in prison (Philippians 4:10,18). In the same way, we have brothers and sisters who labor in difficult places far from home, and they need to know that we are there for them.

And when our time comes to leave this sinful world and go to be with the Lord, we can be assured that a "crown of life" awaits us – our own "medal of honor."

Words To Live By

PATRIOTISM - THE LAST "REFUGE" OF A "SCOUNDREL

"*PATRIE*" IS THE FRENCH WORD FOR "FATHERland." With just a few changes we have the English word "patriotism"— the love for or devotion to one's country. Boswell, the biographer of Samuel Johnson, recorded that on the evening of April 7, 1775, Johnson said, "The last refuge of a scoundrel is patriotism!" In other words, when someone finds himself in retreat because of some unwise or unethical action, his last line of defense is often to claim that he did it out of a sense of "patriotism."

The word *patriot* virtually overflows with emotional significance. I find it hard to believe that any true American would ever refuse to be called a "patriot." To do so would almost be to reject the founders of the American Republic, and the nearly unreachable dreams of those great men who, by signing *The Declaration of Independence*, pledged their very lives and fortunes. To refuse to be called a "patriot" would be tantamount to saying there *is* no "American Dream," that the magnificent experiment called "democracy" is unworkable. In 1776, this was a virtually unknown concept of government, but today nearly every form of despotism is glibly called "democratic."

No word so easily slips from the tongue of a politician as does the word "patriot." There is hardly a politician in Washington who would not identify himself as a "Patriot" with a capital "P." Once upon a time, however, politicians might have wanted to be identified with the name "Christian," but that day seems now to belong to the distant past. Although one might really *be* a "Christian," to actually *be known as such* could mean political death and obscurity. The public disdain for Christian principles and morality might, however, be nothing more than the mirror image of the spiritual temperature of the churches of America. It has always been true that, as children mimic their parents, and as students mimic their teachers, the people mimic their spiritual leaders, be they "priests" or "preachers." Rarely do the people rise above their spiritual leaders; rarely do politicians rise above those who elect them.

It is sad that in today's political climate *selfishness* has replaced *selflessness*, *ideology* has replaced *idealism*, and *avarice* has replaced *altruism*, concern for others. And since, in the eyes of many, our great country has become an undesirable place, patriotism, for many, has lost its primary significance. How can one have "patriotic feelings" regarding a "fatherland" which one does not love?

Of course, the Christian realizes that this land, even "America the Beautiful," is not his permanent dwelling place (Hebrews 11:13). We sing, "This world is not my home, I'm just a passing through," and although we really do mean those words, we also ought to realize that we are connected, in meaningful ways, to this world and to this country of which we are citizens. Paul exhorted Christians to "be in subjection to the governing authorities" (Romans 13:1), to pay their taxes (Romans 13:6-7), and to pray for civil rulers so that "we may lead a tranquil and quiet life in all godliness and dignity" (1 Timothy 2:2). When John warned not to "love the world" (1 John 2:15), he was not saying that we are wrong to love in any sense our earthly "fatherland," the towns or villages where we were brought up, or the homes where so many wonderful memories were made. Rather, he was warning not to be attached to the "worldly" society that is corrupt (Ephesians 2:1-3). He was saying that there is another "fatherland" which should attract us more, which will be ours when comes the time "of our departure" (2 Timothy 4:9). This future "fatherland," this *country* (from the Greek *patria*) which absorbs so much of the Christian's concentration, requires of us a "patriotism" which should far outstrip the sense of "patriotism" which we owe to America.

Can it truly be said of us that we are "patriots"? I hope so. But I also hope that when we call ourselves "patriots" we are telling the absolute truth. And may it be said of us that we are first and last, *Christian* patriots!

Words To Live By

RUNNING WITH THE FOOTMEN

AS A RULE, I HAVE THOUGHT OF MYSELF AS BEING a rather optimistic person. This way of thinking has come from my particular understanding of the word of God. My belief that God answers prayers and cares for His children on planet Earth has led me to believe that in the end, everything will turn out right. However, this line of reasoning has also caused many people to turn against God, since in many instances things do not have a positive conclusion, and instead of peace and harmony, there is hurt and despair.

Job's "friends," some hundreds of years before Christ, appear to have believed the falsehood that good things happen to good people and bad things happen to bad people. They chided Job day and night to confess his sins, to admit that he was not the good man he "pretended" to be. They urged him to "seek God," to "implore the compassion of the Almighty." They perhaps sneered as they mockingly said, "If you are pure and upright, surely now He would rouse Himself for you and restore your righteous estate" (Job 8:5). Many people today believe this idea, but they are in error. The fact remains that Job was indeed a righteous man. God was not *punishing* Job, but He was allowing him to be tested by Satan. For whatever reason, good things often happen to bad people, and bad things often happen to good people, and God allows it to be so.

Because of this, I have also become to some degree a *pessimist*! Do I believe that ultimately all will turn out well for the believer? Yes, of course! As a Christian, I have a hope "that does not disappoint" (Romans 5:5). Jesus Christ, the Son of God, died for me when I was helpless, and made a promise to me which He will not revoke, if I persevere to the end (Hebrews 3:6). *If I persevere to the end!* If I persevere, and "overcome," God will give me a "crown of life" (Revelation 2:10), but if I do not overcome, He will "erase" my name from His "book of life" (Revelation 3:5). And there is the rub!

I control, in part, what the future holds for me, and you are partially responsible for *your* future.

On a special trip to Texas, my wife and I sat reminiscing with a dear friend and former missionary colleague, J Lee Roberts, who passed from this life a short time later. We listened with attention as he described his service in World War II. J Lee told in detail how he had sloshed through mud and snow with other foot soldiers on their way through the Belgian Ardennes, during what Americans call the "Battle of the Bulge." Some soldiers rode in trucks, jeeps, or tanks, but most were "foot soldiers." To be able to endure as a foot soldier, one had to be in top physical condition. In Jeremiah's day, although there was the cavalry – the horsemen – most were foot soldiers. The foot soldiers had to keep up with the more rapid pace of the horsemen. When Jeremiah observed the sad spiritual condition of the people of Judah, he told them in no uncertain terms that they were woefully unprepared to face the hardships headed their way. "If you have run with footmen and *they* have tired you out," he wrote, "then how can you compete with *horses*?" (Jeremiah 12:5). "You will never be able to keep up," God was saying.

This is a valuable lesson for us today. My pessimistic side tells me that evil days are coming upon us. It may not be next week or next year, or even in our lifetime. But come they will, and we must be prepared. We must also prepare our children, because they are the ones who will most likely be affected by the "evil days" of which I am speaking. Who would have thought that North Korea would be a threat to the free world? Who would have predicted the horrible deeds that are being perpetrated against Christians in Africa and in the Middle East? And no one just thirty years ago could have predicted the degree to which America has lost her moral compass. This is not God's doing, no more that it was God who afflicted Job.

Evil days are coming! Will I be ready and able "to endure" them? I will need to have exercised myself morally and spiritually to have the strength to endure. Paul wrote:

Everyone who competes in the games exercises self-control in all things.

> They then do it to receive a perishable wreath, but we an imperishable.
> Therefore, I run in such a way, as not without aim;
> I box in such a way, as not beating the air;
> but I discipline my body and make it my slave,
> so that, after I have preached to others,
> I myself will not be disqualified.
> (1 Corinthians 9:25-27)

Paul essentially said what Jeremiah had said, that without exercise I will not be able to keep up. "If you have run with footmen and they have tired you out, then how can you compete with horses? If you fall down in a land of peace, how will you do in the thicket of the Jordan" (Jeremiah 12:5).

LIFTING THE BUS!

IT WAS MID-MORNING IN EARLY SPRING IN LONDON, England, when an urgent call alerted paramedics to a serious accident during rush hour traffic in the suburb of Walthamstow. A double-decker bus had crashed, running over a cyclist and pinning his legs beneath it. The situation appeared to be hopeless. A large crowd had quickly surrounded the bus, and assessing the dire state of the injured man, someone yelled for everyone to grab the bus and lift it off him. And they did! Within five minutes of the distress call, the paramedics arrived on the scene to find that the injured man had been rescued.

This rescue could not have been done by one man, not even by twenty strong men, but one hundred ordinary people who had been waiting at the bus stop combined their strength and lifted the bus, freeing the injured man. That's the power of the many.

It is true, however, that we must never underestimate the power of one single person, for there are many examples of what a truly determined individual can accomplish. But many such individual achievers are often people who by their example are able to rally others to a cause. In the early twentieth century, Mahatma Gandhi was one such person. But had multitudes of others *not* rallied behind him, Gandhi would have been forgotten.

Solomon wrote about "a certain man without a dependent" who had no heirs. "There was no end to all his labor," he wrote (Ecclesiastes 4:8). This man worked hard every day, deprived himself of pleasures, and amassed a large fortune, but his unceasing labor amounted to nothing in the long run. Then Solomon wrote, "*Two* are better than *one* because they have a good return for their labor. For if either of them falls, the one will lift up his companion" (Ecclesiastes 4:9-10). One person might do much, but "two are better than one." Solomon concluded that thought, saying, "And if one can overpower him who

Words To Live By

is alone, two can resist him. A cord of three strands is not quickly torn apart" (Ecclesiastes 4:12).

While one person can achieve much, some situations demand the cooperative effort of the many. Our Lord Jesus did not entrust the Good News to only one single person, but chose twelve men as His special messengers to the world. Although Christ appointed Paul to be the "apostle to the Gentiles" (Acts 9:15-16), He appointed the gentle encourager, Barnabas, to be Paul's special co-worker for the first missionary journey (Acts 13:2). In all of his subsequent travels, Paul chose other faithful workers to travel with him. Paul mentioned some of these men in his writings. He spoke of Timothy, a "kindred spirit" of "proven worth" who "served with me in the furtherance of the gospel" (Philippians 2:19-22), and of Epaphroditus, "my brother and fellow worker and fellow soldier, who is also your messenger and minister to my need" (Philippians 2:25). To the Romans, Paul spoke highly of Prisca and Aquila, a husband and wife team who were his "fellow workers in Christ Jesus," and who had "risked their own necks" for him (Romans 16:3-4).

What is the point in what I am saying? Is there a lesson here for us? Indeed, there is! There is power and strength in a group, strength enough to accomplish what one person could not accomplish alone. I have seen it many times in France and Belgium, where a single convert lived in a village or city far removed from the nearest congregation, where there was no one else of "like precious faith" (2 Peter 1:1) with whom to worship God on the Lord's Day, and where there was no other child of God from whom to seek encouragement and strength from day to day. And these precious souls scattered here and there, far from other believers, were often like leaves which were broken from the tree and left to dry up and die.

The *Hebrews* writer wrote of some Christians who had fallen into the habit of "forsaking our own assembling together" (Hebrews 10:25). He urged his Christian readers to "draw near with a sincere heart in full assurance of faith," so that might "consider how to stimulate one another to love and good deeds" (Hebrews 10:22-24). Paul wrote, "So we, who are many, are one body in Christ, and individually members one of another" (Romans 12:5). "Members one of another," Paul wrote. Our lives are so intertwined because of our common faith in Christ that we find it very difficult to survive alone. We survive together; we need each other. I need *you* and you need *me*. The person who does not realize this truth is similar to the young man in Christ's parable, who, thinking he would be better off on his own, gathered his belongings and left the security of his father's house only to end up alone, hungry and destitute in a far country (Luke 15:11-17).

Although not impossible, I think it is very hard to go to heaven alone. I believe that is why the Lord purposed congregations of believers. We need each other; we need the group. I cannot lift the bus by myself, but with the combined strength of the many, with God's help, we can!

Words To Live By

"ON THEIR BEHALF"

DON'T WE SOMETIMES LIKE TO JUST SIT AND RELAX, letting others take care of our every need? Maybe it's at a nice restaurant where the servers are constantly passing by our table to refill our tea or coffee. Or maybe it's on a tour where we just follow the professional guide and listen as he or she explains what we are seeing. We don't even have to worry about where we're going next; we just get on the bus when told to and take our seat to the next destination. Everything is done for us.

But while that can be very enjoyable, the inverse can also be great fun. I'm talking about *doing things for others*. Serving those who perhaps cannot afford to do some things for themselves, or who are physically incapable of doing certain necessary things. We could do things *"on their behalf."*

Jesus taught His disciples, both by word and example, unforgettable lessons about service to others. When the Twelve apparently forgot all about common courtesy in their mad dash to get the best seats at their last Passover meal with Jesus, it was the Lord who got up to wash *their* feet (John 13:12-17). Their thoughts that evening were for *self*, not for *others*, not even for their Lord. The Lord therefore became the servant, as Isaiah the prophet had foretold over six hundred years before (Isaiah 52:13ff). He did for the disciples what they should have been doing for Him.

In His great prayer later that same evening, Jesus said to the Father, "I ask *on their behalf*; I do not ask on behalf of the world, but of those whom You have given Me; for they are Yours" (John 17:9). *"For their sakes* I sanctify Myself, that they themselves also may be sanctified in truth. I do not ask on behalf of these alone, but for those also who believe in Me through their word" (John 17:19-20). This, therefore, includes us, you and me. Jesus prayed not only for the Twelve, but for "those also who believe in Me through their word." Jesus died *for you and me*, and for anyone else who comes to Him in humble faith.

"on Their Behalf"

What Jesus did for His disciples on that holy evening serves as an example for us. We should be involved *in service to others*, following that great example. We should be thinking of doing things *"on behalf"* of others.

Before his conversion, Saul of Tarsus had tried to destroy the church, and many godly men and women had suffered at his hands (Acts 22:19-20; 26:9-10). After his conversion, as Paul, the Apostle to the Gentiles, he himself was called upon to suffer for Christ. Paul did not object to this, but instead he said, "I rejoice in my sufferings *for your sake*, and in my flesh I do my share *on behalf of His body*, which is the church, in filling up what is lacking in Christ's afflictions" (Colossians 1:24). Paul suffered *"on behalf of"* the church! He suffered *for their sake*.

Sometimes, in anger or impatience, someone may cry out, "For God's sake, just do it!" The expressions "For God's sake!" or "For Christ's sake!" should not be so lightly used. When we say "for God's sake" we should *really* mean "for the sake of God." In fact, everything that we do should be for "God's sake." That is, "on behalf of" God, or "on behalf of Christ." Paul suffered "on behalf of" the body of Christ.

What about you and me? Do we ever do something "on behalf of" the church? For the "sake of" the church? There are many ways of doing something "for Christ's sake." Consider the following:

- We should obey the laws of the land *"for the Lord's sake"* (1 Peter 2:13).

- We should bear it patiently when we are misrepresented or treated harshly *"for the sake of conscience toward God"* (1 Peter 2:19-20).

- We should be on the lookout for people in need, because when we clothe, provide food or medical assistance for the needy, the poor, or the orphans, we do it *for the Lord* (Matthew 25:40).

- When we faithfully use the "gifts" recorded in Romans 12:6-13, we are *serving the body of Christ*. These gifts include *teaching, encouraging, giving, leading, showing mercy* and *love*.

- We must always be careful to treat our brothers and sisters with proper respect, for "he who in this way *serves Christ* is acceptable to God and approved by men" (Romans 14:18).

The beautiful song *None of Self and All of Thee* concludes with these words:

Higher than the highest heavens,
Deeper than the deepest sea,
Lord, Thy love at last has conquered,
None of self, and all of Thee,

THE "LOWER" LIGHTS

THE VILLAGE NESTLED ON A STEEP INCLINE ON THE shore of the North Sea was home to perhaps a hundred people, mostly fishermen. A small bay with a rocky beach lay below it in a semi-circle. There were no boats at anchor in the bay; all of the able-bodied men and older boys had left early that morning for a long day of fishing. Now it was late and darkness had fallen. The weather had taken a sudden turn for the worst and the gusting winds had begun to howl. Heavy rain was blowing hard and churning waves were rolling into the bay.

The womenfolk of the village were greatly concerned for the safety of their husbands, sons, and brothers, but what could they do? On the point of the cliff high above the village, the lighthouse was sending forth a strong light which even in the storm could be seen for miles, warning passing ships that a dangerous shore was near and that they should keep their distance. This lighthouse also was signaling the fishermen of the village that their home lay in that direction, but in the deep darkness and the harsh blowing rain, how could they determine exactly where lay the shoreline of the bay where they could anchor their boats? The answer lay with the "lower lights."

Every woman who could walk rushed out to the shore of the bay, carrying lanterns. They lined up on the beach around the bay, waving their lights, hoping that the fishermen in distress could see them and be guided to safety. To be sure, the great lighthouse on the hill was important, even necessary, but the "lower lights" were also necessary, since they were the "lights" which would guide the fishermen to the safety of the bay.

A favorite song by P. P. Bliss was based upon such a scenario as I have described:

Brightly beams our Father's mercy from His lighthouse ever-more,
But to us He gives the keeping of the lights along the shore.

Words To Live By

Dark the night of sin has settled, loud the angry billows roar;
Eager eyes are watching, longing for the lights along the shore.
Trim your feeble lamp, my brother! Some poor sailor, tempest-tossed,
Trying now to make the harbor, in the darkness may be lost.

Chorus:

Let the lower lights be burning, send a gleam across the wave!
Some poor fainting, struggling seaman, you may rescue, you may save.

Our Lord Jesus tells us that, as His disciples, we are "the light of the world" (Matthew 5:14). We are the "lights along the shore" that those who are tossed by the angry billows can see and be led to safety. If we do not "trim our feeble lamps," how can those who are lost find their way home? Sometimes, those who call themselves "Christians" do not conduct themselves as Christians should, and the "light" that is in them is "darkness" (Matthew 6:23), compounding the problem for the lost. Those who are supposed to be "guides" are leading them in the wrong direction. If I, for example, trying to lead someone to Christ, am not living as a Christian should, the lost person whom I am trying to influence will very likely be turned away because of my hypocrisy. My actions will speak louder than my words. I will be recognized to be a fake, a sham, and I will have no influence for good.

Paul said we should be "examples" or "illustrations" of *proper* speech, *godly* conduct, *real* love, *fervent* faith, and *moral* purity (1 Timothy 4:12). Peter wrote that we should "keep our behavior excellent among the Gentiles" so that they will be able to "observe" our good deeds and be led to Christ (1 Peter 2:12).

Obviously, we cannot save everybody, but we *can save some*. We can be "lights along the shore" that guide some poor lost soul home to God.

WHO ARE YOUR HEROS?

ALEX RODRIGUEZ, STAR THIRD BASEMAN FOR THE New York Yankees, was suspended for 211 consecutive games because he took performance enhancing drugs. It was in all the news.

I suppose that, as a teenager, I loved baseball about as much as any of my friends did. I played left field in the Babe Ruth League. I could recognize the names of star players in the Major Leagues, and knew the teams they played for. I still enjoy watching baseball, football, soccer, basketball, hockey, and golf, but I do not idolize any of the players. I am thrilled when I see a spectacular play in any of these sports. However, I do not count any sports figure to be a "hero" or "role model" simply because he or she happens to be a great player.

In fact, we must be careful as we search for "role models," whether in sports, politics, military, or even in religion. In all of these categories, there are some "players" who will disappoint us. They are, after all, still human, with "feet of clay."

There are, nevertheless, numerous people who have served as role models for me. Some of these are historical characters, imperfect of course, but still worthy of emulation, still worthy of my admiration. One of these is the great French statesman, Victor Hugo, who stood firm for the Republic, and was for his pains forced into exile. Another, closer home, was George Washington, the "Father" of our great nation, who served two terms without salary, as our first president. Several of my teachers at Freed-Hardeman College, and some colleagues at David Lipscomb University, such as the late Batsell Barrett Baxter, touched my life and served me well as Christian models of faith and humility.

The writer of *Hebrews* provided a list of faithful men and women of Old Testament fame, "of whom the world was not worthy" (Hebrews 11:38), suggesting that we should imitate *their* faith. Then, utilizing a sports analogy, he suggested that in the same way that these godly men and women had faithfully run *their* race, we also should run "with endurance the race that is set before *us*" (Hebrews 12:1). And, of course, the greatest hero of all, Jesus, who "endured the cross," stands at the head of the list as one whom we must admire and imitate. "For consider Him who has endured such hostility by sinners against Himself, so that you will not grow weary and lose heart" (Hebrews 12:3).

Too often, we discover fatal flaws in our human heroes. Too often, they disappoint us. Does that mean that we should not think of men and women today as "role models"? Of course not! Only that we should not elevate them so highly, or place in them so much trust, that if or when they fail us, we are left with nothing. We should learn to imitate the good qualities of a person and reject that which is not good.

On the flip side, we should strive to live in such a way that someone might consider us to be role models. Consider what the apostle Paul said to Timothy: "Let no one look down on your youthfulness, but rather in speech, conduct, love, faith and purity, show yourself an example of those who believe" (1 Timothy 4:12). Although much younger than Paul, Timothy was a grown man, probably in his late twenties or early thirties when Paul wrote this letter to him. As compared to Paul, Timothy was "youthful." And as a "young" man, he might have been esteemed less than if he were older. Young preachers often live "in the shadow" of older, more experienced preachers, so Paul counseled Timothy not to give that a second thought, but to conduct himself in such a way that people would view *him* as an example of what *they* ought to be. "Those who believe" need models of proper speech, models of conduct, models of love, of faith, and of purity. Timothy was called on to serve as such a model.

You and I are also called to serve as models. We should remember that someone is always looking at us, whether at our work place, at the grocery store, at school, or at church. Little eyes are also watching, and little ears are listening as we speak, and are making judgments concerning us.

We are indeed serving as "role models." It is up to us to decide whether we will serve as good models or bad ones.

YOUTH FOR GOD!

IMAGINE JEREMIAH WAS IN ABSOLUTE SHOCK. HE had just learned from Yahweh (Jehovah) about his appointment as a "prophet to the nations" (Jeremiah 1:5). Jeremiah's dismay is revealed by his emotional cry, "Alas, Lord God! Behold, I do not know how to speak, because I am a youth." Just a "youth"! Already listed among "the priests," Jeremiah was certainly no child. Nevertheless, he was young, perhaps in his early twenties, not yet married (Jeremiah 16:1-4). He saw himself as unprepared by reason of experience and age to accomplish what Yahweh was asking of him.

But God chose *him*! Jeremiah was not the first young person to be chosen by God for a great task, nor would he be the last. We remember that God chose young Joseph to eventually be the savior of his family, preserving and training him for the task through various struggles and trials (Genesis 45:5). Joseph, as a young man, did not realize that God was preparing him for service, but he maintained his moral purity and integrity during times of great stress and trial, and God was able to use him in a powerful way.

God would much later use four other men who, as young boys, had been forcibly removed from their families. These young men came to be known in Babylon as Shadrach, Meshach, Abed-nego, and Belteshazzar (Daniel). Young people have been inspired for generations to imitate the great faith and confidence displayed by these young men. Even as young boys, they made up their minds (Daniel 1:8-13) not to "defile" themselves with the food that the Babylonians required them to eat. These were godly young people who, even in difficult circumstances, separated from their parents, and taken to a foreign country and culture, committed themselves to right living and obedience to God.

Then there was the young man Timothy, whose lifestyle and faith were such that the apostle Paul chose him as a missionary companion. Luke writes that Timothy "was *well spoken of* by the brethren who were in Lystra and Iconium" (Acts 16:1-3).

We remember Ruth, Naomi's young daughter-in-law, who faithfully stood by Naomi, choosing Yahweh, the God of Israel, to be her God, and who became an ancestor of Jesus of Nazareth (Ruth 1:16-17; 4:17). There was also the beautiful young Jewish girl, Esther, who was chosen by the Persian King Ahasuerus to be his wife (Esther 2:8-9). Esther's excellent conduct in the palace led to "favor and kindness" on the part of the king, so that when she desperately needed the king's help for her people who were threatened with annihilation, she was able to prevail (Esther 4:13-14; 7:1-7.) The aged King Solomon, perhaps reflecting upon his own youth and regretting his many later errors, urged young people of his day, and us as well: "Remember also your Creator in the days of your youth, before the evil days come and the years draw near when you will say, 'I have no delight in them.'" (Ecclesiastes 12:1). How well I remember hearing Solomon's admonition for the first time. What an impression that made on my young heart! I resolved early in my teens to serve God. To be perfectly honest, I was quite ignorant of the kinds of opportunities that would come my way, and did not know how God might use me, but before I finished grade eleven of high school, I decided I wanted to preach the gospel. Before I went to college, God had provided me several pulpits in south Mississippi in which I developed my speaking abilities. And before my eighteenth birthday, I had decided to be a missionary in French-speaking Europe. God works in mysterious ways! Looking back, I can see how God has used me and my wife in ways we could not have imagined.

I urge young people to commit their lives to God's service, and not to be content just to "come to church," but to choose to serve in specific ways. The church needs godly examples for future young people. The little ones among us will need good role models as they grow up. You may say, "I am just a youth! What can I do?" In the first place, you can do like Joseph and keep yourself morally pure. You can participate in the worship services at your church. You can make a greater effort to really learn God's word in your Bible classes. And you can think about how God might use you as you develop into adulthood. The church will need Bible School teachers, deacons, and elders. If you do not think about these things now, you might be hardened later against them, as Solomon said in Ecclesiastes. I have seen young people who had great promise and ability turn away from God. This world is a dangerous place for the young. Temptations are strong, and many are they who "mess up" their lives even before they become adults.

The psalmist asks the right question and gives the correct answer: "How can a young man keep his way pure? By keeping it according to Your word" (Psalm 119:9). My wish for the youth of the church is that they will be able to say with the psalmist, "With all my heart I have sought You!" (Psalm 119:10).

Words To Live By

A SAD, SAD STORY

I SAT READING FROM "COVER TO COVER" THE *Chester County Independent*, the weekly newspaper that kept me somewhat attached to Henderson, the west Tennessee town we lived in for over twenty years. Suddenly, a name caught my eye in the "Your Right to Know" section. A young woman named "C..." had been arrested and incarcerated in the local jail. How could I not remember the sweet young girl whom I had baptized about eight or nine years previously!

It would be pointless to trace the stained trail of her spiritual descent that led to this result. We saw her grandmother just a few days later and learned still more of her sad story, a story that has affected many people who loved and still love her. I write about it today with a heavy heart.

This morning, in my car, the radio happened to be tuned to A.M. 650, where Conway Twitty was singing a somewhat "lusty" song that I had never heard. "Gotta' be bad to have a good time," he sang. What a sad "philosophy" that is! "Gotta' be bad to have a good time"! Although this philosophy is espoused and followed by multitudes, it is a *bankrupt* philosophy. It leads unfailingly to moral ruin, and life's highway is littered with the spoiled and wrecked lives of those who believe and practice it. Solomon warned his "son" not to accept the invitation of the "adulteress" who "flatters with her words" and tries to seduce him (Proverbs 2:16-20). "Her house sinks down to death," he said. "And her tracks lead to the dead; none who go to her return again, nor do they reach the paths of life." He further said that although her lips "drip honey" and her speech is "smoother than oil," in the end she is "bitter as wormwood" (Proverbs 5:3-4).

Inexperienced young people, especially, are more likely to fall for Satan's great lie – "Gotta' be bad to have a good time." I say, therefore, to the teens among us that it is a *fatal* lie, a *blatant* falsehood, that you can't have a "good time" while being good. The prophet

Isaiah spoke of people who "call evil good, and good evil" (Isaiah 5:20), but that is what is happening today all over America. The folks in Hollywood whose chief goal is to make a lot of money have continually "pushed the envelope" of accepted morality, gradually urging and leading toward a society where nothing is really wrong and nothing is really right, as long as you have no problem with it. It took a generation to accomplish it, but Hollywood has been able to convince America that "bad" is really "*good*," or if not "*good*," it is at least *okay*!

Our society has gone down the path of relativism and has arrived at the brink of a moral precipice, over which many are leaping to their own destruction. The sad thing is that they are often so "loaded" and "stoned" that they don't even know what they are doing. Marriage is no longer considered to be a permanent situation, and by many is even deemed to be an unnecessary bother. People just decide to live together with no real sense of commitment. The result is that many children are raised by single mothers, sometimes never even knowing their dad. Beyond that, liberal politicians have legislated "same sex marriage," laying the foundation for the complete destruction of marriage as we know it. And some states across America are legalizing marijuana, making it available in retail stores, thus sending the message to young people that this "gateway" drug is not harmful.

When "evil" is marketed as being "not so bad," it is not surprising that many people are tempted to "try" it. Just once, they say. They don't intend to become "addicted." "Just a little won't hurt," they think. However, rules exist to prevent us from harming ourselves and others, by doing things "just once." The news reported that a man fell to his death from the South Rim of the Grand Canyon. Yes, there are signs warning people not to get too close to the edge. I don't know why this person fell, but I do know that he got too close to the edge. The Law of Moses functioned somewhat like the signs at the Grand Canyon, warning people not to do certain things, warning them of consequences if they do them anyway. And a lot of people just don't like rules or laws. Rules keep them from "having fun," so they ignore the rules, have their "fun" and often receive tragic consequences.

Words To Live By

Two opposite lifestyles are available to us. We can either set our mind on the "flesh," or on the "Spirit" (Romans 8:5-6). The one brings "death," and the other brings "life and peace." The choice is ours, as individuals. What will be *my* choice? I chose many years ago to follow the lead of Jesus Christ, the Son of God, and I have observed the faithfulness of my Savior.

ARE YOU A GOOD DRIVER?

SEVERAL YEARS AGO, WHILE STUDYING SPANISH IN Cuernavaca, my wife and I decided to visit "Las Grutas," a huge cavern in Mexico reputed to be "the largest cavern in the world." To get there we bought tickets on the Mexican version of Greyhound, called "La Flecha Roja," – the "Red Arrow." Being among the first to board the bus, we took the choice front seats so as not to miss any of the scenery along the way. This was probably a mistake. Since the cavern was in the central Mexican mountains, we were treated to the driver's fantastic skills, as we raced along the narrow highway, making hairpin turns, hardly slowing down. From our front seats, we could literally look straight down into the valley below as the bus made the turns. The seats we occupied were not for sissies! After visiting the impressive caverns, we waited for an hour by the road for a return bus. As we boarded, we found there were no seats remaining. People were standing in the aisle, all the way to the back. Some passengers had chickens and other small animals. My wife had to sit on the motor cover, by the driver, facing the rear, while I stood in the open door of the bus, holding on for dear life! The door was broken and could not be closed. We marveled again at the skills of the man to whom we had committed our lives.

The Bible speaks of life as being a "walk" (Ephesians 4:1), although at times it can resemble the *wild ride* just described. It is also called a "pilgrimage" (Hebrews 11:13; 1 Peter 2:11) or a "journey." Peter tells us to be careful as we travel along, urging us as "aliens and strangers to abstain from fleshly lusts which wage war against the soul." The journey is dangerous, so Peter warns us to "be of sober spirit," to be "on the alert" (1 Peter 5:8), because "the devil" is on the prowl "like a roaring lion, seeking someone to devour." In some ways, we are like drivers on life's highways, rushing here or there. What kind of driver are we? It sometimes seems that we are in such a rush to get to our final destination that we take extraordinary risks.

Words To Live By

Our Mexican driver was responsible for perhaps seventy or more lives that day, but you couldn't tell it by the way he drove. Sometimes, the way *we* "drive," or conduct our lives, might make people wonder if we value life or the lives of those in our care. I learned to drive a car on graveled country roads where one would only occasionally meet another car or truck. Since there was no "driver education" course offered in the schools, our parents or an older sibling would show us how to shift gears, "give it the gas," or put on brakes. So it is that often in life children grow up with little or no instruction on how to live. Their parents learned on their own, so they may offer no corrections, no advice, to their children. They grow up thinking they are "excellent drivers," but the outcomes of their lives say otherwise.

People who abuse alcohol often rationalize their behavior by claiming that they only hurt themselves, but that is not true. Although the drinker's first victim is himself, nearly everyone in the family is harmed to some extent. Marriages are destroyed, even if there is no divorce. Because a parent's example is so strong, either for good or bad, children often imitate the behavior of their parents, becoming drinkers themselves. The same thing can be said of all the other vices. Bad drivers are not good driving instructors; bad character does not breed good character.

From his jail cell in Bedford, England, the preacher John Bunyan sent forth his wonderful book, *The Pilgrim's Progress*, in which he described the adventures of a character named "Christian," as he walked on his way to the Celestial City. From his prison in Rome, the apostle Paul sent instructions to the Christians at Ephesus on how to "walk" on *their* journey. Paul wrote, "I implore you to walk in a manner worthy of the calling with which you have been called, with all humility and gentleness, with patience, showing tolerance for one another in love" (Ephesians 4:1-2). He spoke of the lifestyle of the Gentiles who "walk in the futility of their mind, being darkened in their understanding." These, Paul wrote, are "callous," having "given themselves over to sensuality for the practice of every kind of impurity with greediness." But, says he, "You did not learn Christ in this way" (Ephesians 4:17-20).

We need to examine our lifestyle, our manner of walking as Christians. Everything we do affects our families, our friends, even people we might not know well. How we live is important. *My* misconduct affects not just *myself*, but my spouse, and my children as well. As Paul instructed Timothy, we should also show ourselves as good examples in "speech, conduct, love, faith and purity" (1 Timothy 4:12).

I sincerely doubt that the driver of *La Flecha Roja* thought much about our feelings that day. Was he a good driver? He may have thought so. He did keep the old bus between the ditches, as we say, but he scared the living daylights out of us! What about you and me? Spiritually speaking, how is our "driving"?

Words To Live By

C'MON! IT'LL BE All RIGHT!

FOLLOWING A PERIOD OF TORRENTIAL RAINS, IT was a sunny day. As an insurance agent and registered representative for a brokerage firm, I had an important appointment with a potential client. To avoid the flooding Big Black River, I had taken the long road around through the tiny village of Carlisle, Mississippi. As I slowly drove through the village, I passed a country store on the left, where several smiling teenage boys stood on the porch watching me drive by. Ahead was the railroad, and on the other side I could see the whitewashed Methodist church where, as a child, I had wept during a film showing of the crucifixion of Jesus.

As I drove across the railroad tracks, I was dismayed to see the road ahead covered with water. I stopped my car and stared. Just ahead I could see the one-lane bridge across Bayou Pierre. Suddenly a pickup truck rushed past me, into the water and over to the bridge, where it stopped. One of the boys I had seen earlier motioned to me, shouting, "C'mon! It'll be all right!" So, I drove into the water, pulled up onto the bridge and stopped, terrified! The creek was raging beneath me, just two feet below the car, and on the other side there was water as far as I could see. The road could not be seen. The boys in the pickup were jubilant! They were laughing and having great fun at my expense. "C'mon!" they repeated. I shook my head, in disbelief at my stupidity. My life was in danger. I slowly backed the car off the bridge, and fortunately made my way back through the water to the country store, where my whole body began to shake uncontrollably. I there learned that I actually knew two of those boys, having gone to school with their father and aunt many years before.

Too often, we listen to the seductive voices around us that assure us that "everything will be all right." The prophet Jeremiah spoke of those who assure us of "peace, peace," when there is no peace (Jeremiah 8:11). We hear the smooth, silky voice of Satan as he assured Eve that she could without fear taste the forbidden fruit (Genesis 3:4-5).

The written words of the apostle Paul were sometimes twisted by his enemies to make them mean something totally different from what he intended (2 Peter 3:16), but those who so "twist" the word of God do so at their own peril and to "their own destruction." An example of such "twisting" is found in Romans 3:8. Paul had been teaching that "where sin increased, God's grace abounded all the more" (Romans 5:21), but some people twisted this to make Paul say that it is okay to "do evil" if the result is "good." They said, in effect, "The ends justify the means!"

Peter wrote about the Gnostic sects which sometimes infiltrated Christian congregations with the design to "introduce destructive heresies," in an attempt to deceive gullible Christians. He warned the churches about their "false words" (2 Peter 2:1-3). These people "indulge the flesh in its corrupt desire," Peter wrote. They "count it a pleasure to revel in the daytime." They have "eyes full of adultery that never cease from sin, enticing unstable souls" (2 Peter 2:10-14). But those who are enticed by these people will discover, perhaps too late, that they are "springs without water and mists driven by a storm" (2 Peter 2:17). The "freedom" that they promise disappears like the morning mist, as soon as the light of the sun shines on it. Such deceptive teachers promise what they cannot deliver and those who follow them will perish. "C'mon!" they say! "It'll be all right!" But it is often too late and their followers are enslaved (2 Peter 2:19). Examples of such "enslavement" include drug addiction, alcohol addiction, porn addiction, and gambling addiction. "C'mon," they say. "One time won't hurt you!"

Perhaps the strongest addiction of all is "sexual" addiction, which is why the Bible so often warns the "young man" to avoid immorality. "My son," wrote Solomon, "give attention to my wisdom...For the lips of an adulteress drip honey and smoother than oil is her speech; but in the end, she is bitter as wormwood...Her feet go down to death...She does not ponder the path of life; her ways are unstable, she does not know it." (Proverbs 5:1-6). Solomon told his son that "When your flesh and your body are consumed" you will say, "How I have hated instruction!" "I have not listened to the voice of my teachers" (Proverbs 5:11-13). This is perhaps why Paul wrote: "Flee immorality. Every other sin that a man commits is outside the body, but the immoral man sins against his own body" (1 Corinthians 6:18).

Immorality affects one's body in ways that other sins do not, and for that reason is exceedingly dangerous and difficult to deal with.

The world may say, "C'mon! It'll be all right," but you should beware the rushing floodwaters just below your feet that threaten to overpower you and take your life. The boys who told me, "C'mon! It'll be all right," were just having fun at my expense, but it could have cost me my life.

COULD'A, WOULD'A, SHOULD'A!

HOW MANY TIMES HAVE WE SEEN OTHER PEOPLE perform some spectacular act or deed, and said, "I could'a done that!" I have often joked, "If I had any talent, I could have been a great musician, too!" Right! Maybe and maybe not. Having great talent is no guarantee for success. "Could'a" has no intrinsic worth. All it indicates is *possibility*. The music world is littered with the carcasses of unfulfilled talent. I remember once years ago sitting at our kitchen table, listening with amazement as a young woman sang for us. I think I have never heard a more beautiful voice. Afterward, she expressed some bitterness that others with lesser talent were looked upon as "stars."

On the other hand, there are those with less talent who have accomplished great things. I think of Charles (not his real name), who, in my opinion, had little talent as a preacher. His grammar was atrocious. Yet Charles was a great servant, with much zeal. Perhaps because he could find no congregation in the South that would accept him, He took his family north to a metropolitan area where in just a few years he built a solid congregation. He possessed much more than just "possibility." He had great desire and used his energy to succeed. I had badly misjudged my friend.

Then there are the "would'a" people. "I would'a done it if...." These people believe they were somehow hindered from doing what they think they "could'a" done. They perhaps believe somebody else is the reason they did not succeed. Or perhaps they feel they never got the opportunity to do what *they* believed themselves capable of doing. They don't realize "opportunities" do not randomly occur; they are *made*! If we wait around for opportunities to do good, we will never do the good things of which we are capable.

In fact, opportunities *to do good* abound. While it is certainly true that we cannot take advantage of every opportunity to do good, we are nevertheless able to do *something*. The apostle Paul wrote to the

Colossian Christians, asking them to pray for him and his companions, that God would "open up to us a door for the word" (Colossians 4:3). Paul had his eyes open for opportunities. He believed that the prayers of Christian people would help him as he worked. Then he wrote, "Conduct yourselves with wisdom toward outsiders, making the most of the opportunity" (Colossians 4:5). Every day, we meet people we don't know, in stores, on the street, or at work. Most of the time we just walk on by, and by walking on by, we probably miss opportunities for good. Once I encountered an elderly lady on the street as she stood handing out promotional religious literature to passersby, and I just walked on by without speaking to her. Feeling guilty, I hastily returned, and within a minute I had arranged for Bible studies with her which led not only to her conversion but to that of several of her friends. Open doors that are ignored may never again be opened, and "I would'a" cannot be used as a valid excuse.

I "should'a" is the most heartrending of the three expressions. Many bitter tears have been shed by people who missed opportunities, or who did not make good use of their abilities when they could have, and by those who did not do what they could have done, because they just *would not*! They are now left only with regret that they "should'a" done those things, but didn't, and now it is too late.

"Didn't" is the operative word. I **could' a**, but didn't! I **would'a**, but didn't! I **should'a** but didn't, and the responsibility is all mine. Jesus taught several parables about people who "hear" but do not "act upon" what they hear (Matthew 7:24). He said, "I was hungry, and you gave me nothing to eat; I was thirsty, and you gave me nothing to drink" (Matthew 25:42), and the people answered, "When did we *not* do these things?" Jesus told them that when they "*did not do* these things" to other people in need, they "did not do" them to Him.

They "should have," but they did not. Could'a, would'a, should'a, but didn't. So sad! The Quaker poet, John Greenleaf Whittier, wrote:

> For all sad words of tongue and pen,
> The saddest are these, "It might have been."

EXCUSES! EXCUSES!

THE WEATHER COULDN'T HAVE BEEN WORSE. The snow and ice almost made it impossible to get to the small backwoods church in McNairy County, Tennessee. I was presenting a series of lessons on the book of Revelation, and in spite of the weather a good number of people came out every evening to hear me. The elderly preacher invited my wife and me to have dinner at his home on the following Sunday. Knowing that the good sister was a great cook, we were looking forward to the occasion. Sunday came, and following the morning service with my regular congregation, we went home, ate lunch, and settled in for a leisurely afternoon. An hour or so later, the phone rang. As soon as I heard the voice on the other end of the line, I knew we had forgotten the Sunday dinner. My heart sank. I had forgotten all about it. What could I say? No excuse could possibly ease the disappointment and hurt which was obvious in the voice of the elderly brother. They had invited other guests and family members, but we were to be the guests of honor, and we had forgotten. They had gone ahead and eaten without us. The invitation was not extended a second time and I have never completely gotten over it. How could I have treated these people like that!

Jesus told a similar story. "A man was giving a big dinner, and he invited many" (Luke 14:16-24). When the time for the dinner arrived, the man sent servants to each one of his invited guests, only to hear that each of them had other things to do and could not come. Like me, they had excuses. One of them claimed he needed to check on some land he had bought. A second said he needed to try out some oxen he had recently purchased. A third man said he had just gotten married and could not come. Since the meal was on the table and everything was prepared, the host sent his servants into the streets with instructions to "bring in here the poor and crippled and blind and lame" (Luke 14:21). Since there was still room, he again sent his servants out into the highways and along the hedges where the extremely poor would likely seek some kind of shelter, and to "compel" them to come, "so that my house may be filled." But, the host said, "None of these men who were invited shall taste of my dinner!"

Although I think that *my* excuse ("I forgot about it!") was better than the excuses offered by the men in the Lord's story, the result was the same. *I did not eat the dinner which was prepared for me!* And there was no other invitation.

Oh, we always have reasons for the things we do and even for the things we don't do, but which we were supposed to do. We call them "reasons," not "excuses." "Reasons" sounds better. But most of the time there is really no difference between "reasons" and "excuses." When we talk about other people, we say they offer "excuses," but when *we* try to get out of doing something we don't really want to do, we say we have "reasons" for not doing these things. And, really, when we analyze Jesus' story, we sense that the men who offered excuses really *did not want to go* to the dinner in the first place. The "excuses" they offered were not valid reasons. The fact is they treated the dinner invitation with utter contempt, and the host saw through their false excuses.

Jesus told His story on a Sabbath day while He was enjoying a leisurely lunch with a group of men, among whom were some "lawyers and Pharisees" (Luke 14:3). Having noticed how some of these men had sought out the seats of honor at the table (Luke 14:7), Jesus commented to the host that it would be better to invite to his receptions "the poor, the crippled, the lame and the blind" (Luke 14:12-13), instead of his friends and relatives. Very likely, this comment was not very much appreciated by the host or the other guests, so perhaps sarcastically or perhaps to change the mood, another of the guests spoke up saying, "Blessed is everyone who will eat bread in the kingdom of God!" (Luke 14:15). This was a reference to the Messianic Kingdom of God which many of these individuals believed would be established when the Messiah came. Many of the Lord's fellow guests may have been eagerly watching for the Messiah, believing that His arrival was to occur very soon, but they did not believe that Jesus of Nazareth was the Messiah.

Today, nearly everybody we meet in our area of the country would agree that Jesus is the Christ. Few people would deny this. Yet, there are many vacant seats at the "table of the Lord." The invitation has gone out, "Come to the feast." The Lord's servants have gone out with the news, "The dinner is ready!" Matthew's account of a similar story concludes with the words, "Many are called, but few are chosen" (Matthew 22:14). Excuses! Excuses! Two thousand years later, people are still the same. We want to attend the dinner, but we allow other pursuits to distract us. Many of these "reasons" seem legitimate. Many people are so busy at their jobs they don't have time for the Lord's dinner, and many don't really believe they *need* His dinner. It appears that many members of the church at Laodicea thought they had everything under control and didn't need anything else. Jesus is pictured as standing outside the church door, calling, "Hello! Is anyone there? If you will open the door, I will come in and eat dinner with you." (Revelation 3:20).

The tragedy is that the invitation to dinner often comes only once. If for any reason we miss it or forget to come, we may not be invited a second time.

Words To Live By

"FUHGEDDABOUDIT"

BOB CARR, A MINISTER FOR A CONGREGATION IN New York, encourages Christians to keep on working to bring people to God (*The Christian Chronicle,* May 2014). He says, "God's word doesn't fail. After all, if Jesus would've given up on us, fuhgeddaboudit!" If we can't count on God, we might as well "forget about it!" There is no one else to count on, no other place where we can find relief.

God's promise is clear, and we can depend on God to keep His word. Through the prophet Isaiah, Yahweh said: "So will My word be which goes forth from My mouth; It will not return to Me empty, without accomplishing what I desire, and without succeeding in the matter for which I sent it" (Isaiah 55:11).

God's word will not return to Him "empty." What He says will indeed happen. What God promises, He will provide. A great example of this is given in Genesis 6 – 9. The wickedness of mankind caused God pain and sorrow, so He regretted that He had even made man on the earth (Genesis 6:5,6). "Grieved in His heart," God resolved to wipe the earth clean through a great flood. But He remembered Noah, a righteousness man (Genesis 6:9), a "preacher of righteousness" (2 Peter 2:5), and resolved to spare him and his family.

God told Noah to build a great boat in which not only his family, but animal life, could survive the flood. God gave specific instructions concerning the boat, including its length, width, and height, and the kind of wood to be used. The Bible records that Noah *believed* God (Hebrews 11:7) and immediately set about building the boat (Genesis 6:22). We don't know how long it took Noah and his sons to finish the job, nor are we told in the Bible that anyone opposed his work or even ridiculed him as he worked, although we can imagine that such may have happened. The fact that Noah was called a "preacher of righteousness" might indicate that he attempted to warn other men about what was going to happen to *"fuhgeddaboudit"*

the earth. When Noah had finished his work and the animals were safely inside the boat, the rain began to fall, and the water quickly rose, destroying mankind and all vestiges of man's society. What God had said would happen did indeed happen.

During the reign of King Josiah, of Judah, God revealed to the young priest Jeremiah that unless the people repented of their idolatry and great wickedness, He would allow the kingdom to be overrun by the warlike Babylonians (Jeremiah 1:13-16). For several years, the Babylonians had been swallowing up small kingdoms all around Judah, and were heading toward Jerusalem. The advancing Babylonian army was compared to a tornado, "a boiling pot" swirling down from the north, that would engulf Judah unless Yahweh intervened. "They will fight against you, but they will not overcome you, for I am with you to deliver you," God told Jeremiah. The fierce Babylonians were not sent specifically to punish Judah, but if the people of Judah did not repent and turn back to Him, Yahweh would not intervene on Judah's side to protect them. He told Jeremiah, "Roam to and fro through the streets of Jerusalem, and look now and take note. And seek in her open squares if you can find a man. If there is one who does justice, who seeks truth, then I will pardon her" (Jeremiah 5:1). But Jeremiah found no such man, and in the eleventh year of Zedekiah's reign, the Babylonians burned the "house of God and broke down the wall of Jerusalem," and carried the survivors to Babylon as slaves (2 Chronicles 36:19-20). God did not cause this, but He allowed it to happen.

Jesus, our Lord, calls sinners to Him, saying, "Come to Me, all who are weary and heavy-laden, and I will give you rest. Take My yoke upon you and learn from Me, for I am gentle and humble in heart, and you will find rest for your souls. For my yoke is easy and my burden is light" (Matthew 11:28-30). We do not know how long it will be before the Lord's gracious call will no longer be extended. Like the people before the great flood, it appears that we still may have time to consider and accept His offer of salvation. And like the citizens of Judah, although we can see the storm gathering in the distance, there may yet be time for repentance. But unless there is true repentance, and unless men turn to God, there is no hope for salvation. Christ is the only way to God. On the very eve of His crucifixion, Christ declared, "I am the way, and the truth, and the life; no one comes to the Father but through Me" (John 14:6). Only several months later, the apostle Peter boldly proclaimed before the "rulers and elders" of Israel, on the temple plaza, "There is salvation in no one else; for there is no other name under heaven that has been given among men by which we must be saved" (Acts 4:12).

The promises of God are sure; He *will* keep His word. Believe it! God's word will not fail. Jesus Christ, our Lord, has not given up on us. If we cannot count on God, *"fuhgeddaboudit!"*

DO YOU REMEMBER?

I SOMETIMES THINK I HAVE FORGOTTEN MORE THAN I know. Indeed, it is so easy to forget. You don't have to *try* to forget, but you *do* have to *try* to remember. Forgetting is easy for all of us.

I remember my mother's birthday, and that of my wife and children, but the birthdays of other family members are problematic to say the least. My *worst* problem is with names. I can remember the names of great Protestant reformers of the 16th century, but can't remember the name of the person I just met five minutes ago. This inability to remember names is not the result of dementia, but is one I have wrestled with for half my life.

Some things are important enough, however, that it would be a shame to forget them. How about a short test? What do the years 1776, 1914-18, and 1945 mean to you? Who was the first president of the United States? Does the name Marquis de Lafayette ring a bell? What happened at Pearl Harbor, at Normandy, or at Bastogne? What about 9/11? What is "the Bill of Rights"? Who were Douglas McArthur, Joseph Stalin, and Adolph Hitler? What was the "Holocaust"? Where is Arlington National Cemetery?

My point is that many people will not have a clue regarding most of the previous questions, and that is too bad. When we forget our history – or worse, when we never learn it in the first place – we are often doomed to repeat it.

The last Monday of May, is *Memorial Day*. Originally called "Decoration Day" because people went to the cemeteries to decorate the graves of loved ones who had fallen on the fields of battle. Memorial Day is supposed to be a day of remembrance, a day that celebrates the courage of those who, in President Lincoln's words at Gettysburg, "gave the last full measure of devotion" in the defense of liberty and justice. However, Memorial Day has become for many a day for family, picnics, and fun, rather than a day for remembering.

The only Memorial Day celebration that I can really remember was several years ago in Belgium. We had reserved a section of seats for us and a group of Freed-Hardeman University students at the American Cemetery near the village of Henri Chappelle, not far from the University's Belgium campus. With pride we watched as a contingent of Marines marched through the vast cemetery where over 7,000 young American soldiers lie buried. Our beautiful flag preceded them as they marched to the music of the Marine band. As different dignitaries told stories of valor and bravery, we all wiped away tears. What a wonderful day that I will never forget!

Alas! The story of another procession through the narrow streets of Jerusalem nearly 2,000 years ago has been all but forgotten by many today. They know very little about the Carpenter of Nazareth, some questioning even His very existence as a historical person. For many He is no more than fodder for fiction, a character embellished by second century Christians, a "good" man, but certainly not a "miracle worker." Instead of "God with us," the "Light of the world," the "Way, the Truth, and the Life," Jesus is maligned by some as "the one who invented hell."

The greater tragedy is that many who have been "brought up in the church" no longer attend, and we wonder why. In some cases, I think I can understand why; in other cases, I just cannot understand. I do know, however, that simply "going to church" can often equate to nothing more than a dreary exercise in futility. Unless there is a solid underpinning of genuine faith, based upon a real repentance and regret for past sins, there is little hope for a continuing heartfelt devotion to God. Unless one enjoys reading the words of Christ and learning from Him, one will sooner or later become so involved in other things that the Christian experience will become no more than a distant dream.

Concerning some, the *Hebrews* writer said, "You have become dull of hearing. For though by this time you ought to be teachers, you have need again for someone to teach you the elementary principles of the oracles of God, and you have come to need milk and not solid food" (Hebrews 5:11-12). In other words, these people who had at one time been faithful Christians had *lost their momentum*, and had *regressed* to a state of "babyhood." They had *forgotten* even the "first principles" of the word of God. They needed to be taught again.

Let's take another test. Can you quickly find a Scripture reference that the preacher might suggest during a sermon? Do you know the difference between the Old Covenant and the New Covenant? Do you know why the blood of Christ was required? What do the names Moses, Aaron, Joshua, Jeremiah, Saul of Tarsus, Luke, or Timothy mean to you? Why do we observe the Lord's Supper on Sundays? Could you open the Bible and show someone what people were told to do to become Christians? Could you show someone a verse of Scripture that indicates that we should "sing" during worship?

I certainly know we all are at different levels of knowledge and understanding, and I do recognize that the preacher should be more knowledgeable about the Bible than is the usual person. I have invested nearly sixty years in Bible study, and should certainly possess more Bible knowledge than most. But there are certain facts and elemental concepts that all mature Christians should know and remember.

In the same way that Memorial Day has become for most people just another day off from work, just a day for recreation, Sunday has become for many just another day for whatever one wants to do, just a day off.

Words To Live By

ENOUGH FUEL TO MAKE IT HOME?

IN 1968, LIVING AND WORKING FOR THE LORD IN Verviers, Belgium, our little family took our first vacation since our marriage ten years earlier. We allotted the then huge sum of $200 for this trip. We were going to Rome! We loaded the old car, drove to Cologne, Germany, then up the beautiful Rhine valley, planning to visit an American acquaintance in the university town of Tubingen. The next morning, we continued southward toward Lake Constance, where we rented a room from a German lady who spoke no English. The following day, still in Germany, our old car just gave up the ghost. We had to spend a night not in our budget in a hotel while the car was being repaired, bringing our remaining funds to the danger point. We ditched our plans for Rome, stopping instead in Genoa, Italy, where Christopher Columbus was born. Right away, we located a fellow minister, Truman Scott, who was working with a church in Genoa. I mentioned to him the precarious state of our finances, and since he was leaving on vacation elsewhere, he invited us to stay rent free in his home. We did not make it to Rome, but had a great time in Genoa. To shorten my story, as we were leaving Italy a week later, on the return journey home, we had only enough money for gasoline and a meagre lunch of Italian minestrone. I drove all night non-stop through the lower French Alps, following an interminable line of Frenchmen returning home from vacations, and finally arrived home early in the morning. When I later tried to re-crank the car, it would not start. Out of gas!

In a spiritual sense, as we journey toward the home which the Lord has prepared for us (John 14:2-3), we all face a similar situation, and the question arises, "Do I have enough fuel to make it home?" The writer of *Hebrews* tells about Abraham who, when called by God, obediently left his home in the fertile Euphrates valley, and began a long journey "not knowing where he was going" (Hebrews 11:8). This courageous man of faith believed God, trusting that He would provide for him on his journey. God gave him a vision of a "city which

Enough Fuel To Make It Home?

has foundations, whose architect and builder is God" (Hebrews 11:10). His "fuel" was *his faith*. And Abraham had "fuel" in abundance for his long journey, enough to "make it home."

The question for us today is, "Do *we* have enough fuel to make it home?" Is *our* faith strong enough to provide us the assurance and spiritual strength necessary for our own journey home? All along the way we will face unforeseen difficulties and problems which may cause many to question the reality of that "home" which we have only "seen" through faith.

The *Hebrews* writer tells us that the "city" which God has prepared for us is a "better" place, a "heavenly one" (Hebrews 11:16), but we have not seen it with our own eyes, nor has anyone returned from the dead to assure us of its reality. Indeed, the only "proof" of its existence is the word of God. Jesus told His disciples that He was going "to prepare a place" for them, and therefore for us (John 14:2). The disciples believed Him, and so must we. They had reason to believe Jesus, if not immediately upon hearing those words, but three days later, after His death on the cross, when they saw Him alive, standing in their midst in the upper room (John 20:19-29). Because we, with good reason, believe the testimony of these men who witnessed His death and who saw Him after His resurrection, we have "faith" to sustain us on our journey, faith enough to get us "home." These disciples heard Him speak, saw Him and His nail-scarred hands and feet, and touched Him with their own hands after His resurrection. And they "proclaimed" to us what they saw and heard so that we also "may have fellowship" with them and "with the Father, and with His Son Jesus Christ" (1 John 1:1-3).

But do *we* have enough spiritual "fuel" to get us "home"? Individual Christians who have the misfortune of living where there is no congregation of like-minded believers may have a problem. Peter addressed his second letter to those "who have obtained *like precious faith with us* through the righteousness of God and our Savior Jesus Christ" (2 Peter 1:1). Paul spoke of local congregations as of the "body" of Christ in this or that locality, showing how each person has "gifts" that contribute to the proper functioning of the congregation (1 Corinthians 12:4-31). To the Ephesians, Paul wrote that "the whole body, being fitted and held together by what every joint supplies, according to the proper working of each individual part, causes the growth of the body for the building up of itself in love" (Ephesians 4:16). But a Christian who lives far from any such congregation cannot receive the help of others of "like precious faith" as can those who compose the congregation. Often, such isolated Christians grow weak and "die" for lack of spiritual nourishment. This was a problem we had to deal with in our work in Belgium. When people moved away for health reasons or lived too far away to be active in the congregation, they ran the risk of becoming spiritually "anemic."

This is no doubt why the *Hebrews* writer urged his readers to "hold fast the confession of our hope without wavering" and to "consider how to stimulate one another to love and good deeds, not forsaking our own assembling together as is the habit of some" (Hebrews 10:23-25). Those who do not assemble regularly with other Christians to worship God or contribute what they can to the upbuilding of the family of God, run the risk of actually losing their faith. The *Hebrews* writer says, "Take care, brethren, that there not be in any one of you an evil, unbelieving heart that falls away from the living God. But encourage one another day after day, as long as it is still called 'Today,' so that none of you will be hardened by the deceitfulness of sin. For we have become partakers of Christ, if we hold fast the beginning of our assurance firm until the end" (Hebrews 3:12-14). This is the spiritual "fuel" that each one of us needs to get us "home."

NOT FOR SALE!

THERE IS SOMETHING EXHILARATING AND EXCITING about a sale. My wife loves an auction, and I must admit I do also. The first time, however, that I got up the nerve to raise my hand at an auction, I actually bought a box full of old safety razors, which they were practically *giving* away by the end of the auction. And at yard sales and in antique shops, my wife displays the art of bargaining with more expertise than do most people I know. Sometimes, just for fun, she has bargained with a seller just to see how low she could bring the price down, when she actually did not intend to buy.

It is very sad, I think, to see a home sold at auction, for whatever reason, along with the furniture and all of the prized souvenirs accumulated during many years. Most of us have objects in our homes that we would not want to part with for any price. Precious memories are attached to them and they are just *not for sale!* Yet, we know that at some point, perhaps after we die, these special objects *will* be put up for sale, and the price they bring may be small.

Over the course of human existence, nearly everything imaginable has been bought or sold. The apostle John described the downfall of "the great city Babylon," saying that among the items that would no longer be bought or sold in her markets were *"horses and chariots and slaves and human lives"* (Revelation 18:11-13). "Slaves and human lives"! It is estimated there were more slaves than free men in Rome in the first century A.D. But although the great human tragedy of legalized slavery was finally abolished in the western hemisphere in 1865, a secret, illegal slave trade *still flourishes* in parts of Africa, and Indochina. And perhaps even worse than slavery, in some ways, there is the despicable traffic of "human lives," which John seems to differentiate from "slavery." It is well known that in some nations of the far east poverty-stricken parents often sell their very young daughters into marriage or prostitution.

The apostle Paul described the unsaved person as one who is "of flesh, sold into bondage to sin" (Romans 7:14). Paul wrote that before coming to Christ we were all "slaves of sin" (Romans 6:6), but that having come to Christ through obedient faith, we were set free from that "slavery" and became "slaves of righteousness" (Romans 6:17-18). As a minister of the gospel, Paul was fighting hard for the souls of the very people who were reading his epistle. Some of these people had been set free from sin by Christ, but seemed to have forgotten the One Whom they were supposed to be serving. Some of them were slipping back into the "bondage" of sin, *selling themselves*, as it were, to another master.

"For Sale!" Even today, many of those for whom Christ died seem to have *sold themselves* again to Satan, and for a bargain price. In ancient times, the oldest son received his father's special blessing and, at the father's death, the major part of the inheritance. But Isaac's oldest son Esau cared nothing for such things. He cared only for what the day could bring him. When his brother Jacob offered him a bowl of red stew in exchange for his right of inheritance, he readily agreed (Genesis 31-34). The author of *Hebrews* wrote that "Esau sold his birthright for a single meal" (Hebrews 12:16). What a bargain! Yet, people are making such deals every single day. They are in effect bartering their valuable souls for *pennies*, for a momentary passing pleasure.

Therefore, I ask the important question: *How much is my soul worth to me?* What price would I place on my soul? What would be the lowest price that I would accept for my eternal soul? Jesus taught His disciples that anyone who wished to come after Him would have to *deny himself* and *take up his cross* and follow Him. "What will a man give *in exchange for his soul*?" (Matthew 16:24-26). Jesus is saying that each of us must make the choice – Will I follow Jesus? Or will I follow my own pleasures? To follow Jesus requires that I give up many things that I might want. To follow Jesus requires that I "take up my cross," that I agree to suffer if necessary, and that I follow Him to the very end. So, how much am I willing to give in exchange for the life He offers me? What is my soul worth to me?

Paul described his own commitment when he was converted. He wrote that "Whatever things were gain to me, those things I have counted as loss for the sake of Christ" (Philippians 3:7). He was willing to pay the asking price. Christ asks for our ALL. He will not barter with us. There is no lowest price that He will accept.

As you and I follow Jesus, we will have many close encounters with Satan, our archenemy. Satan has many schemes or tricks by which he seeks to steal what is valuable to us (2 Corinthians 2:11; Ephesians 6:11). He will attempt to bribe us with a moment of pleasure and will creep up during our unguarded moments. If possible, he will rob us of our chastity; he will exchange our innocence for a few casual looks at pornographic images; he will erode our faith through false science and ingenuous, but fallacious, arguments. By promising us earthly wealth and power, he will try to turn our eyes away from Jesus (Hebrews 12:2-3) and distract us from our glorious hope of heaven.

We need to be firm, as was Jesus when Satan tempted Him (Matthew 4:1-11), and let him know without a doubt that there are some things that are NOT FOR SALE!

Words To Live By

HOLD THAT HAMMER CORRECTLY!

MY FRIEND AND BROTHER IN CHRIST, MONSIEUR Noblue (pronounced *NO-Blue- A*) died in the Lord some forty years ago, but I will never forget him. His heart problems wouldn't allow him to exert himself physically, but he watched me as I worked to prepare the new church meeting place in Verviers, Belgium. I was nailing paneling to the auditorium walls when he softly suggested, "You aren't holding the hammer right; hold it *this* way." Now, so many years since then, every time I hold a hammer I remember what he said. "Hold the hammer correctly!"

What my friend said also applies to our use of Scripture. The apostle Paul wrote, "Be diligent to present yourself approved to God as a workman who does not need to be ashamed, accurately handling the word of truth" (2 Timothy 2:15). Too often, some of the most diligent evangelists, the hardest working servants of God, do not "accurately" handle God's holy word. As a result, they misapply and misinterpret God's instructions, not only going astray themselves, but leading others with them. To this point, Peter warned that in the letters of the apostle Paul "are some things hard to understand which the untaught and unstable distort, as they do also the rest of the Scriptures, to their own destruction" (2 Peter 3:16).

When Paul warned Timothy to charge his hearers "not to wrangle about words" (2 Timothy 2:14), he did not mean that "words" were unimportant. His meaning was that they should not "wrangle about empty and trifling matters" (Thayer). He told Timothy to warn Christians to "avoid worldly and empty chatter" and to "refuse foolish and ignorant speculations" (2 Timothy 2:16,23). It is in this context that Paul encouraged young Timothy, a spiritual "church builder," to "hold that hammer correctly."

Paul explained to the Corinthians that God, through the Holy Spirit, revealed His "thoughts" to the apostles (1 Corinthians 2:10-12). The Spirit of God enabled the apostles to "know the things freely given to us by God." Paul said that the apostles "speak" these things, "not in words taught by human wisdom, but in those taught by the Spirit, combining spiritual thoughts with spiritual words" (2 Corinthians 2:13). Without "words" there can be no teaching, no preaching, no Scripture, because "scripture" is something that is *written*. While it is true that the gospel was first taught *orally* by inspired men of God, it is now propagated through the inspired writings. As Paul continued to instruct Timothy, he wrote, "All Scripture is inspired by God and profitable for teaching, for reproof, for correction, for training in righteousness; so that the man of God may be adequate, equipped for every good work" (2 Timothy 3:16-17).

How we interpret individual *words* is very important. We think that because we *speak* English, we automatically know what English words *mean*. But that can be misleading, because the English language, more than French or Spanish, is constantly changing. Words that we dared not use in the 1940s or 50s, not to mention 500 years ago, are commonly used today, with *vastly different meanings*. For this reason, when we read the Bible, we ought to keep a good dictionary close at hand. A good practice is to read from more than one version of the Bible. I recommend the *New American Standard Version*, but there are other very good modern English translations.

Beyond individual *words*, however, it is very important to consider the *context* in which these words are found. Never read just one verse of Scripture; read an entire paragraph. If your Bible does not separate thoughts into paragraphs, read the entire chapter, making an effort to discern the main point of a verse or paragraph. Consider the paragraph "headings," although understanding that these "headings" represent what the editors consider to be the main point. It can also be very helpful to research other places in Scripture where *key words* are used. Use a concordance or the center references of your Bible to find other passages or verses where a word or topic is discussed.

The more one reads the Bible, the better one becomes at reading it. The more practice one gets at Bible study, the better one becomes as a Bible student. Practice doesn't make perfect, but it certainly makes one more proficient and able at whatever one does. If you want to become "a workman who does not need to be ashamed," a student who "accurately" handles the word of truth, you must "be diligent to present yourself approved to God" (2 Timothy 2:15).

I never aspired to be a carpenter, but I did learn how to "hold the hammer."

LOOKING GOOD!

I DON'T SUPPOSE THERE EXISTS A TEENAGE GIRL WHO, as she walks past a group of boys, would not enjoy hearing one of them exclaim, "Looking good!" She might not cast a glance in their direction as she keeps on walking, but she will surely smile the rest of the way home. But let's not kid ourselves! All of us want to "look good" when we go out. And there are those who actually think they do.

We were living temporarily in Vicksburg, Mississippi, with my parents in the summer of 1959. My wife, Virginia, was very pregnant and didn't feel particularly beautiful. She was walking on South Washington Street, on her way back to the house, when an 18-wheeler rolled past. When the driver saw her, he blew several loud blasts on his horn. Needless to say, that made her day, and she has told the story many times since, such an impression it made on her. Someone actually thought she was "looking good" when she wasn't feeling like it.

Even in the prophet Isaiah's day, some 2,700 years ago, people cared how they looked on certain occasions. The prophet noted that "a bridegroom decks himself with a garland," and "a bride adorns herself with her jewels" (Isaiah 61:10). Although times have changed a lot since then, it still matters "how we look" on certain occasions. When I was a young boy, we didn't have much of this world's wealth, but on Sunday, when we went to the Lord's house, we tried to look our best. It was not a matter of pride, because our "best" was almost always very ordinary when compared with what some others possessed. But my Mom insisted since we were going to church that we shine our shoes and comb our hair, and put on our finest shirts, homemade from flower sack cloth. And even today, I find it very hard to "dress down" when I present myself to worship God in the assembly.

The principle pronounced by the prophet Malachi is true, that we should not offer to God a sacrifice that we would be ashamed to offer to a high-ranking government official. Malachi upbraided the people who brought lame and sick animals to the altar of God as offerings (Malachi 1:6-14). He asked, "Why not offer it to your governor? Would he be pleased with you? Would he receive you kindly?" The principle is that we should offer our *best* to God. We should be careful to present ourselves to the Lord of hosts *at our best*. Although the principle goes far beyond what we wear to church, it still applies to some degree. Our relaxed attitudes about "how we look" may mirror relaxed *attitudes* about the worship in which we engage on the Lord's Day. So, while not making a distinction between the "haves" and the "have nots" (James 2:1-7), I would not come before God in dirty, ragged clothes that I would refuse to wear to work, to a job interview, to a wedding, or to a funeral. The principle is that we offer our "best" to God.

Paul wrote that Christians should be instructed to "adorn the doctrine of God our Savior in every respect" (Titus 2:10). For His part, God has demonstrated "His grace" by "bringing salvation to all men," thereby "instructing us to deny ungodliness and worldly desires and to live sensibly, righteously and godly in the present age" (Titus 2:11-12). Paul defines this spiritual "adornment" in his epistle to the Colossians: "So, as those who have been chosen of God, holy and beloved, put on a heart of compassion, kindness, humility, gentleness and patience." And above all of that, he says, "Put on love, which is the perfect bond of unity" (Colossians 3:12-14).

There is an "inner beauty" that is far more important than the physical beauty that so often turns heads. There is certainly nothing wrong with "looking good," but we must not be obsessed with the outward beauty of the body. Peter makes this point while addressing Christian women, but the principle applies equally to men: "Your adornment must not be merely external—braiding the hair, and wearing gold jewelry, or putting on dresses; but let it be the hidden person of the heart, with the imperishable quality of a gentle and quiet spirit, which is precious in the sight of God" (1 Peter 3:3-4). Where the NASB exhorts us to worship God "in holy array," the KJV reads, "in the beauty of holiness" (Psalm 29:2). "Holy array" refers to the "holy garments" which priests had to wear when they worshiped in the temple, and holiness is always beautiful. While we certainly don't want to "show off" before other people, wanting people to notice how "holy" we may think we are, true holiness when worn humbly as "holy garments" should always be the dress of the Christian, in church or out where we live in the world. Indeed, it is more important to "look good" in the spiritual sense than to "look good" physically.

How do we look? Are we paying as much attention to "inner beauty" as we pay to external, physical beauty? Are we "looking good"?

Words To Live By

LOW MAN ON THE TOTEM POLE

A TOTEM WAS A CARVED IMAGE THAT SERVED AS a symbol for many Native American tribes, clans, and families, or even for an individual person. Often, totems were carved from tree trunks to make what we call a "totem pole." While totems may have been objects of worship for some tribes or clans, they often served simply to honor important persons or ancestors. Perhaps for this reason, our English expression "low man on the totem pole" evolved, indicating the person at the "bottom of the heap," the person with the least authority in a company or on the job – the least important person.

When I was in my last year of high school, I sometimes felt that I was "the low man on the totem pole." I was the one who was *not chosen* to do the selected reading at graduation (although I did "try out" for the honor); I was the guy who was *not selected* as "class favorite"; I was the one who did not "wow" the crowd with a great song. My good friend Jimmy did that! I was also the guy who was *not mentioned* for any important achievement. I felt like the proverbial "low man on the totem pole."

But, was I? Actually, contrary to our English expression, the "low man" on the totem pole was *the most important of all*! The "low man" was actually the person *most honored* among the tribe or clan.

One of the most moving events recorded in the New Testament occurred in the rented hall where Jesus and his disciples observed the final Passover of His earthly life (John 13:1-20). The twelve disciples had apparently entered the hall before Jesus arrived. Everything was prepared, and the meal, including the cooked lamb, the bitter herbs, the unleavened bread, and wine, was already on the table (Matthew 26:17-19; Mark 14:16).

The disciples quickly chose their places around the low "table." In those days, one did not sit in a chair to eat; one *reclined* on a cushion. According to Albert Edersheim (*The Life and Times of Jesus the Messiah,* Book V, Chapter 10), the table would have been a long rectangle arranged with cushions around the outside, leaving the front end free for serving. The position of highest honor would have been the second or middle cushion when there were more than two persons at a table. Some of the disciples apparently had hurried to choose the places of honor to the right and left of the seat where Jesus would sit. Judas Iscariot had chosen the position on His *left*, so that as he reclined, he would have been closest to the Lord, but behind Him, since they would be reclining on their left side. John, the disciple "whom Jesus loved" was on the Lord's *right* side, "reclining on Jesus' bosom" (John 13:23). Simon Peter must have been positioned directly across the table from John, so that he could gesture to John, asking for clarification of the Lord's statement that one of them would betray Him (John 13:21-24). John, then, leaned back "on Jesus' bosom" and asked Him to name the person who was going to betray Him. (John 13:25).

Before this, however, as they were reclining at the table, Jesus abruptly got up, laid aside His outer garments, asked for a towel, and girded Himself. As the disciples, no doubt in utter shock, silently watched, the Lord poured water into a basin, and began to wash the feet of the disciples (John 13:4-5). According to Jewish custom, a servant would wash the feet of a guest, but since there was no servant present, and since not one the disciples had volunteered for the task, Jesus Himself set about doing it. Suddenly, Simon Peter realized the incongruity of the situation and, aghast, declared, "Never shall You wash my feet!" But Jesus replied, "If I do not wash you, you have no part with Me." (John 13:6-8).

The disciples had "messed up" in a colossal way. In their haste to get the best seats at the table, they had neglected their most basic responsibility. They badly needed the lesson of the hour. Jesus, their "Lord" and "Teacher," was instructing them by *word* and *example* that if they were to succeed in the great task before them, they would have to conduct themselves as *servants*, not as masters. "If I then, the Lord and the Teacher, washed your feet, you also ought to wash one another's feet. For I gave you an example that you also should do as I did to you" (John 13:14-15).

This was not a *new* teaching; the disciples must have already heard it numerous times. On one occasion, having been invited to a dinner, Jesus had watched the guests as they entered, and had seen how they were "picking out the places of honor at the table" (Luke 14:7). In a parable, He taught those guests the danger of choosing the seat of honor. It could happen that someone "more distinguished" might arrive and the master of the house might ask you to give up your seat to that person, and you would be disgraced in the eyes of all. The Lord taught them to select the "last place, so that when the one who has invited you comes, he may say to you, 'Friend, move up *higher*.'" His main point was, "For everyone who exalts *himself* will be humbled, and he who humbles *himself* will be exalted" (Luke 14:11).

The Lord was essentially teaching that the place of greatest honor in His service is that of a servant. We should therefore pray, "Lord, make me a *servant*!" "Lord, give me the *heart* of a *servant*!" The "*low* man on the totem pole" is truly, in the Lord's eyes, as it should be for us, the place of highest honor.

OLD BROTHER HILL

INDELIBLY STAMPED ON MY MIND IS THE MEMORY of those godly men and women who, in the late 1940s and early 50s, week after week and year after year, met in the small church house in the Midway community where I was reared in my early years. Oh, I realize now that they were far from perfect, but to my boyish mind they were *untouchables*. They were for the most part simple hard-working farmers who had had little opportunity for schooling, but they were good people and could be counted on to be present at every Sunday worship appointment.

Of all the men of that country congregation, the most memorable one was old brother Hill. I can still clearly see brother Jim Hill in my mind's eye, even now, seventy years later. When it came his turn to pray, Brother Hill would move to the aisle and bend his knee to the floor as he led the congregation in prayer to God. I don't remember his prayers, but I remember his *praying*! Brother Hill did not kneel in prayer to be *seen* or to *conform to custom*, but because he was speaking to God. He was above all things a *humble man*. Humility and love were his Christian clothing, two character traits that enriched his life and the lives of all who knew him. His influence was great in the church and in the community. And when the church happened occasionally to go through a rough spot, most often because of someone's peculiar likes or dislikes, people turned to Old brother Hill for his advice – and they listened to what he had to say. How could they not?

In the first recorded "sermon" taught by Jesus, the very first sentence concerned humility. "Blessed are the poor in spirit," He said. (Matthew 5:3). He taught His disciples not to flaunt their prayers and generosity before the public, so as to be seen by others, as did the proud Pharisees (Matthew 6:1-7). To illustrate the lesson, Jesus contrasted a sinful tax collector and a self-righteous Pharisee (Luke 18:9-14). The Pharisee was vaunting his goodness, saying, "God, I thank You that I am not like other people: swindlers, unjust, adulterers, or even like this tax collector." As he spoke he looked disdainfully toward a tax collector who was "beating his breast, saying, 'God, be merciful to me, the sinner.'" Jesus concluded His story, saying, "I tell you, this man [the tax collector] went to his house justified rather than the other; for everyone who exalts himself will be humbled, but *he who humbles himself* will be exalted."

I dare say that of all the character flaws a person may possess, *pride* is one of the worst, and *humility* – the opposite of pride – is *the most difficult trait to develop*. If this were not true, why would the pages of the New Testament urge us at every turn to be *humble*? The apostle Paul teaches us to *"give preference* to one another in honor" (Romans 12:10), and not to "be haughty in mind," but to "associate with the lowly." "Do not be wise in your own estimation," he wrote (Romans 12:16).

Paul wrote also to the Philippians, "Do nothing from selfishness or empty conceit, but with humility of mind regard one another as more important than yourselves" (Philippians 2:3). To the Ephesians, he wrote, "Walk in a manner worthy of the calling with which you have been called, with all humility and gentleness, with patience, showing tolerance for one another" (Ephesians 4:1-2). The KJV reads "meekness" instead of "gentleness," but since people usually mistake "meekness" for "weakness," the word "gentleness" is to be preferred here. In fact, the "meek" person is one who through strength of character is truly able to control himself, whereas the "weak" person has no real control over his feelings or actions. Therefore, only a truly strong person who practices self-constraint or self-control can be truly humble.

Humility is not normal. It is not inherited from one's parents. Although there are always exceptions to every generalization, I think that humility is learned over time, through hardships and troubles. For this reason, humility is more often seen in adults than in the young. Maybe this is why Paul warned the younger man Timothy, urging him to be an example to the believers "in speech, conduct, love, faith, and purity" (1 Timothy 4:12).

Humility has two sisters: wisdom and understanding. Solomon wrote, "When I was a son to my father, tender and the only son in the sight of my mother, then he taught me and said to me, 'Let your heart hold fast my words; keep my commandments and live; Acquire wisdom! Acquire understanding!'" (Proverbs 4:3-5).

Old brother Hill acquired both wisdom and understanding, and without realizing it, he acquired humility.

SATAN'S SCHEMES

MOST OF US DISLIKE PEOPLE WHO ARE ALWAYS trying to control us, manipulate us, or "manage" us by devious, underhanded ways. We don't usually object, however, to honest influences, or to above-board argumentation, and there is a place for discussions in which each person is free to voice his or her opinions without fear of ridicule or rejection.

But Satan is a different matter. He is a schemer and a manipulator from the very beginning. He is by "nature" a liar and "the father of the lie" (John 8:44), as the original Greek text puts it. The very first mention of Satan in the Bible depicts him as a liar (Genesis 3:1-6). He approached mother Eve, a woman who had absolutely no concept of falsehood, of deception, or of "sin," and persuaded her with a lie to eat the forbidden fruit. But, to be honest, what Satan said to Eve was not absolutely false, although it was a lie. When he told Eve, "You surely will not die!" he was saying a "half-truth." God had indeed said if Adam and Eve ate the fruit they would die (Genesis 2:17), but Satan twisted the meaning of the word "die." By the word "die" God had meant one thing, and Satan pretended that He had meant something different. Being "deceived," Eve ate the fruit and "died" immediately, spiritually (1 Timothy 2:14), according to the meaning which God had intended. She began to die physically when she was expelled from the Garden of Eden and separated from the Tree of Life (Genesis 3:22-24).

How then does Satan frame his efforts to deceive?

First, Satan attempts to convince us that "sin" does not really exist. This idea seems to have been accepted by some in the church at Corinth, in Greece. They were saying, "All things are lawful for me" (1 Corinthians 6:12). They appeared to be saying this in the context of morality, that maybe it was acceptable to "be joined to a prostitute" (6:16). Paul referred again to their statement when he discussed how some of these Christians were continuing to "partake of the table of demons" (1 Corinthians 10:23). These new Christians were continuing to frequent the pagan temple while at the same time partaking "of the table of the Lord." We are not told why they kept going up to the pagan temple. Was it simply to eat the food which was "sacrificed to idols" (I Corinthians 10:18-19), or was it to engage the temple prostitutes, as some of them had obviously done before becoming Christians, having considered this to be a religious activity?

Satan has not modified this very successful tactic. Even today, he would have us believe that what one does with one's body is not a problem, that there can be no wrong, no sin, since there is really no such thing as "immorality." Just a few years later, after Paul's death, the Gnostics would begin to propagate the notion that "we have no sin" (1 John 1:8; 2:4), denying that their immoral acts were sinful. They taught that the body physical is evil, but since bodies of flesh were imposed upon us by the Creator, mankind cannot be held guilty by what the body does naturally. Actions done by the body cannot be "sinful." Peter spoke of these false teachers in these words: "Many will follow their sensuality, and because of them the way of the truth will be maligned; and in their greed, they will exploit you with false words" (2 Peter 2:2-3). "For speaking out arrogant words of vanity they entice by fleshly desires, by sensuality, those who barely escape from the ones who live in error, promising them freedom while they themselves are slaves of corruption; for by what a man is overcome, by this he is enslaved" (2 Peter 2:18-19).

Since the early 1940s, we have witnessed a modern revival of this Gnostic error, in what has been called "Existentialism." Jean-Paul Sartre, an atheist and popular French novelist, built his ideas upon the philosophy of Soren Kierkegaard, proclaiming that each individual is free to do as he pleases. According to Sartre, there exists no moral code from God, no right or wrong. "God is dead," he said. His idea was not that God had actually died, but that if He exists, He is not in any way involved in human existence. The Bible has no moral authority for mankind. Each person must make his own choices, and becomes his own moral compass, his own guide. "All things are lawful for me," became their concept.

A second tactic used by Satan is that of *incrementalism*, a philosophy which advocates political and social change *by degrees,* over time. We have certainly seen this over the past few decades in America. Consider, for example, the movies shown today. I can remember when it was taboo to use in a movie even the mildest form of profanity. The producers the great film *Gone with the Wind* decided to risk using the word "damn" at the very end of the film, knowing that it would offend many, but believing that they could get by with it, and get by with it they did! Furthermore, "bedroom scenes" were strictly behind closed doors, hinted at. Today, nothing is left to the imagination, and children are permitted to see almost any movie, with or without parents. But these changes have come *by degrees*, slowly, stealthily, so that we are amazed, almost surprised, at the changes that have occurred.

Jesus taught a parable about how "while men were sleeping" the devil came and sowed "tares" among the "wheat" (Matthew 13:25). Among other things, the Lord was warning us to be vigilant, to be on guard, lest before we know it, Satan will have done his dirty deeds among us, "while we were sleeping."

A third tactic Satan uses is to make evil *look good*. We talk about "sugarcoating" things, and Satan is the super sugar coater. Car dealers use pretty girls in short shorts to promote their cars. "Sex sells!" Lifting up his glass, a party goer exclaims, "Let the good times roll!" Alcohol enlivens and makes a party really rock! I have seen close up, as a child, the so-called "good times" enjoyed by drunks. Satan shows us only the "good times." He doesn't describe the real tragedy that follows closely behind the person who "sleeps around," who uses "recreational" drugs, or who abuses alcohol.

Paul wrote, "We are not ignorant of [Satan's] schemes" (2 Corinthians 2:11). Peter warned us, "Be of sober spirit, be on the alert. Your adversary, the devil, *prowls around* like a roaring lion, seeking someone to devour (1 Peter 5:8).

YOU ARE WHAT YOU EAT

IN A VERY REAL SENSE, I AM "WHAT I EAT." THE CEREAL that I eat in the morning, the hamburger that I may hastily choke down during the noon lunch break, and the delicious medium-rare Texas-sized T-bone steak during a special night out – it all becomes ME as it passes through my digestive system. God arranged it to be so, and it amazes me to think how the vitamins, minerals, fats and acids combine to make all of my unique body parts, while feeding my brain and making my muscles strong. The psalmist David marveled at how God "skillfully wrought" us in the "depths of the earth," starting from an "unformed substance" in our mother's womb (Psalm 139:13-16).

As informed, intelligent adults, we know that some foods are good for us while others are not. We also know that if we over-indulge at the dinner table our bodies will feel the ill effects of it. Some people mistreat their bodies by stuffing themselves with fatty foods that bloat and cause them to be overweight; others abuse their bodies by starving themselves, thinking skinny is better than fat. We all need to become better informed about the foods and beverages we consume, so as to develop healthy bodies.

But the food we eat feeds only the *physical body*. What about the *spiritual* part of man? What feeds the *spirit*? What feeds the *mind*? The body is important, but the *spirit* is of much greater importance, so that what we feed our mind and spirit becomes urgent.

We are also "what we eat" in a *spiritual sense*. Everything around us impacts our minds and spirit, sometimes for good, often for ill. For this reason, Solomon recommended care in the selection of friends and companions. "Do not enter the path of the wicked," he said. "Do not proceed in the way of evil men. Avoid it, do not pass by it; turn away from it and pass on. For they cannot sleep unless they do evil" (Proverbs 4:14-16). Unfortunately, young people especially, inexperienced and a little naïve, often get into trouble because of

Words To Live By

the crowd they happen to be with. For example, when I was young teen, new to city life, I made friends with some boys on our block. These boys introduced me to some conduct that could easily have altered my life in a bad way. Suffice it to say that I would have been in deep trouble if our exploits had been discovered! Although I was unaware of what was going to happen until it went down, I was part of the group and would have shared the consequences. Incidentally, I never told my mother these things, because I knew they were wrong. A rule worth remembering is this: Any conduct that you must hide from your mother is probably wrong.

Jesus taught His disciples that "the worry of the world and the deceitfulness of wealth" can "choke" the word of God so that it becomes "unfruitful" (Matthew 13:22). Although we might hear the word of God at church, and although we might sincerely love God's word, the affairs of the world can render it ineffectual in our lives, if we are not careful. Paul wrote, "Bad company corrupts good morals" (1 Corinthians 15:33), so it is important to have friends who can help us be good and to do right. We should try to be good examples to people who do not know God's word, but we must allow God to control our conduct. I learned very early that it is important to choose worthy friends, because it is easy to be led astray.

Everything that we see, hear, or read affects our mind and spirit in some way, to some degree.

The Lord Jesus compares our *minds* to a "storehouse" which we fill over the course of our life. He uses the word "treasure" or "treasury" (Matthew 12:34-36). The "good" man has filled his "treasury" with good things, while the "evil" person has filled his with evil things. What we fill our minds with is largely up to us. We can fill it with filthy words, dirty jokes, lewd pictures, and evil desire, or we can fill it with wholesome words (Ephesians 4:29), pure and honorable thoughts (Philippians 4:8), and with love which is patient and kind (1 Corinthians 13:4-7). Jesus tells us that what we put into our minds, or what we allow others to put there, will determine what we do and say. "The mouth speaks out of that which fills the heart" (Matthew 12:34). People who use bad language cannot offer as an excuse that they didn't "mean to say that." They are simply bringing "out of their evil treasure" what they themselves have put there over time.

I wish I could have known Gaius, a special friend of John the apostle. While most of us are concerned about our physical health, this blessed man was obviously more concerned with his *spiritual* well-being. John indicated as much when he expressed his joy that Gaius was "in good health" *spiritually* (3 John 1:2). He expressed his hope that Gaius' *physical* health was as good as that of his *spirit*. Gaius was paying more attention to his spiritual health than to the health of his body. And that is how it should be. The body is temporary; the spirit will live on.

We are, indeed, what we eat.

Words To Live By

"THE GRASS IS ALWAYS GREENER OVER THE SEPTIC TANK."

In 1976, humorist Erma Bombeck published her bestselling book, *"The Grass Is Always Greener Over the Septic Tank."* Bombeck might really have believed the idea expressed by her title, and most people would chuckle and quickly agree, but they would be wrong. All it takes is a drought to observe that the statement is fallacious. Very quickly, for lack of water, the grass over the septic tank would begin to die.

Spiritually speaking, the devil wants us to believe that "grass" really does grow "greener" over the septic tank, and that the most fun and amusement can be found "over the septic tank." Satan has many devices, many schemes, by which he attracts those who are looking for a "good time" and "fun." In the devil's amusement park, the bright lights, neon signs, and blaring music attract the attention of the naïve and unthinking crowds, drawing them into the casinos and clubs. Cities like Las Vegas and Reno, with their breathtaking lights, perpetuate the myth that if you are looking for a wonderful experience, you should go there. Many people have swallowed Satan's lie like a fish swallows a lure, and are suddenly taken captive by him.

Several years ago, I sat one evening around a table in North Montreal, Canada, with some twelve or thirteen other people, for the weekly meeting of Gamblers Anonymous. I knew none of these people and they did not know me. Someone opened the meeting with a reading of the "Serenity Prayer" and after a few other brief readings, the participants began to tell their sad stories. One man told how he had stolen money from his wife and had gone to the race track to bet on the horses. He had won big, and lost bigger, finally leaving the track penniless. A woman told how she had gone with her husband to Las Vegas for a short vacation, and after she had lost all of her own money at the casino, she stole her husband's money, losing it as well. These were not "once in a lifetime" experiences for these people;

they had done this many times. They were *addicted*, not to money, but to the thrill of the race, to the thrill of betting. They wanted to win so that they could continue betting, and they would bet until they had nothing left. I remember reading about a Vicksburg native who in one night at a riverfront casino lost his money, his car, and his house, before throwing himself into the river to drown.

Satan's myth is indeed alluring, not unlike the brilliance of the well-crafted lure which the fisherman dangles in the water. It looks so real, so tasty, so sweet! But it is *death* and *ruin* to the person who takes the bait. Each day that passes, someone can be heard hawking some fantastic deal on television. Our mind urges us to exercise caution, but our emotions prevail and we lay our money down, only to learn too late that we have been had.

Worse than losing money is to lose one's *soul*! The woman was walking alone in the beautiful garden, perhaps in the cool of the afternoon shade, admiring the various fruit trees, when suddenly, a quiet voice spoke to her, saying, "Did God really say that you are not permitted to eat from every tree in the garden? What God said is not true. You will certainly *not* die if you just take a taste of it!" The woman believed the sly voice, looked more closely at the fruit of the tree and saw that it was very *beautiful* and must have a *great taste*. She reached up, picked the fruit, and ate it! (Genesis 3:1-6).

Suddenly, in the twinkling of an eye, that woman lost for her and for her husband everything that was good and wholesome. In one thoughtless moment, she brought loss and ruin upon herself, her husband, and her future children. In just the same way, in a moment of stupidity and carelessness, countless men and women have thrown away future happiness for a pipe dream, for promises that were "too good to be true." Thinking they were going to reap happiness and great fortune, they bartered their lives for a moment's pleasure. Allured by the "bright lights," they paid dearly for empty promises. Like children at a county fair, they spend all their money trying to win a cheap toy, or a shiny ring made of plastic and glass. What people perceive as "green grass" often turns out to be an illusion. They believe the devil's lie that the "grass" always grows greener over the "septic tank," where nothing good and wholesome can exist. As Peter wrote, "These are springs without water and

Words To Live By

mists driven by a storm, for whom the black darkness has been reserved" (2 Peter 2:17-19). They have been listening to the devil, the greatest "con artist" of the ages, who, "speaking out arrogant words of vanity," entices people "by fleshly desires, by sensuality," promising them "freedom," but bringing them into the slavery of corruption.

Following His baptism, Jesus left the valley of the Jordan River and journeyed into the desolate, barren Judean wilderness (Luke 4:1). He remained in the wilderness forty days, fasting, and "being tempted by the devil." During that entire period, according to Luke's account, Jesus was tested in every conceivable way, but without yielding. We remember that our Lord was tempted, not as God, but as a human being made of flesh just as are we (Hebrews 2:17-18). He resisted the temptations through His own strength, not through miraculous help from the Holy Spirit. He could have fallen for Satan's lies, but He did not. Jesus knew well the Holy Scriptures which were so ingrained into His heart and mind since childhood that they immediately came to His mind, and these words of God helped Him to resist.

Satan, the devil, is a shyster, a liar from the beginning (John 8:44). He has convinced multitudes that "the grass always grows greener over the septic tank," but it does not! Only those who receive Jesus Christ into their hearts and lives can come to know true happiness, as they "walk in a manner worthy" of Him, seeking to "please Him in all respects, bearing fruit in every good work" (Colossians 1:10).

THE SADDEST WORDS EVER!

As we were returning from church services in Lille, France, we noticed a man lying beside the street, obviously passed out drunk. This was a common sight and there was nothing that we could do. Nevertheless, I have never forgotten that moment, a first for me.

Who was this man whose name I would never know? He was someone's child, someone's brother, perhaps even someone's father. In the distant past, he had perhaps been someone's employee, lover, or friend. But when I saw him on the street, he was alone, a lost person with no past, no viable present, and no future, only a blip on the radar screen of human existence. This is one of my saddest memories.

The Quaker poet, John Greenleaf Whittier, wrote, "Of all sad words of tongue or pen, the saddest are these, 'It might have been.'" What could the man I saw have done differently? What might he have achieved in life, if only….?

The teen grandchild of a friend was having a great time with another teen as they sped down the two-lane road in the pickup. My friend's grandson leaned his body out the truck window and waved his arms, shouting and laughing. The teen driver, distracted, lost control of the truck and they plunged into a wooded area. I would speak a few days later at the saddest funeral I have ever endured. A young life was lost in a moment of foolish "fun." So much "future" was lost that day; so much sadness was caused in a single unthinking, careless moment.

Nevertheless, that is often the way things are in life – an unexpected, unsought, accidental occurrence that changes everything in the blink of an eye. No one ever sits down to plan "how I can wreck my life" or "how I can cause my loved ones pain," or "what will be the best way to assure that I am a failure in life." Certainly, no sane or thinking person would intentionally decide to ruin his chances for advancement at work or to destroy his family's happiness.

We get married and bring children into the world; we work to provide a living for our family. We watch our children as they go off to school and grow into adults, hoping all will be well with them and that they will be happy and secure. Most parents really want more than anything else to see their children succeed in life and be happy.

However, many of us thoughtlessly allow ourselves to be involved in situations which have the potential of ruining our future. Even preachers are not immune to this. For this reason, I follow a rule not to counsel a woman without my wife being present. The devil can and does use innocent circumstances to cast a shadow of suspicion over one's reputation and diminish his influence for good.

Parents often trust that their inexperienced boys and girls will always do what is right. For this reason, Paul encourages parents to "bring them up in the discipline and instruction of the Lord" (Ephesians 6:4). The word "discipline" sometimes indicates "punishment," but in this context, refers principally to the "leading" of the child by the parent. The parent "leads" the child in a variety of ways, the most important being his personal example. If a dad demonstrates genuine love for his wife, his sons will learn to show proper respect for girls. If the mother shows love for her husband, her daughters will likely follow her example. If the parent uses bad language, the child will probably use it; if parents are dishonest, the children may very likely be dishonest; if the parent is lukewarm with respect to the church, the child will usually follow his example. Paul says we should *point our children toward God* from an early age, teaching them good principles with our *words* and demonstrating the meaning of obedience by our own obedience to God's word. It is very sad to learn of the sudden death of a child, taken from his or her family by a tragic accident or dread disease. We think of all this person might have been able to accomplish in life, but it is sadder still when a person falls prey to the devil's lie.

Jesus taught the parable of the "prodigal" son, who "squandered his estate with loose living" (Luke 15:13). This young man wasted his life and was eventually reduced to the position where, working with the pigs, he was forced to eat what the pigs ate in order to survive.

While it is true that he eventually repented and came back home, we wonder what he could have accomplished in life if only he had remained in his father's household.

God stands by the garden gate, as it were, watching and waiting for one erring child to return home. Oh, how He wishes that His child had stayed at home! Truly, "Of all sad words of tongue or pen, the saddest are these, 'It might have been.'"

Words To Live By

WHAT IS *YOUR* "WORLDVIEW"?

YOU DON'T HAVE A "WORLDVIEW"? SURELY YOU do! Everybody has one whether he knows it or not. One's "worldview" is the sum total of one's *beliefs*, how one views life. One's "worldview" involves one's ideas about morality, God, the past, the present, and the future, and about the *meaning* of life or its lack of meaning.

One of the greatest problems faced by foreign missionaries is that of different worldviews. Missionaries often experience "culture shock" when they enter a country where the customs of the people are very different from those at home. What we call "customs" includes every facet of life in a particular region or country, including religion, marital practices, childcare, food, personal relations, work ethic, and morals. For example, some "world religions" (Hinduism, Taoism, Buddhism) have "no personal, supreme, all-powerful deity but rather a formless, timeless reality," according to Eugene Nida, a well-known missionary anthropologist (*Customs and Cultures*, 171). Adherents of many oriental and African religions view life as "cyclical," meaning that the life of a person may be represented as a *circle* which has neither a beginning nor an end. When "death" occurs, the individual is believed to be "reincarnated" into something else, perhaps an animal or a plant. Christians, however, view life as a *straight line*, with a beginning and an end. The Christian's worldview includes belief in an all-powerful God who, at some point, created the universe, the earth, and everything that populates it. This worldview includes belief that at some point in the future, God will summon all men before Him to be judged, after which He will destroy the heavens and the earth (Hebrews 9:27; 2 Peter 3:3-7).

The apostle Paul encountered a completely different worldview when he turned from the Jews to the Gentiles. The Greeks and Romans believed in many "gods." *Jupiter* (or *Zeus*) was the chief deity, but there was a god for every human emotion. Indeed, these "gods" reflected every human frailty and moral defect, and humans who believed in them mirrored, in their turn, the defective

What Is Your "worldview"?

characters of their gods. It would have been easy for Paul to attack these people for their immoral lives, but instead he always began by teaching them about the "true God." He did this when he preached to the Galatians at Lystra (Acts 14:15-18), to the Athenians on the Areopagus (Acts 17:22-34), and to the Roman governors Felix (Acts 24:24-26) and Festus (Acts 26:1-26).

Even in "Christian" America, there are many people who do not believe in God. Atheists are prominently in the news as they seek to remove every symbol of Christianity from our courthouses, our state houses, our military cemeteries, our mottos, and even our currency. We can expect that their worldview will gain in momentum as they increasingly resort to lawsuits to achieve their goals.

Many teachers and professors in our schools and universities are teaching our children that instead of having been created by God, mankind evolved from lower creatures and that we are but distant cousins to the apes. While, in all fairness, these academics may often be good people who profess a high moral belief, they do not base that belief on the Bible. Their system of morality, based on human understanding, changes with the shifting sands of "custom" and "political correctness." Recently, for example, an abortion advocate asserted that until a baby bonds with its mother, it is not really a "human person," and that even after being born alive, it would be permissible to destroy the baby. That person's worldview obviously differs greatly from mine which holds that even a child in the womb is a real person, deserving the same protections that we all cherish. Many people believe they are permitted to do anything they desire, whenever, and wherever they might wish. The Christian worldview, however, is totally different. "Do you not know," says Paul, "that your body is a temple of the Holy Spirit who is in you, whom you have from God, and that you are not your own?" (1 Corinthians 6:19).

The Christian worldview includes the belief that at the end of time there will be a final judgment day when evildoers will be punished and the righteous rewarded. We believe that there will be a "day of wrath" (Romans 2:5) for the wicked, as well as a day when those who do the will of God will receive "glory and honor and peace" (Romans 2:10).

Each one of us needs to examine his "worldview." What do I believe? Why do I believe what I say I believe? What is my worldview?

Words To Live By

"YOU MAKE ME SO MAD!"

BEDLAM ROYAL HOSPITAL, FOUNDED IN LONDON, England, in 1247, developed over time into an institution for the mentally insane. The name "Bedlam" has for many years served as a synonym for "madness." The word "mad" meant "insane," and people who were "mad" were sent to Bedlam Hospital, usually never to return to sane society.

Have you ever gotten so mad that you couldn't think straight? I am sorry to confess it, but I have. Married for only a few months, my wife and I were driving home on a curvy two-lane road, when two kids passed our car and purposely drove very slowly, always preventing me from passing them. I saw red and as soon as I was able to pass, I forced them to stop, got out and threatened to whip both of them on the spot. My excuse for this behavior was that these boys were putting my bride in danger, but my "madness" that afternoon so long ago put her in even greater danger.

James, the Lord's brother, wrote, "The anger of man does not achieve the righteousness of God" (James 1:20). The apostle Paul wrote, "Let all bitterness and wrath and anger and clamor and slander be put away from you" (Ephesians 4:31). This is not to say that *emotion* is bad. The Lord Jesus, Himself, was furious at the people who were making His Father's house a den of thieves (Mark 11:15-17). But Jesus did not "lose His temper" when He was angry. As Paul urges, "Be angry, and yet do not sin" (Ephesians 4:26). When we do not check our anger, we "give the devil an opportunity" (Ephesians 4:27). In a very real sense, unchecked anger is similar to "temporary insanity," or "madness."

Sometimes, friendly "discussions" devolve into unfriendly "arguments," often because someone will not listen calmly to what the other is saying. Recognizing this tendency, James urges us to "be quick to hear, slow to speak, and slow to anger" (James 1:19). "Argument" is not, of itself, a bad thing, but it is important to learn *how to argue*. It is necessary to assume that the other person in the discussion is honest and that his point of view may have validity. Before jumping to conclusions, one should ask questions in an effort to completely understand what is being argued. A person who will not take the time to listen and understand what the other is saying will misunderstand and draw a wrong conclusion. From that point, the discussion can become heated and people become angry.

The wise man Solomon wrote, "He who restrains his words has knowledge, and he who has a cool spirit is a man of understanding" (Proverbs 17:27). And again, "He who is slow to anger has great understanding, but he who is quick-tempered exalts folly. A tranquil heart is life to the body. But passion is rottenness to the bones" (Proverbs 14:29-30). Solomon was saying that a quick-tempered person is more apt to commit foolish acts (Proverbs 29:22), but that the "even-tempered" person who practices self-control is less likely to suffer a heart attack from a fit of passion. "A fool," said Solomon, "always loses his temper, but a wise man holds it back" (Proverbs 29:11).

Self-control does not come naturally. The apostle Peter urged Christians to diligently apply themselves to the development of seven cardinal virtues, the third of which is "self-control" (2 Peter 1:6). When a person, for whatever reason, loses control of his mind, he is apt to lose control of his actions. He raises his voice, begins to accuse, and says things he may later regret, and to that extent becomes "mad." At the conclusion of a Super Bowl game, tempers flared, and in anger, blows were exchanged. The antidote to this kind of behavior is love, according to the apostle Paul: "Love is patient, love is kind and is not jealous; love does not brag and is not arrogant, does not act unbecomingly. It does not seek its own, is not provoked, does not take into account a wrong suffered, does not rejoice in unrighteousness, but rejoices with the truth; bears all things, believes all things, hopes all things, endures all things." (1 Corinthians 13:4-7). An old hymn says it well:

> Angry words! O let them never from the tongue unbridled slip;
> May the heart's best impulse ever check them ere they soil the lip.
> Love is much too pure and holy, friendship is too sacred far,
> For a moment's reckless folly thus to desolate and mar.

Words To Live By

Angry words are lightly spoken, bitt'rest tho'ts are rashly stirred,
Brightest links of life are broken by a single angry word.
"Love one another," thus saith the Savior;
Children, obey the Father's blest command.
(H.R. Palmer)

ONE MORE NIGHT WITH THE FROGS!

I T WAS EARLY SPRING IN THE EGYPTIAN DELTA, IN THE year 1446 B.C. and Pharaoh Thutmose III was the probable ruler over Egypt. Moses, then eighty years old, a swarthy, sun-browned goat-herd shepherd from the wilderness country of Paran, was agitating among the Israelite slaves. The older Egyptians no doubt recognized Moses as being the man who had been known as the adopted son of Thutmose's daughter, who had reared and educated him as a royal Egyptian.

But now this Moses was agitating for the release from slavery of the entire Israelite population, so that they could go and worship their God, *Yahweh* (Exodus 3:15). At God's command, Moses had stood unafraid before Pharaoh Thutmose and demanded, "Let My people go!" When Pharaoh refused, as God had said he would, Moses met him the next morning on the bank of the Nile River, and raising his rod toward the Nile, he shouted, "Thus says *Yahweh*, 'By this you shall know that I am *YAHWEH*'; behold I will strike the water that is in the Nile with the staff that is in my hand, and it will be turned to blood!" (Exodus 7:17). But court magicians convinced Pharaoh that this was but a magician's trick.

A week later, Moses was sent by God a second time to Pharaoh's court (Exodus 8:1) with the same request, "Let My people go, that they may serve Me." This time, Moses told Pharaoh that Yahweh would "smite your whole territory with frogs" (8:2). The frogs would "swarm" across the land and would be in every house, in every room, and even in their beds. Frogs would be in their ovens and the kneading bowls in which they prepared their bread. Pharaoh refused to listen to Moses, and the frogs came! When frogs died, they rotted in heaps and "the land became foul" with the stench from millions of decayed frogs.

Finally, Pharaoh begged Moses to ask *Yahweh* to get rid of the frogs and he would let the Israelites go. Moses replied, "The honor is

Words To Live By

yours to tell me when" (Exodus 8:9). Personally, if I had been in Pharaoh's shoes at that moment, I would have immediately said, "NOW! Get rid of them now!" But the words apparently stuck in Pharaoh's throat. He was too proud to give in so readily, so he said, "Tomorrow." (8:10).

John Sydney's hit song "*Manana* is good enough for me" might have been a hit for Pharaoh Thutmose III. He was certainly saying, "Not today. Tomorrow will be soon enough." One more night with the frogs will be fine.

Too often, people put off until "tomorrow" things they ought to do today. When I tried to support myself while serving fulltime as a minister, I sold life insurance for a year or two. The first question I would ask a potential client was, "Do you have a will?" Inevitably, the answer came back, "No, not yet." Every responsible person ought to have a valid, up-to-date will, but most people put it off. They intend to do it, but "not today," tomorrow!

The same thing is unfortunately true with spiritual concerns. Too often, an individual who hears the invitation to come to Christ, will put it off. "I'll do it later," he says. "Let me think about it." "I know I ought to do it, but not today." I have often heard these statements. The Roman governor Felix phrased it slightly differently. When pressed by Paul, Felix said, "Go away for the present, and when I find time I will summon you" (Acts 24:25). Felix did have further interviews with Paul, but he had lost the concern that he felt at that first interview. And this is the very point we need to realize. The gospel message will touch the heart and we are thrilled to hear it, but when we put off doing what it tells us to do, it becomes easier to ignore it. And eventually, God's message no longer produces the same effect. We have been lulled into thinking that we really don't need to get upset about it. When Saul of Tarsus was confronted by Ananias and heard what God was requiring of him, he may have appeared at first to protest, but Ananias quickly interjected, "Now, *why do you delay*? Get up and be baptized, and wash away your sins, calling on His name" (Acts 22:16).

Why spend one more *minute* "with the frogs"? Why spend one more hour with one's *sins*! *Manana* is not "good enough" for what ought to be done *today*!

One More Night With The Frogs!

Why do you wait, dear brother. O why do you tarry so long?
Your Savior is waiting to give you a place in His sanctified throng.
What do you hope, dear brother, to gain by a further delay?
There's no one to save you but Jesus, There's no other way
but His way.
Do you not feel, dear brother, His Spirit now striving within?
O why not accept His salvation, and throw off thy burden of sin?
Why do you wait, dear brother? The harvest is passing away;
Your Savior is longing to bless you;
There's danger and death in delay.
Why not? Why not? Why not come to Him now?
(G. F. Root)

Words To Live By

REMEMBER LOT'S WIFE!

NEARLY TWO THOUSAND YEARS BEFORE CHRIST, Abraham left Ur of the Chaldeans, travelling northward with a large clan led by his father, Terah. This move was in obedience to a command of God to Abraham (Acts 7:2-4). The large company would stop for an extended period when they reached the slopes of the Lebanon Mountain Range which extends southward through Palestine. They would leave there a town named for Abraham's brother, Haran. Having heard from God a second time (Genesis 12:1-4), at age seventy-five, Abraham and his clan, including Lot and his family, left their kinsmen and journeyed southward.

As both Abraham and Lot acquired great wealth in the land of Canaan, conflict eventually caused problems between them. Their extensive herds of livestock required large grazing pastures, and quarrels arose between their herdsmen (Genesis 13:5-7). Abraham wisely said to Lot, "Please let there be no strife between you and me, nor between my herdsmen and your herdsmen, for we are brothers" (Genesis 13:8). Being the older man, Abraham could have settled the matter in his own best interests, but he chose to let Lot make the choice. Standing perhaps on the summit of one of the rolling hills near Bethel, north of Salem, Abraham pointed towards the hill country on his right, then to the lush valley of the Jordan River on his left, and said to Lot, "Is not the whole land before you? Please separate from me; if to the left, then I will go the right; or if to the right, then I will go to the left" (Genesis 13:9).

Lot then demonstrated his own mindset, choosing for himself what he considered to be the best land – the "well-watered" valley of the Jordan. Lot's apparent self-serving attitude would ultimately be his downfall. Moses recorded that this episode occurred "before the Lord destroyed Sodom and Gomorrah" (Genesis 13:10). So, Lot moved his flocks and herds down into the valley of the Jordan. As time passed, he approached closer and closer to the very wicked cities located near the shallow waters of the southern part of the

Remember Lot's Wife!

"Salt Sea," later called the "Dead Sea." Surely, he had heard of the evil reputation of these cities, but that did not deter him. Closer and closer he moved, until finally he moved his family into the city of Sodom. Lot eventually even sat "in the gates of Sodom" (Genesis 19:1), indicating that he participated in the government of the city. Although Lot is described by the apostle Peter as a "righteous man" oppressed by the "sensual conduct" of the "unprincipled" citizens of Sodom (2 Peter 2:7-8), it does not appear that he gave much thought to how his actions would affect his family.

One hot day, three messengers from God approached Abraham, near Hebron, while he was resting under an oak tree (Genesis 18:1-2). They were bringing bad news. God had had enough! He was going to utterly destroy the cities of the plains, including Sodom and Gomorrah. At Abraham's pleading, God sent two of these angels to Lot's home to warn him to leave the city immediately (Genesis 19:1-2). Learning that Lot had male visitors, a large band of men, young and old, surrounded his home, demanding that he put these two men out so that they could "have relations with them" (Genesis 19:5). During the remaining hours of the night, the angels urged Lot to flee the city with his family, but Lot "hesitated" (Genesis 19:16). Finally, the angels "brought them outside the city," commanding them to run for their lives, and not to "look behind" them as they went (Genesis 19:17).

As they hurried away from the city, Lot's wife, for whatever reason, "from behind him, looked back, and she became a pillar of salt" (Genesis 19:26). Jesus urged his disciples to "remember Lot's wife" (Luke 17:32).

What should we learn from this story? Several life-lessons are apparent, the first of which involves the decisions we make. Lot, for example, was told by Abraham to decide where he would take his family. In making his decision, he did not consider what he owed his uncle Abraham who had allowed him to come with him to Canaan. He thought first about himself, and what would benefit *him* the most. He did not hesitate. Instead of allowing his uncle Abraham to choose, *he chose* to his eventual regret what he considered to be the best part of the land.

The second lesson we can learn is to consider the future, to make intelligent, informed choices, instead of just reacting to circumstances that arise. Lot seems to have "moved his tents" toward ever greener pastures for his flocks, eventually "as far as Sodom" (Genesis 13:12). Lot did not *suddenly arrive* at Sodom, but he approached it by degrees, step by step. And this is how most of us get into trouble, slowly, not suddenly. There can be little doubt that Lot had heard of the evil reputation of Sodom and the "cities of the valley." It is possible that he reasoned that this reputation had been grossly overstated and that Sodom couldn't possibly be that bad. Whatever might have been Lot's reasons, he did move his wife and daughters into a wicked environment, a decision that would bring terrible consequences. We should learn, as parents, to consider how our decisions might affect our family. Christian parents are told to "bring up" (educate) their children "in the discipline and instruction of the Lord" (Ephesians 6:4), and this requires some serious thought and planning.

A third lesson we should learn from Lot's wife is not to "look back." Her action of "looking back" involved more than just a turn of the head. Instead of just a glance over the shoulder to see the rain of destruction behind her, her backward look implies *regret* that she was leaving her home in Sodom. The implication is that Lot's wife would have preferred to remain in Sodom, in spite of the wickedness there. Even Lot had been reluctant to leave it, although his "righteous soul [had been] tormented day after day by their lawless deeds" (2 Peter 2:8).

We must remember Lot's wife, learning by her example not to "look back," but to "lay aside" the former lifestyle which was "corrupted in accordance with the lusts of deceit," and to be "renewed in the spirit of [our] mind," putting on a "new self, which in the likeness of God has been created in righteousness and holiness of the truth" (Ephesians 4:22-23).

As Christ said, "Remember Lot's wife. Whoever seeks to keep his life will lose It, and whoever loses his life will preserve it" (Luke 17:32-33).

THE "NOT" IN THE DEVIL'S TALE

As Eve walked through the garden on that fateful day, she found herself standing before the forbidden tree of which God had spoken. He had called it "the tree of the knowledge of good and evil" (Genesis 2:17). But what did Eve know of "good" or "evil," having never experienced "evil"? Obviously, "evil" was something to be avoided and God had added the threat: "In the day that you eat from it you will surely die." That certainly sounded ominous, but what did Eve know of "death"? Had she perhaps seen an *animal* die? We have no idea how long Eve and Adam had already been in the garden, and certainly nothing in Scripture indicates that the animals and plants created by God never *died*. Eve must have known what *death* was, since otherwise God's instructions would have meant nothing to her. As she stood before the tree, contemplating perhaps its natural beauty, a serpent spoke to her, saying, "Indeed, has God said, 'You shall not eat from any tree of the garden'?" (Genesis 3:1-6). Eve seems to have calmly responded that God had given permission to eat the fruit of any tree except this particular tree – the "tree of the knowledge of good and evil" – adding that if she even touched the tree or its fruit she would "die." The serpent then said to her, "You surely will *not* die!" (Genesis 3:4). Satan's tale was certainly different from the *Lord's* story! This "NOT" in Satan's tale would have far reaching effects. God had told the couple they would surely die if they ate this fruit, but Satan, contradicting God, said they would NOT die!

It is interesting, and for some perhaps a little disturbing, to reflect that this forbidden tree did not just suddenly appear in the garden of its own accord. Indeed, God Himself had created it and placed it there, within easy reach of Adam and Eve. To many people, it is troubling that God should thus appear to be the devil's *accomplice* in the seduction of our first parents, but they are in error to so judge.

I do not presume to know everything about the unfathomable Being whom I worship. Since I believe the Bible to be true, I believe that

Words To Live By

God created all things, "both in the heavens and on earth, visible and invisible, whether thrones or dominions or rulers or authorities," and that "all things have been created through Him and for Him" (Colossians 1:16). Nor do I presume to know everything about God's purposes when He created humans. I do, however, believe, as Paul wrote, that humans were "created...*for* Him." Whatever else that phrase may mean, it certainly means that mankind was created "for" God, for *His* glory, for *His* purposes. When we examine the Scriptures, we discover that God created man, as He had also created the angels, to be creatures of *free will*, creatures with the ability to *choose* to do right or wrong. Without the ability to choose, we would be nothing more than robots, without conscience, without the ability to do right or wrong.

In order to *choose*, one must have a *choice*. God provided our first parents with a choice when He created the "tree of the knowledge of good and evil." He clearly warned them not to eat the fruit of that tree, or even to touch it. When they believed the devil's lie, they acted upon their freedom to choose, and ate the forbidden fruit. Actually, as Paul wrote, only the *woman* was "deceived" (1 Timothy 2:14). *Adam's* sin was different from that of Eve (Romans 5:14), since knowing full well what he was doing, he ate the fruit. Adam's sin was *deliberate*, therefore, in a sense, *worse* than that of Eve. The result, however, was the same in both instances – death!

The commandments of God are "holy, righteous, and good," wrote the apostle Paul (Romans 7:12). They were not given out of a desire to "trip up" weak humans. Their purpose was "to result in life" (Romans 7:10), to "lead us beside still waters," to "guide us in paths of righteousness," and to "restore" our souls (Psalm 23:2-3). The commandments of God are not difficult to grasp or to obey. God said through Moses, "This commandment which I command you today is not too difficult for you, nor is it out of reach" (Deuteronomy 30:11). Certainly, the simple commandment given to Adam and Eve was not hard to understand, but Eve chose to believe the devil, when he said, "You will NOT die!"

The devil's "NOT" brought disobedience into the world, and disobedience resulted in a deluge of grief and sadness, affecting every man, woman, and child, in every nation under heaven. God tells us that our "body is a temple of the Holy Spirit" (1 Corinthians 6:19); Satan, on the other hand, argues that "it's *your* body" to do with as you wish, that "nobody can tell you how to use *your* body." If we buy into the devil's lie, we will certainly inherit the resulting "whirlwind" of grief, and will have to stand someday, without benefit of counsel, "before the judgment seat of Christ" to receive the ultimate recompense for how we have misused our body, according to what we have done, "whether good or bad" (2 Corinthians 5:10).

Do not believe the "NOT" in the devil's tale!

Words To Live By

"MY ENEMIES WITHOUT CAUSE"

JEREMIAH WAS A YOUNG PRIEST, THE SON OF Hilkiah, also a priest. When God called him to be his prophet, Jeremiah answered, "Alas, Lord God! Behold, I do not know how to speak, because I am a youth" (Jeremiah 1:1-6). At times during his prophetic ministry, he tended to disagree with how God was treating His people. From Jeremiah's point of view, God was destroying the very work that He had created (Jeremiah 12:2-4). He complained to the Lord, "How long is the land to mourn?"

But God patiently answered His young prophet, saying, "If you have run with footmen and they have tired you out, then how can you compete with horses? If you fall down in a land of peace, how will you do in the thicket of the Jordan?" (Jeremiah 12:5). God effectively told Jeremiah that he had better get into shape, because the competition was going to get tougher very soon. In fact, King Jehoiakim's eleven years' reign (609-598 B.C.) had hardly begun when God told Jeremiah to stand in the "court of the Lord's house" and to preach repentance to the multitudes that had come to worship. Jeremiah must have preached a fiery sermon, since it infuriated the priests and the unfaithful prophets, who immediately seized him, planning to put him to death (Jeremiah 26:2-9). Although cooler heads were able to save Jeremiah on that occasion, his enemies continued to plot against him throughout the reign of Nebuchadnezzar's puppet king Zedekiah. Near the end of Zedekiah's reign, when Nebuchadnezzar's army temporarily moved away from Jerusalem (Jeremiah 37:11-16) to confront an approaching Egyptian army, Jeremiah's enemies became emboldened against him. They arrested him, beat him, and threw him into a prison cell, where he stayed "many days." Soon afterward, deciding to kill him, they dropped him by ropes into a cistern. There was no water in the cistern, "only mud," and Jeremiah sank deeply into it. He would have died there but for the secret intervention of an Ethiopian eunuch, who counseled the king to rescue him (Jeremiah 38:7-16).

As Jeremiah had prophesied, Jerusalem was again besieged by the Babylonian army and, in 586 B.C., her walls were breached. Solomon's magnificent temple was torched, the houses of the city were burned, and the formidable city walls were broken down. The riches of the city were carried away to Babylon and some 4,600 Jews were led away into exile, never to return to Judah (Jeremiah 52:7-30). King Zedekiah, attempting to flee, was captured in the plains of Jericho. Before having his eyes blinded, he was forced to watch as his sons and all the princes of Judah were slaughtered by the king of Babylon. He was then taken bound to Babylon where he would languish in prison until the day of his death (Jeremiah 52:8-11).

Following these events, Jeremiah was permitted by the Babylonians to remain a free man in Judah, where he intended to continue living (Jeremiah 39:11-14; 42:19), but he was forced by a group of desperate Jews to flee with them to Egypt. He seems to have spent his last years in Egypt (Jeremiah 43:1-7), and according to Jewish tradition, he was murdered there by stoning. Hebrews 11:37 may be a reference to this. It was perhaps in Egypt that Jeremiah composed the beautiful, moving poem titled *Lamentations*. He recorded in verse his memories of those horrible days (Lamentations 3:48-56):

> My eyes run down with streams of water
> Because of the destruction of the daughter of my people.
> My eyes pour down unceasingly,
> Without stopping,
> Until the LORD looks down
> And sees from heaven.
> My eyes bring pain to my soul
> Because of all the daughters of my city.
> My enemies without cause
> Hunted me down like a bird;
> They have silenced me in the pit
> And have placed a stone on me.
> Waters flowed over my head;
> I said, "I am cut off!"
> I called on Your name, O LORD,
> Out of the lowest pit.
> You have heard my voice,
> Do not hide Your ear from my prayer for relief,
> From my cry for help.

Jeremiah's was a tragic story. His enemies "without cause" were many, hunting him down "like a bird," silencing him "in the pit" where "waters flowed" over his head (Lamentations 3:52). Although many of us have also seen tragedy and suffering, few could rival that of this faithful man of God. Nevertheless, tragedy is tragedy, hurt is hurt, and sorrow is sorrow, regardless of its scope. Jeremiah's example has been preserved for us to follow. As he remained faithful through tremendous trials, so may we. As he continued to listen to God's voice, so should we.

Even good people can become depressed and question whether God cares. But He is still there! He is still speaking to us through His holy book, the Bible, if we will but open it, read it, and abide by its teachings. The great prophet, Habakkuk, Like Jeremiah, sometimes questioned what God was doing. Nevertheless, Habakkuk ended his oracle with a hymn of hope in poetic form:

> Though the fig tree should not blossom,
> And there be no fruit on the vines,
> Though the yield of the olive should fail
> And the fields produce no food,
> Though the flock should be cut off from the fold
> And there be no cattle in the stalls,
> Yet I will exult in the LORD,
> I will rejoice in the God of my salvation.
> The Lord God is my strength,
> And He has made my feet like hinds' feet,
> And makes me walk on my high places.
> (Habakkuk 3:17-19)

PRAISE THE LORD!

THE PSALMIST WROTE, "PRAISE THE LORD! SING TO the LORD a new song, and His praise in the congregation of the godly ones" (Psalm 149:1). Music, both vocal and instrumental, has been a part of the human experience almost since the beginning of time. According to the Bible, the "father of all those who play the lyre and pipe" was Jubal, a descendant of Cain (Genesis 4:21). Poetry and song have been highly regarded by every culture, from the most rudimentary to the most highly civilized. The ancient Greeks believed poets were inspired to write by divine beings they called "muses."

The children of Israel were scarcely free from Egyptian oppression when Moses led the congregation in songs of praise to God for their deliverance (Exodus 15:1). It was a celebratory song of victory for what God had done for them. In his song of triumph, Moses focused on God, calling Him by His name YHWH ten times. Probably less than a year earlier, on the slopes of Mount Horeb (Exodus 3:13-15), God had revealed to Moses His divine name YHWH, meaning "I AM" or "I AM WHO I AM." The God of heaven is the ONE WHO IS. Without vowels, the original pronunciation of this name has been lost, but vowels have been supplied in English, rendering it *Jehovah* or, perhaps better as *Yahweh*.

Nothing is said of music or song in the divine worship until the days of David, king of Israel. Even as a young boy, David had enjoyed music (1 Samuel 16:18), and we can visualize him sitting on a boulder on the hillsides overlooking Bethlehem, his home village, playing his harp as he watched over his father's flock. It was perhaps in such a setting that David composed the Twenty-third Psalm, which begins,

The LORD [YHWH or Yahweh] is my shepherd,

> I shall not want. He makes me lie down in green pastures;
> He leads me beside quiet waters.

> He restores my soul;
> He guides me in the paths of righteousness
> for His name's sake.

It would be David, the warrior King, who organized the joyous musical reception when the Ark of the Covenant was finally brought back to the tabernacle after having been held captive for a long time by the Philistines (1 Chronicles 15:16-24). And, it would be the aged King David who organized an elaborate orchestra and chorales for the festivals and worship in the future temple to be constructed by Solomon, his son (1 Chronicles 25:1-7).

The very first hymn of praise found in the New Testament was sung ("said") by Mary, the mother of our Lord (Luke 1:46-55). "My soul exalts the Lord," she sang, "and my spirit has rejoiced in God my Savior." We can assume that the Lord Jesus, Himself, brought up by such a deeply spiritual mother, would have regularly participated in the choral praise in the local synagogues of Galilee, as well as during the festivals such as Passover. In fact, it was at the Passover meal with his disciples, the night of His arrest, that Jesus sang with His disciples the group of hymns known as the *Hallel* (Psalms 115-118). Psalm 117, the shortest of the *Hallel* psalms, begins and ends in Hebrew with the word "Hallelujah," and reads as follows:

> Praise the LORD, all nations;
> Laud Him, all peoples!
> For His lovingkindness is great toward us,
> And the truth of the LORD is everlasting.
> Praise the LORD.

It is also evident that first century congregations of the Lord's church included singing in their worship, as mentioned by Paul in 1 Corinthians 14:15, "I will pray with the spirit and I will pray with the mind also; I will sing with the spirit and I will sing with the mind also." In this verse, Paul is regulating the worship, instructing them not to pray or sing in languages not known by the congregation, unless translation was provided (1 Corinthians 14:13). To the Ephesians, he wrote that they should "speak" to one another "in psalms and hymns and spiritual songs, singing and making melody with your heart to the Lord" (Ephesians 5:19). Similar instruction was given to the Colossian church: "Let the word of Christ richly dwell within

Praise The Lord!

you, with all wisdom teaching and admonishing one another with psalms and hymns and spiritual songs, singing with thankfulness in your hearts to God" (Colossians 3:15). In all of these references, Paul stresses that while we are singing "to the Lord," praising Him and thanking Him, we are also "teaching and admonishing one another."

According to the writer of *Hebrews*, when we pray or sing, we are offering "up a sacrifice of praise to God" (Hebrews 13:15). Under the Law of Moses, worshipers brought animals or fowls to be slain as "sacrifices" to God. We, however, bring to God "the fruit of lips that give thanks to His name," with the assurance that "with such sacrifices God is pleased" (Hebrews 13:16).

Our Father in heaven is worthy of our praise; so is His Son! "Worthy are You, our Lord and our God, to receive glory and honor and power; for You created all things, and because of Your will they existed, and were created" (Revelation 4:11). "Worthy is the Lamb that was slain to receive power and riches and wisdom and might and honor and glory and blessing" (Revelation 5:12). A favorite hymn concludes:

> Praise God, from whom all blessings flow;
> Praise Him, all creatures here below;
> Praise Him above, ye heav'nly host;
> Praise Father, Son, and Holy Ghost.
> Amen.

Words To Live By

PRAISE IS BECOMING!

THE PSALMIST WROTE, "PRAISE THE LORD! FOR IT is good to sing praises to our God; for it is pleasant and praise is becoming" (Psalm 147:1). The dictionary defines "becoming" as "suitable" and "attractively fitting."

The things God requires of us are always for our *good*, never for our *hurt*. Since music can have a calming effect, the young shepherd David would play on his harp when King Saul was "terrorized" by an "evil spirit" and "Saul would be refreshed and be well" (1 Samuel 16:23). Because *singing* requires words, *singing* is even more helpful than music without words. The apostle Paul tells us to "make melody *with your heart*" (Ephesians 5:19), *plucking the heartstrings,* as it were. To the church in Corinth, Paul wrote: "I will sing with the spirit and I will sing with the mind also" (1 Corinthians 14:15). J. H. Thayer, in his Greek Lexicon, paraphrased these words: *"I will sing God's praises indeed with my whole soul stirred and borne away by the Holy Spirit, but I will also follow reason as my guide, so that what I sing may be understood alike by myself and by the listeners."* The point is that when I sing, I should be *spiritually focused*, desiring to worship God, while at the same time also speaking words of encouragement and hope to others in the congregation who are doing the same for me.

Paul told believers to sing *"psalms"* (Ephesians 5:19; Colossians 3:16). It is well documented that during the Passover supper, Jews sang "psalms," specifically those which made up what was called the *"Hallel"* or the *"Great Hallel"* (Psalms 111-118). Each of the psalms of the "Hallel" begins with the Hebrew word *"Hallelujah,"* which is translated "Praise JAH," or "Praise Yahweh." Jesus and His disciples would no doubt have followed at Passover the same practice as other Jews. Matthew (26:30) and Mark (14:26) wrote that before leaving the upper room, Jesus and His disciples "sang a hymn." They both used a *verb* (*hymneo*) that says simply that they "sang." The noun form for "hymn" is not used by either Matthew or Mark, although

Praise Is Becoming!

the verb they used suggests that they sang "a hymn," or "hymns." Jesus did not forget to praise God, even when He knew what terrible things were about to occur. Like Jesus, we should remember to praise our God, since "praise is becoming." There is no doubt that some of the psalms of the Old Testament served as a first hymnal for the early church. Our hymnals today include a number of psalms, among them a perennial favorite, *"Hallelujah, Praise Jehovah"* (cf. Psalm 148). Also popular is "Let the Words of My Mouth," which consists of only one verse (Psalm 19:14).

Paul also tells us to sing *"hymns."* Thayer defines the word *"hymn"* [*hymnos*] as "a sacred song." A *"hymn,"* like a *"psalm,"* takes its character from the Holy Scriptures. Whereas a "psalm" would likely be sung as written in the book of Psalms, a *"hymn"* would be a modern composition, although it, too, would be a song of praise based upon Scripture. One such hymn that we sing today is *"Seek Ye First the Kingdom of God,"* based on the words of Jesus in Matthew 6:33. Another would be the short hymn often sung at the beginning of worship, *"The Lord is in His Holy Temple,"* based on Habakkuk 2:20. One of my favorite hymns is *"Rock of Ages,"* which never fails to thrill me:

> Rock of Ages, cleft for me,
> Let me hide myself in Thee.
> Let the water and the blood,
> From Thy wounded side which flowed,
> Be of sin the double cure.
> Save from wrath and make me pure.
>
> While I draw this fleeting breath,
> When my eyes shall close in death
> When I rise to worlds unknown,
> And behold Thee on Thy throne,
> Rock of Ages, cleft for me,
> Let me hide myself in Thee.

Paul instructed the church to "teach and admonish" one another with "spiritual songs." A "spiritual song" seems to differ from "psalms" or "hymns" in that it addresses a host of ideas that can encourage and strengthen the congregation. Many "spiritual songs" address our hope that, after death, we will be in heaven with Christ and the saints who have preceded us. Many other songs deal with Christian conduct in the present time. "*O, Master, Let Me Walk With Thee*" is a favorite. Another is "*O, To Be Like Thee!*" Still others serve to invite to Christ those who have not yet committed their lives to Him, such as "*Almost Persuaded*," or "*Just as I Am*."

When we assemble to worship God, we would do well to include selections from each of the three categories of songs, but I think we should place more emphasis on songs that *praise God*. After all, that is our chief purpose when we worship. Robert Grant's magnificent hymn urges us to "worship the King!"

> O worship the King, all-glorious above,
> And gratefully sing His wonderful love;
> Our Shield and Defender, the Ancient of Days,
> Pavilioned in splendor and girded with praise.
>
> Frail children of dust, and feeble as frail,
> In Thee do we trust, nor find Thee to fail;
> Thy mercies, how tender! How firm to the end!
> Our Maker, Defender, Redeemer, and Friend!

UNRIGHTEOUS JUDGES

While I was preaching in Jones County, Mississippi, in the mid-1970s, a certain judge of long standing in Hattiesburg was forced out of office for gross misconduct. He accepted bribes in return for favorable opinions and obliged women to provide sexual favors or face long prison terms. As is often the case, this judge had "friends" who were able to keep him in office for many years.

Too often in our society we read in the papers or hear on the national news about corrupt judges who release the criminal who has money and influence, but incarcerate those who cannot pay. Many judges have political biases which result in bizarre judgments and the overturning of age-old societal concepts of morality.

David began Psalm 58 with the question, "Do you indeed speak righteousness, O *gods*? Do you judge uprightly, O sons of men?" It is obvious that in this context the Hebrew word e*lohim,* here translated "gods," refers to officials who hear evidence and render judgments in courts of law.

The prophet Samuel had served as the high judge in Israel before the institution of the monarchy, and each year he rode the circuit "to Bethel and Gilgal and Mizpah," returning then to Rama, where he lived (1 Samuel 7:15-17). He was a righteous judge, but his sons who became judges after him were dishonest, taking bribes and perverting justice (1 Samuel 8:1-3).

King David himself often sat as a judge in Israel, and knew well the temptations that faced such judges. David's most difficult problem, however, was in judging himself. But having a tender heart, he was able to accept his guilt when the courageous prophet Nathan confronted him in the affair of Bathsheba and her husband. Regarding this, he wrote, "I know my transgressions, and my sin is ever before me. Against You, You only, I have sinned and done what is evil in Your sight, so that you are justified when You speak and blameless when You judge" (Psalm 51:3-4).

Human judges will always be flawed, but the Judge of all men is Yahweh, the Creator. He is all powerful, present everywhere and at all times. His gaze penetrates the innermost recesses of our mind and soul. It is He who should strike terror in our hearts as we contemplate our sins, recognizing that He knows our hearts and that we cannot hide anything from Him. His swift judgment will not delay. As David wrote, "Before your pots can feel the fire of thorns He will sweep them away with a whirlwind, the green and the burning alike" (Psalm 58:9). And men will say, "Surely there is a reward for the righteous; surely there is a God who judges on earth!" (Psalm 58:11).

Therefore, in view of the certain coming of Yahweh's judgment, the apostle Paul urged Christians to make sure they are ready for it. He wrote,

> Test yourselves to see if you are in the faith;
> examine yourselves! Or do you not recognize
> this about yourselves,
> that Jesus Christ is in you – unless indeed you fail the test?
> But I trust that you will realize that we ourselves
> do not fail the test.
> Now we pray to God that you do no wrong;
> not that we ourselves may appear approved,
> but that you may do what is right,
> even though we may appear unapproved.
> (2 Corinthians 12:5-7).

The *Hebrews* writer, speaking of the "word of God," observed that it is "living and active and sharper than any two-edged sword" and is "able to judge the thoughts and intentions of the heart" (Hebrews 4:12). As we "examine" ourselves, we would do well to consult God's word as the standard by which we should judge. If I compare my present deeds to my past deeds, I might feel good about myself, but it would be far better to compare myself to the image of what *I ought to be*. That "image" is presented in the word of God.

HATCHING EGGS WHICH YOU DID NOT LAY

THE LAW OF "UNINTENDED CONSEQUENCES"! We all think what we are doing is the right thing, something that will produce good results. But sometimes, after we have invested much time and effort in a project, we learn it will not turn out the way we hoped or believed it would. Maybe we just did not think it through before we started. Perhaps we did not study the problem from every angle, or did not consider what might happen if we did this or that.

The prophet Jeremiah recorded a proverb of his day: "As a partridge that hatches eggs which it has not laid, so is he who makes a fortune, but unjustly" (Jeremiah 17:11). The partridge has been accused of sometimes "stealing" the eggs of other birds, and hatching them, but it may be that, because the partridge builds its nest on the ground, other birds may actually lay eggs in the nest of the partridge, which then hatches them. Either way, the partridge gains nothing, since the resulting chicks will not be partridges. Jeremiah applied the proverb to a man who unjustly makes a fortune which, "in the midst of his days," he loses. Like the partridge, this conniving person gains nothing.

When King David stood upon his roof one evening gazing upon the beautiful Bathsheba as she bathed in her apartment (2 Samuel 11:2), he did not for a moment contemplate the far-reaching consequences of his lust. David intended his tryst with Bathsheba to be only a moment of pleasure, but this woman belonged to Uriah the Hittite, a model soldier who would willingly die for his king. The results of the king's action that night would be disastrous to say the least. He had intruded on a "nest" that was not his and he would pay a price he could not foresee. The results of his moment of illicit pleasure would stretch far into the future. When Bathsheba informed the king that she was pregnant with his child, David was terrified. Knowing that his sin would soon become known, David devised a plan to have Uriah return home on a short furlough, thinking that he

Words To Live By

would sleep with his wife and think he was responsible for her pregnancy. When that plot failed, the king arranged for the unsuspecting husband to be killed in the heat of battle. So far, so good, he may have thought, as he took Uriah's widow for his wife. The child was born and all seemed well, but David had left God out of the equation. David had not been alone on his rooftop or in his bedroom that fateful night. The invisible, all-seeing, ever-present God had been there as well, and in time, God sent his prophet Nathan to knock on David's door. Nathan came to inform David that his innocent "love child," was going to die – an unintended consequence! Furthermore, Nathan informed the king that "because of this deed you have given occasion to the enemies of the Lord to blaspheme" (2 Samuel 12:14).

God did not hide the sins of David, but laid them out before us in sad detail, in all of their ugliness. Yet David really loved God, and God loved David. He was said to be a man after God's own heart (1 Samuel 13:14). It is easy for us to stand at a distance and criticize David, thinking perhaps that we would never do what David did, but we all have faults and have at time nourished our own "secret sins." There is not one of us who can claim to be a "perfect" Christian. We too must do our best to keep our feet in the way of righteousness.

Paul told his young assistant Timothy to "show" himself "an example of those who believe" and to teach others to do the same (1 Timothy 4:11-12). In the same epistle, Paul wrote, "The sins of some men are quite evident, going before them to judgment; for others, their sins follow after. Likewise also, deeds that are good are quite evident, and those which are otherwise cannot be concealed" (1 Timothy 5:24-25). David's sin was kept secret for a while, but if he thought that what he did in secret would remain hidden forever, but he was mistaken. Paul warned that "secret sins" tend somehow to be discovered. When our sin becomes known, not only are we embarrassed, but the church is shamed and God's name is blasphemed. And, of course, there is always the judgment by the "all-seeing" God who does not sleep.

Paul wrote to the Colossians: "Whatever you do, do your work heartily, as for the Lord rather than for men, knowing that from the Lord you will receive the reward of the inheritance. It is the Lord Christ whom you serve. For he who does wrong will receive the consequences of the wrong which he has done, and that without partiality" (Colossians 3:23-25). Our actions, whether good or bad, always bring unintended consequences. Ella Wilcox, in a poem entitled *My Ships*, penned the following words regarding such consequences. Referring to these actions as to "ships at sea." She wrote:

> If all the ships I have at sea
> Should come a-sailing home to me,
> Ah, well! The harbor would not hold
> So many ships as there would be
> If all my ships came home from sea.

It may be that you and I have "ships" at "sea" which we hope and pray will never come home to us. May your "ships" and mine be laden only with *good* freight, with nothing that might cause shame for us, for the Lord's church, or for our God! And may we not "hatch" any "eggs" we did not "lay."

Words To Live By

THE PARABLE OF THE BOILING POT

FOR MANY YEARS, JUDAH HAD BEEN A BATTLEground between the Egyptians and the ruling powers of the Mesopotamian region, first the Assyrians, then the Babylonians. Jerusalem served first the one, and then the other, as it was necessary. Finally, in 597 B.C., the great army of Nebuchadnezzar pushed the Egyptian forces out of the area and subdued Jehoiakim, who was reigning in Jerusalem as a puppet king of Pharaoh Neco. Jehoiakim's son Jehoiachin was carried away to Babylon, along with some 10,000 other citizens (2 Kings 24:10-16). Among these captives was a young priest named Ezekiel (Ezekiel 1:3). He had lived in Babylon with his wife, in relative freedom, when God called him to be His prophet and spokesman, in July, 593 B.C. (Ezekiel 1:1). He would faithfully fulfill these duties for the next twenty-two years.

Much of Ezekiel's book is difficult to understand, but interesting. A great deal of it concerned his beloved Jerusalem which would be destroyed in 586 B.C., and her national restoration, which he would not live to see. Chapters 34-37 contain a mixture of symbols, many of which relate to the future spiritual kingdom of the Messiah (the *church*, Colossians 1:13-20), in which a faithful "remnant" would participate, ruled over by "My servant David" (Ezekiel 34:23-31). The reign of "My servant David" is more fully discussed, and more readily understood, in Ezekiel's parable of the "valley of dry bones" (Ezekiel 37).

On January 15, 588 B.C., "in the tenth month, on the tenth of the month" (Ezekiel 24:1), the prophet Ezekiel saw his vision of the "boiling pot." He was told by God to set a pot of water on an intense fire, bringing the water to a "vigorous" boil. In the pot, he was to place "the pieces, every good piece, the thigh and the shoulder," and to "fill it with choice bones," the "choicest of the flock" (Ezekiel 24:3-5). These "pieces" which were placed in the boiling pot represented the inhabitants of Jerusalem who thought themselves safe, who had been permitted to remain in the city, instead of being deported

The Parable Of The Boiling Pot

as had been Ezekiel and others. The message of the parable of the "boiling pot" was that God would soon judge the city of Jerusalem, because their evil conduct had continued with no sign of repentance. The "pot" was boiling and nothing could prevent what was about to happen to the "rebellious house." God said through the prophet Ezekiel, "You will not be cleansed from your filthiness again until I have spent My wrath on you. I, the LORD, have spoken; it is coming and I will act. I will not relent, and I will not pity and I will not be sorry; according to your ways and according to your deeds I will judge you." (Ezekiel 24:13-14).

As I contemplate Ezekiel's parable, I think about our beloved America. Founded on principles drawn from the word of God, our great nation has long stood as a beacon for freedom and democracy, but it seems now to be in decline in many ways. I recognize that America is not a direct parallel of Israel. Whereas Israel began as a "theocracy," reigned over by the Lord God, America was never a "theocracy." Although to some degree founded upon "Judeo-Christian" principles, America was a human creation whose laws have never been perfect and whose administration has never been guided directly by God.

We have witnessed a steep decline in morality, even when compared with only a generation ago. Right and wrong used to be, at least in theory, polar opposites. In less than fifty years, it seems, moral guidelines and rules of conduct that date from hundreds, and in some cases, even thousands of years have quickly eroded, and "right" has been turned upside down. The line between right and wrong has been blurred by a philosophy of moral relativism similar to that described in Judges 17:6, when "every man did what was right in his own eyes." One recalls the prophet Isaiah's language, "Woe to those who call evil good, and good evil; who substitute darkness for light and light for darkness; who substitute bitter for sweet and sweet for bitter!" (Isaiah 5:20).

The Roman governor Felix trembled when Paul spoke to him about "righteousness, self-control and the judgment to come" (Acts 24:25). We should also tremble as we contemplate the "boiling pot" that could be awaiting our nation, and indeed, the whole world. The apostle Paul wept as he penned his epistle to the Philippians, as he contemplated the fate of those who "are enemies of the cross of Christ, whose end is destruction, whose god is their appetite, and whose glory is in their shame, who set their minds on earthly things" (Philippians 3:18-19). As he wrote to the Corinthians about fornicators, idolaters, adulterers, effeminate, homosexuals, thieves, covetous, drunkards, revilers, and swindlers, Paul reminded us that "such were some of you, but you were washed, but you were sanctified, but you were justified in the name of the Lord Jesus Christ and in the Spirit of our God" (1 Corinthians 6:9-11).

We live in the world, but let us not allow the world to dictate for us what our conduct should be. The "pot" may be boiling even now for us as individuals and as a nation.

THE TWO DAUGHTERS OF THE LEECH

THE LOWLY LEECH IS PERHAPS ONE OF THE MOST despised of all the animals created by God. I remember a movie in which a fugitive from the law was wading at night through a swampy area, when he suddenly realized that some ugly little creatures were attached to his body, sucking his blood. In fact, because leeches are blood suckers, they were valued by medical doctors since the ancient Greeks. Medical leeches could be found in many apothecaries because doctors believed that "bleeding" the patient was often an important part of treatment. The Medieval theory of physiology regarding "Four Humours," or *fluids,* in the human body, held that illnesses resulted from an "imbalance" that "bleeding" could correct. A doctor might apply a leech or two, or use a special cutting tool, in order to rid the patient of the "bad blood." It is believed by many that our first president, George Washington, might have survived the ailment that took his life, if the doctors had not "bled" him. After scientists disproved this ancient medical theory, the use of leeches fell into disrepute.

In recent years, however, the leech has made an unexpected comeback, as doctors have learned that when a leech attaches itself to an animal to get nourishment, it secretes something into the wound that thins the blood. Doctors have recently learned that leeches could indeed be useful with some illnesses, and on January 23, 2011, the U. S. Food and Drug Administration approved their use as *medical devices.*

Several hundred years before Christ, the wise man Agur, the son of Jakeh, coined a proverb based on the leech: "The leech has two daughters," both named *"Give"* (Proverbs 30:15). These "daughters" of the leech share the chief characteristic of their father – neither will ever say "Enough." Their appetite will never be satisfied.

Agur's proverb addressed man's insatiable desire for riches, his inability to be content with what he has. Jesus echoed this bit of ancient wisdom when He said, "Do not store up for yourselves treasure on earth, where moth and rust destroy, and where thieves break in and steal" (Matthew 6:19-20). The Lord's emphasis, however, was not on the *amount* of wealth that one might "store up," but on the *importance* one might place on such things. Jesus was warning His disciples that earthly treasures cannot be guaranteed against loss, and that those who strive for material wealth have their hearts in the wrong place (Matthew 6:21).

Another great lesson taught by Agur's proverb is that we should be less interested in getting stuff and more interested in sharing with others. The "daughters" of the leech are aptly named, for the only word in their vocabulary is "Give!" But the leech's daughters are interested not in giving to others, but in other people giving to them.

Christians should not be characterized by greed or stinginess. The rich man in one of Christ's parables was stingy (Luke 16:19-31). He had great wealth, but shared none of it with those who were less fortunate than he. Every day, as he left his mansion, he seemed not even to notice poor Lazarus as he lay near the gate. He could have been a blessing to this man, but chose not to be. An early Jewish Christian, Joseph of Cyprus, was aptly nick-named Barnabas, "the Son of Encouragement" (Acts 4:36-37). Luke recorded that Barnabas "was a good man, and full of the Holy Spirit and of faith," adding that through him "considerable numbers were brought to the Lord" (Acts 11:24). We think also of the wonderful Christian lady, Tabitha, better known as Dorcas, of whom Luke wrote, "This woman was abounding with deeds of kindness and charity which she continually did" (Acts 9:36).

During what he thought might be his final visit with the elders of the church of Ephesus, Paul spoke these words: "I have coveted no one's silver or gold or clothes. You yourselves know that these hands ministered to my own needs and to the men who were with me. In everything I showed you that by working hard in this manner you must help the weak and remember the words of the Lord Jesus, that He Himself said, '*It is more blessed to give than to receive.*'" (Acts 20:33-35). Finally, Paul shared with us a virtue that he "learned" during his lifetime, a lesson that the "daughters of the leech" could never appreciate, that of being able to be content. "I have learned," said Paul, "to be content in whatever circumstances I am" (Philippians 4:11).

Let us also learn to "be content" in every circumstance of life, striving to be *givers*, instead of *getters*. And "the God peace will be with" us (Philippians 4:9).

GOD IS MY WITNESS!

PAUL WROTE TO THE ROMANS, "FOR GOD, WHOM I serve in my spirit in the preaching of the gospel of His son, is my witness" (Romans 1:9). The apostle often called on God to be his witness. "For God is witness," he wrote to the Philippians, "how I long for you all with the affection of Christ Jesus" (Philippians 1:8). He recognized that God was watching from heaven and was aware of his actions.

The Biblical word for "witness" (*martus*) often carries with it a legal sense. "*Martus* is sometimes used of a legal proceeding as well as nonlegal proceedings that nevertheless carry legal connotations" (Mounce, 797). Indeed, God who *is aware of our actions*, will one day sit as our judge, "so that each one may be recompensed for his deeds in the body, according to what he has done, whether good or bad" (2 Corinthians 5:10). Our consolation lies in the fact that God's Son, Jesus Christ, will act as our court appointed "Advocate," assuring that, though *guilty*, we will be pronounced *justified* (1 John 2:1). The "debt" of sins which weighs so heavily against us will have been "canceled out," "taken out of the way," having been *nailed to the cross* of our Lord Jesus (Colossians 2:14).

The Old Testament counterpart of the New Testament word "witness" is mostly used in the legal sense, as it is illustrated in the Ten Commandments: "You shall not bear *false witness* against your neighbor" (Exodus 20:16). Although to tell a lie is a grievous sin and is also forbidden, the *focus* of the Ninth Commandment given by Moses is more precisely that *one should not bring false charges against another person* in a court of law. The commandment is re-stated in Exodus 23:1-2: "You shall not bear a false report: do not join your hand with a wicked man to be a *malicious witness*."

When Paul called on God to be his "witness," he was aware that God would one day be his judge, but he was also certain that God knew his works. He was not afraid to have God as both his witness and

God Is My Witness!

his judge. Paul did not lie when he wrote to the Romans about his evangelistic efforts, or when he assured the Philippians that he loved them dearly and prayed often for them. He did not lie; he told the truth. And he was happy that God was his faithful witness.

We cannot hide from God. Although we might conceal our actions from other people, even from family and friends, we cannot keep secrets from God. David wrote, "Even before there is a word on my tongue, behold, O Lord, You know it all" (Psalm 139:4). When Hagar had been driven from Abraham's home by her mistress, Sarah, she fled into the desert and was hiding in an oasis near a well of water. God saw her there and told her to return to Sarah and that He would take care of her and her offspring. Hagar returned to Sarah, but in recognition of her encounter with God, she named the well "*Beer-lahai-roi*" – the "well of the God who sees" (Genesis 16:13). God is, indeed, *lahai-roi*, the "God who sees," and this is why Paul called on Him to be his witness. He knew that God saw all of his actions. God also sees everything that *we* do.

But God is not the only witness to our actions. Other people, whether known by us or not, know who we are, and they observe our behavior. That is why Peter wrote: "Keep your behavior excellent among the Gentiles, so that in the thing in which they slander you as evildoers, they may because of your good deeds, as they observe them, glorify God in the day of visitation" (1 Peter 2:12). Other people observe our behavior, but God sees everything, and knows every secret.

In like manner, we are witnesses of the deeds of other people. One dark afternoon, I was returning home from Bible study appointments near Namur, Belgium. The narrow, winding road crossed the plateau region of central Belgium, high above the Meuse River valley. I began to notice that the car directly ahead of me was weaving back and forth across the middle line, sometimes nearly leaving the pavement. Recognizing that the driver was probably drunk and obviously a public danger, I stopped at a roadside pub and dialed the gendarmes. A week or so later, I received a visit from the police, informing me that they had located the inebriated driver and requesting that I appear at his trial. Standing before the judge, I was instructed to tell him what I had seen. I was *a witness* and was sworn to tell the truth. The drunk driver was found guilty *in absentia*, since he did not even show up at his own trial. He never saw the person who had witnessed his actions.

We are instructed by God's word to "walk in a manner worthy of the calling" with which we have been called (Ephesians 4:1). This "worthy" conduct involves *every aspect of our lives*: how we conduct ourselves when we participate in sports, how we behave as spectators at games, how we behave in restaurants, how we treat the servers, how we discipline our children at Walmart, and on and on we could go. In addition to all the other people who see our actions, *Lahai-roi*, "The God who sees," is also a silent spectator.

When we worked with the church in Lachine, Canada, a Christian man who had been sober for twenty-five years suddenly "went off the wagon." On a cold, snowy night I stood with Benoit Lacombe on the sidewalk, trying to persuade him to return home and go to bed, but he refused. I walked with him to the tavern and sat across the table from him while he had his drink, so that I could get him back home. But he just sat there, looking at the bottle. When I asked Benoit why he wasn't drinking, he said, "I can't drink it with you watching!" Isn't it strange that we seem to care more whether people see us doing wrong, than we care about whether *God* sees us?

God is the witness that really counts!

ONLY GOD!

> A tree that looks at God all day
> And lifts her leafy arms to pray;
> A tree that may in summer wear
> A nest of robins in her hair;
> Upon whose bosom snow has lain;
> Who intimately lives with rain.
> Poems are made by fools like me,
> But only God can make a tree.
> (Joyce Kilmer)

A SCIENTIST MAY DESCRIBE ON THE PAGES OF THE *National Geographic* the intimate details of how a leaf may function, but in the final analysis, "only God can make a tree." Or, for that matter, a *leaf*! While it is true that, through cross-pollination, accidental or intentional, new trees may develop over time, the first ones did not just *evolve*; they were *created* – by GOD. Only God can create.

In an otherwise interesting *National Geographic* article about plant leaves, author Rob Dunn wrote: "Chloroplasts, fed by sun, water, carbon dioxide, and nutrients, do the leaf's work. They evolved about 1.6 billion years ago when one cell, incapable of using the sun's energy, engulfed another cell – the reds, blues, indigos, and violets – are trapped" (October 2012, page 54). I have no doubts about the truthfulness of the *scientific data* Mr. Dunn describes. This is material that should be introduced to our children in their science classes in high schools and colleges across the land. What I object to here is the *unscientific* content of Dunn's statement – the assertion that chloroplasts "evolved about 1.6 billion years ago…" My objections involve two things: (1) that chloroplasts "evolved," and (2) the assertion that this "evolution" would have taken place "about 1.6 billion years ago." The second assertion cannot stand unless the first be proved true, and evolution has not been proved to be true. To say that it is true is to perpetuate a falsehood.

Science and assertions are two quite different things. "Science" describes processes and data that can be proved. "Assertions" are statements which may or may not be true. For example, intelligent men asserted for thousands of years that the sun revolved around the earth, and observation seemed to demonstrate that the assertion was valid. We still say "the sun sets and rises," although science has proved it is the earth that turns on its axis and revolves around the sun. Therefore, Mr. Dunn's statement that chloroplasts "evolved about 1.6 billion years ago" is nothing more than an assertion, one that he truly believes, but at the end of the day, it remains only an assertion. Its truthfulness cannot be demonstrated by scientists. We call such assertions "theories." A "theory" is a *possible explanation* of a phenomenon, but it is not a truth that one must accept.

The theory of human evolution is an explanation of how life *may have developed* on planet earth. This theory has come to be accepted by many, if not most, scientists. But there are also many prominent scientists who reject the theory. Of course, those who accept the Theory of Evolution reply that the Bible explanation about how life on earth came about is itself an assertion, and they are correct. The Bible writers did not offer any "scientific proofs" for how the earth or life on the earth came to be. They simply asserted that God created the heavens, the earth, and all life (Genesis 1-3). The New Testament says that "by Him [Jesus Christ] all things were created, both in the heavens and on the earth, visible and invisible, whether thrones or dominions or rulers or authorities – all things have been created through Him and for Him" (Colossians 1:16).

We who believe in God, the Creator, do not reject true science, but we do not base our faith on human science. Human science cannot prove there is no God, and it cannot prove that, if God exists, God did not create all things. In fact, many of the world's greatest scientists have believed in God, and many scientists believe in a Creator. They also reject the theory that life "evolved" or had its origins billions of years ago in some "Big Bang."

Our government has spent billions of dollars in attempts to find evidence of water on Mars, believing that if there has been water, there could have been life on Mars. They spent this money freely because they believe the Theory of Evolution that teaches that the

Only God!

first protein molecule evolved in water, and that, therefore, human life itself sprang from water. Scientists have worked unsuccessfully for years trying to recreate a single living cell. The secret of life still eludes them, and, I believe, will always elude them. As it was written nearly three thousand years ago in the Bible, "I saw every work of God, [and] I concluded that *man cannot discover the work* which has been done under the sun. Even though man should seek laboriously, he will not discover; and though the wise man should say, 'I know,' he cannot discover" (Ecclesiastes 8:17).

There are things that only God can do, and this includes the act of creation. Man can *modify* the raw materials that he finds on earth, but he cannot *create them*. Man can manipulate the human egg or sperm and generate a baby, but he cannot create the life that is inherent within the baby. God is the One who "breathed into" our first parents "the breath of life" and caused them to be "living beings" (Genesis 2:7). The only "scientist" able to accomplish such a feat was Mary Shelley's fictional Dr. Frankenstein.

I stand in awe of the wonderful things modern science has done and can do. Things of which we could only dream a hundred years ago are now things we think we could not live without. Although it may seem to us that there are no limits to what humans can know or do, we would be mistaken to place our confidence and hope in humans or in human science. But there are no limits to what God can do. When Job and his friends were arguing about what was or was not true, God interrupted them, saying: "Where were you when I laid the foundation of the earth? ... Have the gates of death been revealed to you? ... Have you understood the expanse of the earth? Tell Me, if you know all this ... Who has put wisdom in the innermost being or given understanding to the mind? ... Who prepares for the raven its nourishment when its young cry to God and wander about without food? ... Is it by your understanding that the hawk soars, stretching his wings toward the south?" (Job 38-39).

We sing Stuart Hines' majestic hymn,

> O Lord my God! When I in awesome wonder
> Consider all the worlds Thy hands have made,
> I see the stars, I hear the rolling thunder,
> Thy pow'r throughout the universe displayed,

> Then sings my soul, my Saviour God to Thee;
> How great Thou art, how great Thou art!

The American poet Joyce Kilmer wrote:

> I think that I shall never see
> A poem lovely as a tree.
> A tree whose hungry mouth is prest
> Against the earth's sweet flowing breast.

HELP FROM THE SANCTUARY

THE PROPHET ELISHA HAD A VERY CLOSE RELATIONship with Yahweh, the God of heaven. He knew that Yahweh was ever present with him, and he knew that when he spoke with Him, He listened. Elisha's prayers were to the point, a real conversation with God, not a dry work of art directed more toward men than toward God. His close relationship with Yahweh is shown in that he knew without question that He would answer his prayers.

The story recorded in 2 Kings 6 finds Elisha in the hill village of Dothan, early in the morning, just arising from his bed. His servant who had just left the house on some errand was suddenly confronted with a situation that terrified him. The quiet village was surrounded by "an army with horses and chariots" (2 Kings 6:15). Enemy soldiers! Danger on every hand! The servant rushed back into the house, no doubt yelling at the top of his voice, "Alas, my master! What shall we do?"

Elisha did not for an instant lose his calm. He simply replied, "Do not fear, for those who are with us are more than those who are with them." I doubt, however, that this response did much to calm the nerves of Elisha's servant. Since the servant obviously needed some proof that all was indeed well, Elisha immediately spoke to God, saying, "O LORD, open his eyes that he may see." And God "opened the servant's eyes and he saw, and behold, the mountain was full of horses and chariots of fire all around Elisha" (2 Kings 6:17).

Elisha and his servant were the only two people in the village who could see God's army, which apparently had been there the entire time, unseen. The enemy soldiers had orders from the king of Aram (Syria) to seize and perhaps even to kill the prophet. When they came down to him, Elisha prayed again, saying, "LORD, strike this people with blindness, I pray" (2 Kings 6:18), and immediately it was done.

The soldiers from Aram could not see the "horses and chariots of fire" that filled the mountain upon which the village of Dothan was built, but they were as real as their own. Elisha's own servant was not even aware of them until God opened his eyes. Nevertheless, they were there. The unseen "spiritual reality" is as real as the physical realities which we humans can see. The fact that we cannot see them with our physical eyes does not mean they are not real, that they are not there.

Many years before Elisha was born, King David wrote: "May the LORD answer you in the day of trouble! May the name of the God of Jacob set you securely on high! May He send you help from the sanctuary and support you from Zion!" (Psalm 20:1-2). "Sanctuary" is another word for the Most Holy Place, the second room of the Tabernacle, which housed the Ark of the Covenant and the Mercy Seat. The "Sanctuary" of the Tabernacle was a symbol of God's heavenly throne room where the prophet Isaiah, in a vision, "saw the Lord sitting on a throne, lofty and exalted," the "train of His robe" filling the temple (Isaiah 6). It was in the temple's "Sanctuary" that God occasionally met with Moses and spoke with him.

The Lord Jesus instructed His disciples to pray, "Our Father who is in heaven" (Matthew 6:9). To do this, one must *believe in his heart* that there is indeed a "Father" who is in heaven. Jesus often lifted his face toward the sky and prayed audibly, so as to be an example for those who heard Him (John 11:42). Jesus did not *pray to an imaginary God,* and neither do we. In the Bethany cemetery, standing before the tomb which sheltered the dead body of His good friend Lazarus, the Lord's heart was breaking as he saw the sincere grief of His dear friends who had prematurely lost a brother. The "beloved disciple" John records that on this occasion, "Jesus wept" (John 11:35). Different from the loud "weeping" of the mourners, the Lord's "weeping" was quiet. He "shed tears." He was "deeply moved" (John 11:38).

Jesus wanted His disciples at Bethany to know that there is a spiritual reality that they were missing. All they could see at that point was that their friend Lazarus was dead. Jesus wanted them to look beyond physical death and see "life" that they were thus far incapable of comprehending. How could they have known that Jesus

Himself was "the resurrection and the life" (John 11:25)? It is so difficult to see beyond the stark reality of physical things, things that we can touch and hold in our hands. But if Christianity is to be real for us, we must understand, not only with the head, but with the heart, that what is unseen is also real, perhaps more real, more enduring than is the physical.

So, as Elisha had done for his servant, Jesus had to demonstrate this truth for His disciples. He turned to the cave where His friend's body lay, then four days dead, and demanded that the stone be removed. Then He cried with a loud voice, "Lazarus, come forth!"

"Help from the sanctuary!" It is from the "Sanctuary" that our help must come. David wrote, "May He grant you your heart's desire and fulfill all your counsel! We will sing for joy over your victory, and in the name of our God we will set up our banners. May the LORD fulfill all your petitions!" (Psalm 10:4-5). The apostle Paul wrote: "In the same way the Spirit also helps our weakness; for we do not know how to pray as we should, but the Spirit Himself intercedes for us with groanings too deep for words; and He who searches the hearts knows what the mind of the Spirit is, because He intercedes for the saints according to the will of God." (Romans 8:26-27). And God who is in heaven will grant us "help from the Sanctuary!"

PROVIDENCE

WE OFTEN USE THE WORDS "PROVIDENCE" AND "providential" when we talk about God, but did you know that the English word "providence" occurs in the Bible only once, referring not to God but to a Roman governor (Acts 24:2)? In that context, the word signified the governor's benevolent planning and wise decisions. The Greek term is again used in Romans 13:14, translated "provision." The framers of the American *Constitution* and the *Declaration of Independence* often used the word "Providence" as a synonym for "God." As I here use the word, I refer to *God's* benevolent purposes regarding His people.

We often illustrate God's "providence" by citing how He used Joseph to save the family of Jacob during a long period of famine, or a young Jewish girl, Esther, to deliver the Jewish exiles from the evil intent of wicked Haman. The important thing to remember about "providence" is that it can only be recognized after the fact. Joseph, for example, did not know that God would use his troubles to fulfill His divine purpose. He could not have known how the years that he spent as a slave in the house of Potiphar (Genesis 39:1) or in an Egyptian prison would fit into the puzzle of God's grand design. It would only be when his family came to buy food during the famine that Joseph finally understood that "It was not you who sent me here, but God; and He has made me a father to Pharaoh and lord of all his household and ruler over all the land of Egypt" (Genesis 45:8). And Esther had no idea that her elevation to royalty was the work of God (Esther 4:13-14).

In the 1960s, a young missionary named Lynn Camp was smuggling Bibles into Hungary, then controlled by the Soviets. On one trip to Budapest, he visited a large Protestant church and became acquainted with a man named Ivan, a bank executive whose job required him to travel to Vienna about twice each year. On these visits he and Camp would get together and discuss the Bible. On one such visit Camp met Ivan at the West Station and immediately sensed that something terrible had happened. Ivan explained that during the train ride from Budapest, Communist border officials had inspected the contents of his briefcase, and upon seeing his Bible, immediately hurled it through the open window of the moving train. "What is a man in your position doing with a Bible?" he yelled. But this Bible was like a close personal friend to Ivan and he was deeply saddened at its loss. He went back later to that area searching for the Bible, but without success.

Two years later, Camp was again meeting Ivan at the West Station, but this time Ivan was as upbeat as he had been downcast before. He quickly told how just a few days earlier the postman had delivered a package to his house. Sitting at his kitchen table, he opened it and there was his Bible and with it a letter of apology! The letter explained that some of the children of the village had been playing one day along the railroad tracks and found the Bible. Ivan's address was plainly visible inside. Not knowing what it was, one of the children took it to his grandmother who recognized it as a Bible. The news about this Bible had spread rapidly throughout the village. Although older people knew what the Bible was, nobody had one, since the Communist government had banned the sale or possession of Bibles. The writer of the apology letter explained, "We decided to conceal the discovery while those who so desired would make handwritten copies. That joyful task lasted two years. Please forgive our keeping your Bible so long. But you might like to know that we are now a secret band of about thirty who have baptized each other and seek to follow Jesus in our daily lives."

Providence— God's secret work behind the scenes! Paul wrote to the Romans: "Oh, the depth of the riches both of the wisdom and knowledge of God! How unsearchable are His judgments and unfathomable His ways!" (Romans 11:33). The One who had watched as the nomad Ishmaelite caravan stopped by the pit where young Joseph had been placed by his brothers (Genesis 37:25-28) was also watching as the Hungarian child at play by the railroad tracks picked up the strange book. And in the same way that young Joseph would be His tool in the salvation of ancient Israel in Egypt, God would work behind the scenes to present His word to sincere seekers in that unknown Hungarian hamlet.

What about you? Or me? Do you think that God might be able to use us for some great purpose? A purpose that we might never be aware of, but which might benefit others whom we may never know? I believe God can and does use us, although I could not prove it to be so. Maybe this is what Paul meant when he wrote, "God causes all things to work together for good to those who love God, to those who are called according to His purpose" (Romans 8:28). Sometimes, however, even God, the divine Potter, cannot make with a particular lump of clay the beautiful work of art that He would like to create (Romans 9:20-22; Jeremiah 18:3-4), because the clay would "spoil" in His hand.

We can, however, be confident of this, that God will use us if we *want to be used*, and if, willing to be used by Him, *we prepare ourselves*.

"SO HELP ME GOD!"

CADETS AT THE U.S. AIR FORCE ACADEMY HAVE traditionally been required to make the following pledge: "We will not steal or cheat, nor tolerate among us anyone who does. Furthermore, I resolve to do my duty and to live honorably, so help me God." Recently, an attempt was made to remove the ending phrase "so help me God," as being offensive to those who do not believe in God. The resulting controversy has apparently led the Academy to make the offending phrase optional. Those who do not believe in God will not be forced to recite the phrase.

While the Academy's action is only one more indication that the forces of evil are continuing their offensive against anything that smacks of Christianity, Christians ought not be offended by the compromise. To force people to commit to something they do not believe would serve no good purpose, and would simply multiply the number of hypocrites that might already be among us. And, to be candid, Christians should feel no need to append "so help me God" to such a pledge.

For many years, trial witnesses have been required to place their right hand on the Bible and swear to "tell the whole truth and nothing but the truth, so help me God," but I think that now they can just say "I do." Regardless, however, of what the courts might require people to say, it has always been true that some witnesses have been willing to present false testimony if they thought they could get away with it. The "so help me God" phrase has probably never influenced anyone but a believer to stick with the truth; rather it is the fear of punishment that compels most people not to commit perjury. It is for this reason that James, the Lord's brother, wrote, "But above all, my brethren, do not swear, either by heaven or by earth or with any other oath; but your "yes" is to be yes, and your "no," no, so that you may not fall under judgment" (James 5:12).

The Christian's word should be his bond. There should be no need to make elaborate "oaths." As the Lord said, to add other words to a simple, sincere promise does not make one's promise any more certain or sacred. Jews were accustomed to swearing by heaven, by the earth, by Jerusalem, or by their own head, but these things were all beyond their control (Matthew 4:33-37). James' injunction not to swear at all really refers to the kind of swearing that goes beyond the simple promise to tell the truth and to keep one's word.

It is appropriate for the Christian to ask for God's help in every endeavor. In fact, God does help the believer in many ways, and in all kinds of circumstances. Peter wrote: "The Lord knows how to rescue the godly from temptation" (2 Peter 2:9), and to "protect" us by His power (1 Peter 1:5). David wrote, "God is our refuge and strength, a very present help in trouble" (Psalm 46:1). God's children may certainly believe and trust that the God who so often came to David's aid also stands ready to help us today, perhaps in ways that we cannot understand:

> Behold, the eye of the LORD is on those who fear Him,
> On those who hope for His lovingkindness,
> To deliver their soul from death
> And to keep them alive in famine.
> Our Soul waits for the LORD;
> He is our help and our shield.
> For our heart rejoices in Him,
> Because we trust in His holy name.
> (Psalm 33:18-21)

"KISSING UP" TO THE BOSS

I DON'T THINK I HAVE USED THE PHRASE "KISSING UP" more than twice in my entire life. The coarser expression "brown nosing" is another phrase often used to describe the same action as "kissing up." Both of these expressions connote "conniving," shameless self-seeking, underhanded efforts to win approval from someone in authority.

We don't really like people who "kiss up to the boss." These are people who try to advance or get ahead by hook or crook, using whatever method they can, instead of hard work and dedication. Bosses may sometimes tolerate such "boot lickers" whom they might in turn exploit to their own advantage. And those who "kiss up to the boss" often do advance more rapidly, filling the bureaucracy with dishonest and inept self-seekers. The world is full of such people.

Solomon wrote that "the devious are an abomination to the LORD" (Proverbs 3:32). A "devious" person is one who will "kiss up to the boss," showing himself willing to do whatever the boss wants him to do. But as willing as he is to please his manager, he will just as quickly change directions whenever it is to his advantage to do so. Morality matters little to such a person; he is always "testing the wind," ready to do whatever appears best for himself. Solomon said that instead of "lying" to get ahead, it is "better to be a poor man" (Proverbs 19:22), and while there are many who "proclaim" their loyalty, it is often very hard to "find a trustworthy man" (Proverbs 20:6). He suggested that "wealth obtained by fraud" is often *lost*, while that "gathered by labor" *increases* (Proverbs 13:11). Many people presently serving time in federal prisons are there because they illegally and immorally abused the system in order to gain wealth. A prominent example of such is Martha Stewart, who spent a few years in federal lockup, convicted (rightfully or wrongfully) of "insider trading." And who can forget Bernard Madoff, whose name became synonymous with "Ponzi" scams? A recent great recession

Words To Live By

came about largely because of the unethical manipulation of huge sums of money by a relatively few powerful persons.

There were also some "devious" persons who "kissed up" to our Lord in efforts to entrap Him. During His final week before the crucifixion, He was approached by "spies who pretended to be righteous," sent by the scribes and the chief priests who hoped to "catch Him in some statement" (Luke 20:19-20). Imagine for a moment that you were in that crowd, standing near Jesus, in the very shadow of the temple, as He stood teaching the people. They said, "Teacher, we know that you speak and teach correctly, and you are not partial to any, but teach the way of God in truth" (Luke 20:21). The gross hypocrisy of these people astounds us. They called Him *"teacher,"* but believed in their hearts that He was a fraud! They called Him a *teacher of righteousness*, but meant not a word of their praise. They said He was "not partial to any" but they were lying. Jesus, however, "detected their trickery" and reduced them quickly to silence (Luke 20:26).

In an often-misunderstood parable, Jesus referred to an *unethical steward* who had been "squandering" the possessions of his boss for his own advantage. When he was caught and ordered to give an accounting of his mismanagement, he quickly began a *second round* of fraud, by reducing the amounts owed to his boss by various persons (Luke 16:1-8). These people, happy to be able to pay less to get their debts resolved, quickly complied. Therefore, when the unethical steward was shown the door, he was able quickly to find employment with his new-found "friends." In this parable, Jesus was not praising the unethical steward, nor was He telling His disciples to imitate him. He was, however, clearly and without disguise telling the listening "Pharisees, who were lovers of money," that because they "have not been faithful" even in the use of "unrighteous wealth," they should not expect to be entrusted with "the true riches." Turning to the Pharisees, looking them in the eye, Jesus said to them, "You are those who justify yourselves in the sight of men, but God knows your hearts; for that which is highly esteemed among men is detestable in the sight of God" (Luke 16:14-15).

A Greek word, similar to the English expression "kissing up," but with a completely opposite meaning, is the word *"proskuneo,"* the most common word in the New Testament for "worship." This word literally means "to kiss the hand towards" someone. A person would literally fall to his knees and touch the ground with his head in an attitude of humility and reverence. The magi from the Orient thus "fell to the ground and worshiped" the baby Jesus (Matthew 2:11). The disciples, having seen Him walking on the water, "worshiped Him, saying, 'You are certainly God's Son!'" (Matthew 14:33). In John's vision of God's throne, the angels, the "living creatures," and the "elders" "fell on their faces before the throne and worshiped God" (Revelation 7:11). In some instances, however, even the word "worship" has been used in self-serving ways. Satan, for example, asked Jesus to "fall down and worship" him (Matthew 4:9). In effect, he was suggesting that Jesus "kiss up" to him if He wanted to receive the devil's rewards. Jesus, of course, refused. Then, there was the case of the "mother of the sons of Zebedee" who, "bowing down" (*proskunousa*) before Jesus, asked Him to grant special favors to her sons (Matthew 20:20). Her "bowing down" seems to be a kind of "kissing up" in order to gain a favor.

Indeed, *false* piety or *pretended* godliness has often been practiced as a means of obtaining wealth and power. We must, therefore, be careful that our worship be from the heart, sincere and true. The Lord Jesus emphasized that "true worshipers" must "worship the Father in spirit and truth" (John 4:24). When we bow the knee, "kissing the hand towards" our Savior and God, let it be with sincerity, seeking to please God, not self.

Words To Live By

WHOM SHOULD GOD SAVE?

AS MY MIND STROLLS THROUGH THE TWISTING hallways of human history, I notice the names of certain individuals who are certainly LOST. No doubt about it! If the majority opinion is correct about the horrors of hell, these people deserve the hottest fire that demons could possibly cook up! Remember, however, that the majority is rarely right about anything, so we perhaps need to exercise a little caution.

In this brief writing, I am not talking about whom should God *condemn*, because according to the Bible "*all* have sinned and fall short of the glory of God" (Romans 3:23), and *everyone*, therefore, deserves to be lost. Since we can't "work our way" to heaven, if we are to escape the wrath of God, it will be because of His grace (Ephesians 2:8-9).

So, how do we answer the question, "Whom should God *save*?" Actually, the Bible answers this question. To the Jews who believed that salvation could not be extended to Gentiles, Paul observed that the choice is altogether *God's* choice! God told Moses, "I will have mercy on whom I have mercy, and I will have compassion on whom I have compassion" (Exodus 33:19), and Paul applied the statement to God's decision to save *Gentiles* by faith, in the same way that He saves *Jews* (Romans 9:15). If I should decide that God cannot possibly save a particular person who, in my opinion, is too evil to be saved, I would be guilty of talking back to God (Romans 9:19-20) and resisting God's supreme will. Yet, when I have walked through the exhibits in the Nazi death camps at Dachau and Buchenwald, or in the Holocaust Museum in Israel, I have thought within myself that surely *there are people* beyond the scope of God's marvelous grace!

Somewhere recently, I heard it said that "God is not *picky* about whom He saves." Jesus said, "Come to Me, *all* who are weary and heavy-laden, and I will give you rest" (Matthew 11:28). He also said, "*Any* sin and blasphemy shall be forgiven" (Matthew 12:31). "But," we reply, "Surely he doesn't mean...?" And we begin listing those who, in our opinion, deserve God's wrath. Yet, Jesus said, "It will be more tolerable for the land of Sodom in the day of judgment" than for those "religious" bigots who refused to believe after having witnessed many miracles (Matthew 11:24). In a letter to the Christians at Corinth, Paul made a long list of sinful actions that would merit punishment from God, but then he added that "some" of the Christians at Corinth had themselves been guilty of those same heinous sins (1 Corinthians 6:9-11). Guilty but saved!

Jesus was regularly seen in the presence of "sinners" (Luke 15:1), and was therefore condemned by the Pharisees and Scribes. The Lord replied that He was sent to find the "lost sheep" (Luke 15:4). The "good" people aren't as "needy" as are the "sinners." The story about the young man who took his inheritance and squandered it "with loose living" (Luke 15:11-32) ought to cause all of us to stop and think about ourselves. Each one of us can see himself described in this story, either by the *younger* son, who really describes a lot of us, or by the *older* son, who thought he was better than his brother. When we read this story, we may tend to admire the wasteful, loose living younger brother who repented, more than we admire the "faithful" older brother who did not do all of those bad things. And, although many of us tend to be more like the *older* brother, we tend to blame *him* and admire the younger! We have a great problem seeing ourselves as we truly are. Paul, the apostle, saw himself objectively, as "formerly a blasphemer and a persecutor and a violent aggressor" (1 Timothy 1:13). He understood that Jesus had saved him, not because he was such a "good" person, but because of God's incredible mercy. He wrote, "The grace of our Lord was more than abundant, with the faith and love which are found in Christ Jesus" (1 Timothy 1:14).

James, the Lord's brother, wrote that each one of us needs to look into the mirror of God's word and examine how we "look" (James 1:23-25). We need to conduct this examination honestly and carefully. An occasional glance at the mirror is not enough; careful scrutiny should be done regularly, and often. An effort must be made to make changes where changes are needed. Simply to "think" oneself to be "religious" is not sufficient (James 1:26), but righteous activity must result from that visit to the mirror (James 1:26-17).

Words To Live By

No, God is not "picky" about whom He saves. He saves *sinners*! He transforms broken souls and restores spiritual deadness. He causes the "blind" to see and the "lame" to walk. He gives *purpose* to those who stumble blindly in the darkness of evil, and gives hope to the hopeless. He saves *whoever comes* to Him in faith. The church that the Lord began to build on that spring day in Jerusalem (Acts 2) was not intended to be a *refuge* for the good or the righteous, where they could be separate from the sinful and evil. Rather, it was intended to be a *haven* where all who fear God and believe in Jesus, His Son, could find forgiveness and hope. No one who believes in Him, confesses Him, and commits to Him will be refused by Him (Mark 16:15-16). There is no sin so horrendous that the blood of Jesus cannot wash away and forgive.

The words of the wonderful hymn *"Christ Receiveth Sinful Men"* were written by a German Lutheran preacher in Hamburg, Germany, in 1718.

Sinners Jesus will receive; Sound this word of grace to all
Who the heavenly pathway leave, All who linger, all who fall.
Come, and He will give you rest; Trust Him, for His word is plain;
He will take the sinfulest. Christ receiveth sinful men.

Now my heart condemns me not; Pure before the law I stand;
He who cleansed me from all spot, Satisfied its last demand.
Christ receiveth sinful men, Even me with all my sin;
Purged from every spot and stain, Heav'n with Him I enter in.

Chorus:
Sing it o'er and o'er again,
Christ receiveth sinful men;
Make the message clear and plain:
Christ receiveth sinful men.

ON "BROKENNESS"

JEREMIAH, THE "WEEPING PROPHET," WAS PERHAPS standing on a public square in Jerusalem when he cried out, "My sorrow is beyond healing, my heart is faint within me! Behold, listen! The cry of the daughter of my people from a distant land: 'Is the LORD not in Zion? Is her King not within her'?" To this, God responded, "Why have they provoked Me with their graven images, with foreign idols?" Jeremiah answered, "Harvest is past, summer is ended, and we are not saved. For the brokenness of the daughter of my people I am broken; I mourn, dismay has taken hold of me. Is there no balm in Gilead? Is there no physician there? Why then has not the health of the daughter of my people been restored?" (Jeremiah 8:18-22). But there *was* a "balm" in Gilead, and God, the greatest "physician," was near at hand. The problem was that God's people were not interested in consulting Him.

Jeremiah used the word "brokenness" when he referred to the "health" of God's people. And he "mourned" and wept as he contemplated this "brokenness." Jeremiah yearned for the people of God who had forsaken the true God, preferring instead the graven images of the Gentile nations around them. He yearned for the salvation and restored spiritual health of God's people. He asked, almost in despair, "Is there no balm in Gilead? Is there no physician there?"

As we look about us, we wonder at the "brokenness" we see on every side. Who has not had a family member or friend who suffers from drug or alcohol addiction? Who does not know families that have been broken by spousal unfaithfulness or abuse, whether physical or mental? Who among us has not witnessed the results of anger? On and on we could go. We might even in our own neighborhood be led to question if there is a "balm" available that could cure or heal the "brokenness" which we observe about us.

Jeremiah was dismayed that Israel had not consulted God for "healing." History reveals that Israel's brokenness was not healed. In only a short time Jeremiah would witness the complete destruction of Jerusalem and the deportation of the entire Jewish people to exile in a foreign land. Most of these would never return to their homeland.

Fast forwarding to our time, we discover that we do have a "balm" that can cure our ills and a "physician" who knows our problems and is able to heal us. Although Jesus never called Himself the "Great Physician," He hinted that He was. One day, as He entered Capernaum, His "own city," Jesus saw Matthew the tax collector, sitting at his toll booth. Because many tax collectors were dishonest, they were all thought to be so, but Jesus saw in *this* man someone who might be redeemed. So, the Lord invited Himself to dinner in Matthew's own house (Matthew 9:9-11). Other tax collectors and "sinners" were also in the house, sitting with Jesus at the table. The Pharisees were shocked to see Jesus in the presence of these terrible sinners, and mocked Him for it, but Jesus answered, saying, "It is not those who are healthy who need a physician, but those who are sick" (Matthew 9:12). The Lord's purpose was to restore the sick to health and to heal their "brokenness."

The first thing the Great Physician does for the sinner who comes to Him is to wash away the dirt, the spiritual filth, that has accumulated over the years (1 Peter 1:2, 19-23). He so thoroughly cleanses the repentant believer who comes to Him that in spite of his physical age he is like a newborn baby (1 Peter 2:2).

Having washed and cleansed the sinner thoroughly, the Great Physician then performs organ transplantation. Ezekiel prophesied that after cleansing His people of their "filthiness," God would give them "a new heart and put a new spirit" within them (Ezekiel 36:25-26). The Lord Jesus properly diagnosed the greatest health problem of mankind as "hardness of heart" (Mark 3:5), hearts that were filled with "evil" (Mark 7:21). The apostle Paul wrote about spiritual "surgery" called "circumcision...of the heart, by the Spirit" (Romans 2:29).

Following the "washing" and the acquiring of a "new" heart, there must come an extended period of spiritual growth and development.

On "brokenness"

Peter said that the "newborn babies" must "grow in respect to salvation." "Keep your behavior excellent among the Gentiles," he wrote, "so that in the thing in which they slander you as evildoers, they may because of your good deeds, as they observe them, glorify God in the day of visitation" (1 Peter 2:2-3). Paul wrote of this growth period as one during which the forgiven sinner "learns Christ" (Ephesians 4:20), a period of "transformation" during which one "renews" his mind (Romans 12:2).

The Gospel of Christ is indeed a "balm" or *medicine* for the weary, a means for healing "brokenness." In the Lord's famous "Sermon on the Mount," we find what we might call nine "doses" of spiritual "medicines," guaranteed to provide *blessing* and *happiness* (Matthew 5:3-11). Christ spoke first of a strong dose of *humility* and *sorrow for sin* (Matthew 5:3-4). Then He prescribed *gentleness*, an attitude that soothes and calms rather than aggravates (Matthew 5:5; cf. James 3:17-18). A healthy dose of *"hunger and thirst for righteousness"* is needed (Matthew 5:6). *Mercy*, *purity* of heart, and *peacemaking* should be a daily exercise (Matthew 5:7-9). If the preceding "medicines" have been zealously applied, the Christian should be able to *suffer persecution and insults* without complaint (Matthew 5:10-11).

It is also imperative that one remain in constant contact, through prayer, with Him who can "render powerless" the devil, and who is "able to come to the aid" of His people (Hebrews 2:14-18).

> Bring Christ your broken life, so marred by sin.
> He will create anew, make whole again.
> Your empty, wasted years He will restore,
> And your iniquities remember no more.
> (L.O. Sanderson)

ARMISTICE DAY

Do you remember "Armistice Day"? Many Americans might not remember it. Nevertheless, long before November 11 was renamed "Veterans Day," it was called "Armistice Day."

On June 28, 1914, a Serbian anarchist assassinated Archduke Franz Ferdinand, heir to the throne of the Austro-Hungarian Empire, and set in motion a chain of events that soon culminated in what is still called in France "La Grande Guerre"— "the Great War." Although many nations were involved, we remember it best as a war of aggression by Germany. When the United States entered the war on April 6, 1917, on the side of France and Britain, the German advance was halted. Fighting had devolved into a virtual stalemate, with long rows of trenches from which the opposing armies continued to fight for many months, and it became clear to many that no one could win a clear victory. Hostilities officially ended on the western front with the signing of an "Armistice" agreement, at the 11th hour of the 11th day of the 11th month of 1918.

Twenty years later, in 1938, November 11 was designated a legal holiday, "Armistice Day," in Europe as well as in America. On June 1, 1954, the name of the holiday was changed, in America, to "Veterans Day," to honor all who have served in our armed forces.

The "Great War" ended with an "armistice," not a complete and undisputed defeat of the enemy. The opposing armies agreed to cease hostilities and return to their homes. Although it was clear to most observers who had won and who had lost, the aggressor German armies were able to return home with some degree of dignity. The Second World War (1939-45) would end differently, in *victory*, not with an *armistice* and there is a vast difference between the two.

Armistice Day

When we consider the *spiritual war* in which Christians are engaged against the forces of evil, it is important to know the difference between "Armistice" and "Victory." Paul wrote that we are at war "against the rulers, against the powers, against the world forces of this darkness, against the spiritual forces of wickedness in the heavenly places" (Ephesians 6:12). We are told to "take up the full armor of God," so that we will "be able to resist in the evil day, and having done everything, to stand firm" (Ephesians 6:13). To "stand firm" means to be *victorious*. Never does God's word indicate that there exists any other option but victory. There is only victory and defeat; there is no place for "armistice."

In the world of politics, there is some place for "negotiation," and the Lord taught that children of God should act wisely in their worldly affairs with others. He taught that "if you are presenting your offering at the altar, and there remember that your brother has something against you, leave your offering there before the altar and go; first be reconciled to your brother, and then come and present your offering" (Matthew 5:23-24). He tells us to "make friends quickly" with an "opponent at law" before problems get to the point of no return and our "opponent" signs a warrant against us and takes us to court (Matthew 5:25-26). There is certainly something to be said for "negotiations."

But when it comes to our relationship with Satan, the Devil, there can be no negotiation, no compromise, no "give and take." Satan's sole aim is to conquer, to destroy, and to corrupt. It is not a wise move to negotiate with Satan or to agree to an "armistice" with Satan. Paul wrote, "You cannot drink the cup of the Lord and the cup of demons; you cannot partake of the table of the Lord and the table of demons" (1 Corinthians 10:21). The concepts of "righteousness" and "lawlessness" are diametrically opposed to one another, so that there can be no "partnership" between them (2 Corinthians 6:14-15). Because we have nothing "in common" with "Belial," we can have no "fellowship" with the principles of "darkness" (2 Corinthians 6:15). This does not mean that we cannot have friends who are not Christians or "believers." And it does not mean that a Christian cannot marry or be married to a non-Christian, since there were many such unions, even in the Corinthian church (cf. 1 Corinthians 7:12ff). It does mean, however, that the Christian must not surrender his principles for the sake of such unions or friendships. Rather, the Christian should be careful to influence for good his non-Christian friend or spouse (1 Corinthians 7:14; 1 Peter 3:1-4).

The story is told of a hiker in the woods who suddenly found himself face to face with a huge grizzly bear. The hiker knew he could not outrun the bear, nor was he strong enough to defeat him in a fight, so he decided to negotiate. The result of the negotiation appeared to benefit both the hiker and the bear. The bear got himself a good meal, and the hiker a fur coat.

There is no substitute for victory! There can be no "armistice" agreement between the Christian and Satan. But we have been promised the victory if we hold fast. Peter wrote, "Be of sober spirit, be on the alert. Your adversary, the devil, prowls around like a roaring lion, seeking someone to devour. But resist him, firm in your faith" (1 Peter 5:8-9). James tells us, "Submit therefore to God. Resist the devil and he will flee from you" (James 4:7). Count on this, that Satan has no power over you except that which you *permit* him to have.

D-DAY, AGAIN!

MY WIFE AND I TOOK THE TRAIN FROM PARIS IN the early morning, heading for Normandy, getting off at the Bayeux station. We got lodging in the small Hotel de la Gare, just across from the station, and signed up for a tour of the Normandy beaches on the following day. We would explore the German fortifications on the cliffs, walk on the beaches where so many had died, visit the World War II museum, and spend precious time in the American Cemetery overlooking Omaha Beach. It was a sobering experience to walk among the thousands of shining white crosses and Stars of David and to reflect that these young soldiers had died to ensure the survival of liberty in the Western World.

For months the Allies had been planning an invasion of German-held France, hoping to end what we call World War II. General Eisenhower finally decided it was time to just do it. In spite of overcast skies, in the dark of night, a fleet of over 6,000 ships and some 150,000 soldiers left England for the Normandy shores.

D-Day! Invasion Day! A secret plan to turn the tide of the war and achieve victory against the entrenched Nazi forces! The day had arrived when Eisenhower's mighty army would debark on the heavily fortified beaches of Normandy. Preceding the arrival of these vessels in the early dawn of June 6, 1944, thousands of paratroopers jumped from planes into the darkness behind the enemy lines. Many of them were shot dead before they reached the ground; others landed in trees, and were murdered where they hung, but most landed safely, enough to do their assigned task. The Germans had been caught off-guard, and within twenty-four hours the American-led invasion forces had secured the beaches and were moving inland. From that moment on, the German armies were in retreat.

Now, let us look backward in time, to another great Debarkation Day, to plans that God was preparing, an event that had great implications for mankind. God had planned "things which eye has not seen and ear has not heard, and which have not entered the heart of man, all that God has prepared for those who love Him" (Isaiah 64:4; 1 Corinthians 2:2). Isaiah was referring to something God would do in the distant future that would astound both men and angels. God's plan which involved an "invasion" of great importance was cloaked in secrecy, although prophets had hinted at it across the centuries. This "invasion" did not begin with a large fleet of warships or with powerful armies. It began instead with the birth of a boy in a humble dwelling in an insignificant village of the Judean hills. There was, indeed, some degree of "fanfare" which caused a group of shepherds to leave their sheep and head for the village (Luke 2:8-15), where they discovered the child lying in the manger where animals were fed.

It is safe to say that the "enemy" forces were also taken by surprise by this "invasion." In fact, according to the historical records, this baby boy grew into manhood, reaching the age of thirty (Luke 3:23) before a single "shot" was fired. On that day, Jesus of Nazareth left his carpentry shop and went down to the Jordan River where His cousin John was baptizing penitent people. Very soon after this, Satan the devil approached Jesus, attempting to lure Him into some sinful action (Luke 4:1-8). Even at this time, however, there is no indication that Satan, the "ruler" of this world (John 12:31), truly understood what Jesus' mission was. Of course, as Jesus methodically revealed Himself through His many signs, within three years, Satan's understanding grew to the point that he recognized that *this* Man had to be eliminated! Satan "entered into Judas" during the Passover supper (Luke 22:3) and used that weak disciple as his tool to bring about the murder of Jesus.

Did Satan think that by killing Jesus he could bring His mission to an end and avert his own defeat in this spiritual conflict, this greatest of all "wars"? Did Satan *not know* that by killing Jesus he would be fulfilling the ancient prophecies (Psalm 22; Isaiah 53)? How could Satan have known God's great design, since he was not privy to God's thoughts? In fact, the prophets themselves did not understand the meaning of their own prophecies, and the "angels" also longed to look into these things (1 Peter 1:10-12).

In fact, the apostle Paul wrote that "none of the rulers of this age" had understood God's "hidden wisdom," for "if they had understood it they would not have crucified the Lord of glory" (1 Corinthians 2:8). Neither Satan nor his worldly followers could have known anything about how the Divine Being we worship as Lord and Christ (Acts 2:30) would lay aside "equality with God," "empty Himself," and "take the form of a bond-servant" on planet Earth. Surely, such a One would not be expected to die as a criminal on a Roman cross!

The goal of this greatest of all "invasions" was to give sight to the spiritually "blind," to enable the spiritually "lame" to walk, to cleanse spiritual "lepers," to enable the spiritually "deaf" to hear, to raise to a new life those who are spiritually "dead," and to announce good news to the poor who rarely receive anything good (Matthew 11:5). Christians have been called to participate in this conflict, to "put on the full armor of God" and to perform as spiritual soldiers, fighting against "the rulers, against the powers, against the world forces of this darkness, against the spiritual forces of wickedness" (Ephesians 6:10-12). If we are to be properly equipped for this great calling, we need to "take up the full armor of God" (Ephesians 6:13), and prepare to "stand firm." The enemy is real; he is strong; but with God we can and will overcome!

INDEPENDENCE DAY

July 4, 2017, marked the 241st anniversary of the signing of the *Declaration of Independence* by the Continental Congress of the thirteen American Colonies. In 1776, on July 4, following a secret agreement to separate from England, fifty-six patriots began the signing process. All of those brave patriots pledged their lives, property, and sacred honor to the task before them, knowing full well that they would be considered by British authorities to be traitors. Many of these men lost their lives and their fortunes during the ensuing struggle against what was then the most powerful nation in the world. To this day, July 4 has been a special holiday for Americans. Following the Revolution, the congress of the new nation constructed a Constitution which would guide the nation from that day on.

Looking further back in history, we remember two other similar events of tremendous importance, which would radically affect the future of mankind.

The first of these great events was when an Israelite named Moses, in order to fulfill God's purpose in his own life, rejected the riches of Egypt, refusing to continue to be regarded as a son of Pharaoh's daughter (Hebrews 11:24-25). Moses had put his life at risk in order to defend an Israelite who was being beaten by an Egyptian slave master. Called by God to lead the Israelites out of Egypt, Moses instructed the people to eat one final meal in Egypt, a meal called "Passover," replete with symbolism, which would be repeated at the same time each year from that time forward (Exodus 12:14-20). Then he struck a course directly toward the Red Sea, where by God's help he parted the waters and led the multitude across on dry land, out of bondage into freedom. Having successfully escaped the slavery of Egypt, Moses, at Mount Horeb, delivered to the Israelites a set of laws, a "covenant," which would stand as a sacred "Constitution" governing every aspect of their lives (Deuteronomy 5:1-21).

Independence Day

A second historical event of even greater importance occurred 1400 years later when Jesus, a carpenter of Nazareth, was crucified just outside the walls of Jerusalem, during the governorship of Pontius Pilate. Like Moses, Jesus had refused to serve as an earthly monarch (Matthew 4:8-9), preferring to be "king" over a "kingdom" that was "not of this world" (John 18:36), choosing the "shame of the cross," willingly accepting a cruel death in order to "bring many sons to glory" (Hebrews 2:10). This He did for us so that "we would no longer be slaves to sin" (Romans 6:6).

On a Thursday evening, in A.D. 29, after sundown on the 14th day of the Jewish month of Abib (Nisan), Jesus of Nazareth gathered with His twelve disciples in an upper room in Jerusalem to celebrate the Passover. The first Passover had been the last meal eaten by the Israelites before leaving Egypt; it would also be the last Passover meal eaten by the Carpenter from Galilee, before leading His disciples into a spiritual "kingdom" over which He would reign from heaven. Paul wrote: "For He rescued us from the domain of darkness, and transferred us to the kingdom of His beloved Son" (Colossians 1:13). Passover had been a "farewell" for Israel, as it would be a "farewell" meal for Jesus and His disciples.

With the exception of Judas Iscariot, the men who sat at the table with Jesus that evening were deeply troubled (Luke 22:14-22), not only because their Master had been telling them of His approaching suffering and death, but also because they too would be called to die for Him (John 16:1-4). Like the brave men and women who followed Moses out of Egypt and across the Red Sea, and like the American patriots who at their own peril would sign the *Declaration of Independence*, the disciples of Jesus knew well that they would very likely share the sufferings of their Lord. And so did they all!

When Jesus Christ rose from the dead three days later, He also, like Moses, delivered to His followers, through His apostles, a "Covenant," a Constitution, which was meant to serve them from that day forward. It was a "new" covenant which was "better" than the covenant Moses had delivered to Israel (Hebrews 8:6). The covenant given through Moses was "ratified" by the blood of bulls and goat, but the covenant Christ gave *His* disciples was "ratified by the blood of the Son of God" (Hebrews 10:12-14). This covenant is the sacred

"Constitution" which was intended to govern the lives of Christians even today.

Independence Day! For the Israelites, independence and freedom from Egyptian oppression were *achieved* through Moses, but had to be *maintained* through the centuries by the faithful observance of the Covenant. For Americans, independence from England and freedom came through the heroic courage and effort of those early patriots who signed the *Declaration of Independence* and fought to achieve it. But freedom must be *preserved*. Like ancient Israel, who eventually *lost* both their *state* and their *freedom*, American freedom is not guaranteed; it must be preserved by the careful observance of our great Constitution. In the same way, although Jesus Christ, through His death on the cross, purchased our freedom from the slavery of sin, every individual man or woman is actually "set free from sin" when he or she "becomes obedient from the heart to that form of teaching" spoken of by Paul (Romans 6:17). Following that initial victory over sin, each individual Christian must then faithfully follow God's instructions as they are set forth in the gospel of Christ.

Freedom is not free. It is almost always bought at a tremendous price, which makes it worth being preserved.

PURIM - A GOOD DAY FOR REJOICING

ONLY EIGHTEEN YEARS OLD, I WAS IN NASHVILLE to attend a weeklong sales school, learning to sell books as a summer job. Alone for the first time in a big city, after attending worship at a large congregation on West End, I hitchhiked to Centennial Park. It was a warm, sunny spring day, and I found a place where I could sit undisturbed and read from the Bible. I read first the book of *Ruth*, then for the first time the book of *Esther*, and was enthralled by the story of the courageous young queen who risked her own life to save the Jewish people from extermination by wicked Haman, Mordecai's sworn enemy. Toward the end of *Esther*, the anonymous writer explained the origin of the annual two-day Jewish festival of *Purim* (Esther 9:17-19).

A person unacquainted with *Esther* might search in vain in the writings of Moses for a mention of *Purim*. The Law of Moses, however, established only three annual feasts (or festivals) for Israel, as we learn from Exodus 23:14-17; Leviticus 23:4-44; and Deuteronomy 16:1-17. The first of the feasts ordained by Moses was the *Feast of Unleavened Bread,* which began with Passover and lasted eight days in all. This feast took place in the early spring, in March or April. The second feast was the *Feast of Harvest,* also called the *Feast of Weeks* or, in the New Testament, *Pentecost.* This feast took place at the beginning of the barley harvest, fifty days after the Sabbath of the Passover week. The third feast established by the Law was the *Feast of the Ingathering,* a seven-day festival occurring at the time of the harvest of the orchards and vineyards, in the early fall, September or October. This festival is also called the *Feast of Booths* or, in the KJV, the *Feast of Tabernacles.*

The *Feast of Purim*, however, dates from 473 B.C., some 900 years after Moses, when the exiled Jews of Persia had successfully defended themselves against the genocidal holocaust organized by wicked Haman (Esther 3 & 9). The original celebration of this Jewish victory took place first in Susa, the Persian capital city, and then in the rural areas, on two successive days (Esther 9:17-19). Unlike the feasts ordained by Moses, *Purim* was not primarily a worship event. Rather, it was a festival where the people rejoiced and feasted as they remembered the events of those dark days.

The word Purim is a plural, the *im* ending corresponding with "s" in English. A *pur* means a "lot" and refers to the "casting of lots." This was much like our "rolling of dice" or "drawing straws" to make a decision. For example, Joshua cast lots to decide who was the guilty party at their defeat at Ai (Joshua 7:14-17), and the apostles "cast lots" to choose a replacement for Judas as a twelfth apostle (Acts 1:26). In *Esther*, it appears that astrologers in Haman's service "cast the lots" before him to decide which month would be the most favorable for the accomplishment of his evil designs (Esther 3:7). It is ironic that Haman conceived his plot and that his astrologers began casting lots in the month of *Nisan* (also called *Abib*), the month of Israel's departure from Egyptian bondage.

Purim is never mentioned in the New Testament. The unidentified "feast of the Jews" mentioned in John 5:1 could not be *Purim*, since it was a Sabbath day (John 5:9), and such a celebration could not have been observed on a Sabbath.

If you have never read *Esther*, or even if you have, take your Bible and read this wonderful story. I believe that you will be enthralled with it just as I was when I first read it. Although the writer never used the word "God" nor ever referred directly to Him, one cannot read *Esther* without feeling the Divine Presence throughout. One cannot help but be stirred and moved by Mordecai's faithfulness to his much younger cousin, Esther, or by Esther's own courageous actions.

As you read Esther's story, take a little time to reflect on how you, yourself, ought to react when faced with problems which may even be life changing for you and your loved ones. Often, we think only of *self* in such situations, of what the consequences might be for *ourselves*, if we should try to help the situation or try to prevent a problem. I do not mean that we should jump pell-mell into situations that don't involve us, or that we should *meddle* in the lives of others, but there are times when we should forget about self and do what we can, trusting in God Who is always there, even if we cannot see Him. This is what Mordecai advised his young cousin, Esther, whom he had raised as his own daughter: "Do not imagine that you in the king's palace can escape any more than all the Jews. For *if you remain silent at this time*, relief and deliverance will arise for the Jews from another place and you and your father's house will perish. And who knows whether you have not attained royalty for such a time as this?" (Esther 4:13-14). I believe God used Esther to save the Jews; but Esther was an active participant in God's hands.

As I look back on my own life, I believe I see God's active hand at work. Maybe He is at work in your life, using you in ways you cannot now imagine. But we must do our part as active agents in His hands.

Words To Live By

HANUKKAH

THE ANNUAL JEWISH FESTIVAL OF *HANUKKAH* IS not mentioned in the Old Testament, since it originated some two or three hundred years after the last Hebrew prophet wrote. Nevertheless, Hanukkah has been observed by Jews from before the birth of Christ, and reminds them and us of an important moment in the history of the Jewish people. It is mentioned, in the New Testament, but not by name, as we shall see shortly.

The origin of *Hanukkah* is the celebration of victory over one of the most sadistic tyrants of ancient times. The Greek monarch Antiochus IV, called "Epiphanes," ruled over an area which included what we know today as Syria. Daniel called him the "king of the north" (Daniel 11:5-6). Antiochus hated the Jews and wanted their land. In a brutal campaign against them, Antiochus ravaged Palestine. In 175 BC, he issued decrees forbidding many of the religious practices of the Jews. About eight years later, in 168 BC, he entered Jerusalem, compelling the Jews on pain of death to disobey the Law of Moses and selling Jewish women and children into slavery. He erected an altar to the Greek god Zeus (Jupiter) on top of the main altar in the Jewish Temple and sacrificed "unclean" animals – including pigs – in honor of Zeus. This enraged the Jews, provoking them to revolt against Antiochus. The leader of the ill-equipped Jewish army was Judah, one of the sons of Mattathias, a priest. Greatly outmanned and with inferior arms, Judah led his small army in guerrilla warfare, hitting the enemy in swift, hard blows, at their weakest points, earning for himself the name of *Maccabeus*, the "hammer." After nearly four years, the vastly outnumbered Jews defeated Antiochus' army. On the 25[h] day of Kislev (December 24, 164 BC), the priests purified and rededicated the temple, restoring the worship as prescribed by the Law. Since that date, Jews observe an annual celebration of the event, called the Feast of Dedication, the Feast of Lights, or *Hanukkah*. This interesting and exciting story can be read in the apocryphal books of *1 and 2 Maccabees*, written during the second century before Christ, and in the *Antiquities* of Flavius Josephus, written some fifty years after the death of Christ.

Hanukkah is mentioned only once in the New Testament, in John's gospel. "At that time the Feast of the Dedication took place at Jerusalem; it was winter and Jesus was walking in the temple in the portico of Solomon" (John 10:22-23). Although this feast was not a holy day prescribed by the Law of Moses, it was highly regarded by the Jews. Its mention by John in connection with Jesus' visit to the temple implies that Jesus, himself, had gone there specifically for this feast.

The prophet Daniel also foretold the events of this period. The "king of the North" (Daniel 11:7) would fight against the "king of the South" (Daniel 11:5) for the control of "the Beautiful Land" (Daniel 11:16). Eventually the "king of the North" would "desecrate the sanctuary" and "do away with the regular sacrifice," setting up "the abomination of desolation" in the temple (Daniel 11:31). The "king of the South" is an obvious reference to the Egyptian monarch, and the "king of the North" is the Syrian king who desecrated the temple. This came to pass exactly as it was prophesied by Daniel and makes the history of *Hanukkah* of particular interest to the Christian, since it demonstrates the accuracy of the prophecies of Daniel. Liberal scholars, who deny miracles or divine inspiration, date Daniel's writing later than the Maccabean wars, in about 164 BC, claiming that Daniel *describes* history instead of *foretelling* it. But recent scholarship has demonstrated that the arguments of the liberal scholars are tainted with a bias against predictive prophecy, and that there is no valid reason why Daniel should not be dated in the sixth century BC, as we also believe.

The fact of *Hanukkah*, therefore, stands as a reminder of God's power to reveal what *will be* before it happens.

Words To Live By

"MAGNA CARTA"

AN EARTH-SHAKING EVENT THAT WOULD FOREVER alter the course of history occurred in the spring of 1215, eight hundred years ago. Tyrannical King John, the younger brother of Richard I, the "Lionheart," ruled England with an iron fist. Richard, the legitimate king, had been away from England for several years engaged in the Crusades and no one knew if he was alive, dead, or in some distant prison.

King John's word was law and he allowed no dissent. Anyone who dared cross him was subject to torture and death, as well as seizure of all his property. "In 1208 John fell out with a close associate named William de Braose and pursued his family to destruction, starving to death William's wife and eldest son in the dungeons of his castle," while William died in exile in France. (Dan Jones, *Smithsonian Magazine*, July 2015). In the spring of 1215, tired of John's criminal rule, a large number of Barons led an army against John, taking control of London, and forcing him to agree to the terms of a document which would become known as the *Magna Carta*.

Although most people today might be unable to identify this famous document, the framers of our own Constitution were certainly aware of it. "Clauses from *Magna Carta* were written into statutes governing the American colonies from as early as 1639. Later, when the people of Massachusetts rebelled against the Stamp Act, they pointed out that it violated the core principles of the great Charter" (Jones, 27). Clauses 39 and 40 of the *Magna Carta* are the basis for Articles III, V, and VI of our *Bill of Rights*.

During the three years of His earthly ministry, Jesus often spoke of the "Kingdom of Heaven" (Cf. Matthew 13), even promising to give Simon Peter the keys of this "kingdom" (Matthew 16:19). His references to this kingdom were so well known that when He was brought before the Roman governor Pontius Pilate, even Pilate asked Jesus, "So you are a king?" To this perhaps "tongue-in-cheek" *"magna Carta"*

question, Jesus answered with an unequivocal affirmative, "You say correctly that I am a king. For this I have been born, and for this I have come into the world, to testify to the truth. Everyone who is of the truth hears My voice" (John 18:37). Jesus said He had come "to testify to the truth." It then follows logically that the "truth" alluded to by Jesus *exists,* and since it *must* "exist," what does it include and where is it found?

Although the words "constitution" or "Magna Carta" are never used in the Bible, it is clear that God's word through his appointed prophets and apostles must be considered to be God's law for His people. I have heard it said that the New Testament is not "law," since John wrote, "For the Law was given through Moses; grace and truth were realized through Jesus Christ" (John 1:17). However, John certainly was not saying that the word of Christ does not have the effect of law, for Jesus Himself said "You are my friends if you do what I command you" (John 15:14). The apostle Paul, while addressing the idea of "Christian liberty," wrote that "freedom" in Christ does not mean that one is no longer amenable to "law." He argued that although he was not under the Law of Moses, he was nevertheless not "without law," since he was "under the law of Christ" (1 Corinthians 9:21). The major difference is that the Law of Moses demanded perfect obedience, something that was impossible for sinful man, whereas the "law of Christ" takes into account the impossibility of perfect obedience. In Christ, we are encouraged to strive for perfection, but are covered by the blood of Christ when we fail (Ephesians 2:8-9).

With His own blood, Christ signed our spiritual "Magna Carta," which gives us God's will both for individuals and congregations (Hebrews 9:15; 10:9-10). Jude, probably a brother of Jesus (Jude 1:1), wrote of "the faith" which "was once for all handed down to the saints" (Jude 1:3). Jude was obviously talking about the "gospel," the "body of truth held by believers everywhere" (*Notes*, NASB). James called it "the law of liberty" (James 2:12) by which citizens of Christ's kingdom will "be judged." Paul referred to it as being "the doctrine of God our Savior" (Titus 2:10), calling it "sound doctrine" that preachers are exhorted to preach "in season and out of season" (2 Timothy 4:2-3). Paul's comment follows on the heels of his statement that "All Scripture is inspired by God and profitable for teaching, for reproof, for correction, for training in righteousness" (2 Timothy 3:16). This body of sacred writings called "the gospel" or the "new covenant" is contrasted with the law that had been written "on tablets of stone" (2 Corinthians 3:3). Paul wrote that the Law of Moses, the "old covenant," was a "ministry of death" and "condemnation," whereas the "new" covenant is a "ministry of righteousness" (2 Corinthians 3:7-9). It is only in Christ that one finds true "liberty" or freedom from sin (2 Corinthians 3:17).

The writings which define the "gospel" were given by revelation, through "His holy apostles and prophets in [by] the Spirit" (Ephesians 3:2-5). The method of inspiration is clearly set forth by Paul. God had a message for mankind; He revealed this message to Paul and other apostles and prophets, who wrote it down. When we read their writings, we can understand God's message.

The writings of the apostles constitute the spiritual "Magna Carta" of Christ's kingdom, His church. Only through the writings of the apostles can we learn about Christ, the kingdom of God, and the true pathway to righteousness, and it is only in these writings that we can find Christ's instructions regarding His kingdom. The written gospel of Christ stands, therefore, as our "Constitution," written by the finger of God just as surely as He inscribed the Law of Moses on the tablets of stone. Any attempts by men to change or add to this divine "Constitution" must be resisted.

"FULL OF THE SPIRIT"?

Following Peter's sermon in the temple area on Pentecost (Acts 2), the number of believers in Christ had grown rapidly. From a hundred twenty persons (Acts 1:15) before Pentecost, the number quickly passed three thousand baptized believers (Acts 2:41). Within a short time, the number of men, not counting the women, numbered more than four thousand (Acts 4:4), including "a great many of the priests" (Acts 6:7).

The rapid growth of the church inevitably brought problems. Since Pentecost was one of the annual feasts of the Jews, there were in Jerusalem large numbers of Jews from many parts of the empire (Acts 2:8-11), and many of these were becoming converts. A major emerging problem concerned the cultural differences between "native" or Palestinian Jews, called "Hebrews," and those called "Hellenistic" or "Grecian" (KJV) Jews, from outside of Palestine. An organized effort was apparently being made by those in charge of distributing daily food (Acts 6:1) to needy widows. It is obvious that the Hebrew servers were prejudiced against the "Hellenistic" widows and were neglecting them in favor of "Hebrew" widows. When the apostles learned what was happening, they set in motion a plan to correct the abuse. Seven well qualified men were chosen to be in charge of food distributions. The fact that all of these men had Greek names, indicating that they were Hellenistic Jews, would certainly reassure everyone that the food would be distributed equitably.

In addition, the seven men chosen were to be "of good reputation, full of the Spirit and of wisdom" (Acts 6:3). Instead of choosing these men *themselves*, the twelve apostles had told the church to do the choosing. The apostles obviously believed that the church was equal to this task. Although almost everyone had only recently been converted, they were fully capable of discerning who was "of good reputation, full of the Spirit and of wisdom," and this, apparently without any miraculous assistance from God.

Words To Live By

Of the three qualifications required for this service, the first and third presented no problems. They knew what it meant to have a "good reputation" and to be "full of wisdom." In fact, these two qualities must be present in those we select to serve as "elders" or "overseers" of local churches. Paul wrote to Timothy that the "overseer" must be "above reproach," having "a good reputation with those outside the church" (1 Timothy 3:2,7). Prospective elders must demonstrate "prudence" in their conduct (1 Timothy 3:2). Prudence is another word for wisdom. And it is the local congregation that must be knowledgeable and wise enough to decide which men have these qualifications.

But the second of the qualifications demanded by the twelve was perhaps more difficult. What does it mean to be "full of the Spirit"? We know what it means to be "full" of a substance. We know when a container is full of milk or orange juice, but the Spirit of God – the Holy Spirit – is not a "substance." How then does one measure "fullness"?

Someone might say that to be "full of the Spirit" indicates the ability to perform healings or miraculous deeds, such as Stephen and Philip were doing later, after being chosen and after the apostles "laid their hands on them" (Acts 6:6,8; 8:6-7). But there is no evidence that Stephen and Philip were doing any of these things *before* being chosen to serve. They appear to have been no different from the other church members. I think, then, that to be "full of the Spirit" must mean something less spectacular. Nevertheless, the church was certainly capable of observing people and deciding who was "full of the Spirit," else the twelve would not have given them such a charge.

In fact, according to the apostle Paul, the Holy Spirit dwells within every child of God. Paul wrote, "But if anyone does not have the Spirit of Christ, he does not belong to Him" (Romans 8:9). In the context of Paul's statement, there is no difference between the "Spirit of God" and the "Spirit of Christ." Both expressions refer to the Holy Spirit. Every Christian, male or female, in the Judean church had the Spirit of God dwelling within him. This same Spirit of God made their bodies His holy temple just as He dwells in us today (1 Corinthians 6:19).

"full Of The Spirit"?

The question is, therefore, are we "full" of the Spirit of God? The Judean church was instructed to choose men who were "full" of the Spirit, implying that some Christians, although "dwelt in" by the Spirit, were NOT "full" of the Spirit. To be "full of the Spirit" does not equate "perfection." No Christian is perfect in the sense of being without fault or sinless. All have sinned and fall short of what God wants us to be (Romans 3:23). God does not require perfection of any person; He does, however, require that we fight against the evil desires of the flesh and submit to the Spirit of God, to be led by Him (Romans 8:5-10).

Are we being led daily by God's Spirit? Are we following what the Spirit of God instructs us to do in the Gospel? The apostle Paul wrote to Christians at Rome, imploring them, urging them, not to "be conformed to this world, but (to) be transformed by the renewing of (their) mind" (Romans 12:2). He wrote these words to people in whom the Holy Spirit of God was dwelling. That Paul could write this shows that not every Christian is "full of the Spirit," although that should be the goal of every child of God. Peter urged Christians to "grow in respect to salvation" (1 Peter 2:2). Paul encouraged the Philippians to "prove" themselves "to be blameless and innocent, children of God above reproach in the midst of a crooked and perverse generation" (Philippians 2:15).

People who come to God do not start out "full of the Spirit," but they grow as they are led by Him. Paul urges us to "test" ourselves, to "examine" ourselves. This is not an easy thing to do, but without such self-examination there can be no growth. How "full of the Spirit" do you perceive yourself to be?

"BE CAREFUL, LITTLE TONGUE, WHAT YOU SAY!"

WISE KING SOLOMON WROTE 3,000 PROVERBS (1 Kings 4:32), a small number of which are included in the Biblical book of *Proverbs*. These wise sayings still ring true to the modern reader. Many of Solomon's proverbs concern human relationships and how the tongue can affect these relationships for good or evil. Consider the following: "A gentle answer turns away wrath" (Proverbs 15:1). "A man has joy in an apt answer, and how delightful is a timely word" (Proverbs 15:23). "Pleasant words are a honeycomb, sweet to the soul and healing to the bone" (Proverbs 16:24). "Like apples of gold in settings of silver is a word spoken in right circumstances" (Proverbs 25:11).

Most lessons given on the use of the tongue concern its inappropriate or bad use. I want to concentrate on the great power for good for which our tongue can be used. While it is true that "gossip" can hurt and destroy friends, gentle speech, appropriate words, can build up and encourage. And, how great is our need for encouragement!

While it is true that a harsh rebuke or an angry word spoken or written will remain for years in someone's memory, it is equally true that a kind word, a gentle word of commendation, will also be remembered and appreciated. When we compliment someone sincerely for some good quality possessed, it will build him up and encourage him. If we tell a friend how much we appreciate him, he will not forget it. It will encourage him to know that someone notices, and nearly everyone has some quality that we might honestly and sincerely admire. A kind, encouraging word spoken might start a spiritual fire, or fan a flickering flame that could become capable of much future good.

"Be Careful, Little Tongue, What You Say!"

The great poet Longfellow must have been thinking of the unseen good that a "song" or "word spoken in right circumstances" can do, when he penned "The Arrow and the Song."

> I shot an arrow into the air,
> It fell to earth, I knew not where;
> For, so swiftly it flew, the sight
> Could not follow it in its flight.
>
> I breathed a song into the air,
> It fell to earth, I knew not where;
> For who has sight so keen and strong,
> That it can follow the flight of song?
>
> Long, long afterward, in an oak
> I found the arrow, still unbroke;
> And the song, from beginning to end,
> I found again in the heart of a friend.

One word of encouragement, one sincere compliment or gentle commendation might seem to us as nothing. But the person thus influenced for good will never forget.

Words To Live By

PARDON MY FRENCH?

OFTEN, WE HEAR SOMEONE SAY, JOKINGLY, "Pardon my French, but ...." Then he goes ahead and uses a word that is not used in polite society. It is as though "Pardon my French!" somehow makes it okay. When I hear someone say this, I think, "That is certainly not French!" My point is that when we want to say or do something we know we shouldn't, we should take responsibility for it. Why even in jest blame it on the French or someone else?

It is generally true that we just don't like to take responsibility for what we do. King David sinned grievously, with far-reaching life consequences which adversely affected not only his family, but the entire nation of Israel (2 Samuel 12:10-11). When the prophet Nathan forced him to really examine himself, David exclaimed, "I have sinned against the Lord" (2 Samuel 12:13). However, David's admission of guilt could not erase or prevent the dire consequences of his actions, and in later life, his conscience would be haunted by the recollections of his misdeeds. He wrote, "Be gracious to me, O God, according to your lovingkindness; according to the greatness of Your compassion blot out my transgressions. Wash me thoroughly from my iniquity and cleanse me from my sin. For I know my transgressions, and my sin is ever before me" (Psalm 51:1-3).

Every action, good or bad, brings consequences. Bad personal decisions or actions on my part not only hurt me but potentially everyone that I love, and may bring reproach on my family and on the church of God. As Paul wrote, "Whether, then, you eat or drink or whatever you do, do all to the glory of God. Give no offense to Jews or to Greeks or to the church of God" (1 Corinthians 10:31-32).

A commonly used Latin expression is *"Caveat emptor,"* a legal term meaning "Let the buyer beware." If you buy a used car, "Caveat emptor!" If you purchase property sight unseen, "Caveat emptor." If you access risky sites on the Internet, "Caveat emptor." If you decide to try methamphetamines or marijuana even "just one time," "Caveat emptor." If you think you have the winning hand at poker and you "bet the farm" on it, you may very well wind up with no farm. "Caveat emptor!" You are responsible, and the consequences could be severe. Your actions might cost you an opportunity to advance in your job; you might even *lose* your job, your health, your house, or your family. Believe me, I have seen it happen many times, sometimes to people who were very close to me. "Play with fire and you may be burned" is a true statement, and that's neither French nor Latin.

Another Latin expression we often hear is *"Carpe diem,"* which means "Seize the day!" Used in a positive sense, this is a good expression. Indeed, we should recognize opportunities that come our way in life. Sometimes, we let financial success slip through our fingers because we fail to seize an opportunity that comes our way. The story was told of a contest, in which people were to walk through a corn field, looking for the biggest ear of corn. They could only choose one ear; the person who emerged from the field with the largest ear of corn would be the winner. Some contestants passed by many large ears, thinking that surely there would be one larger a little farther on, but as they approached the finish line, they had to choose a small ear or have nothing. Many college students graduate, expecting to find a place at the top of the ladder, but find jobs in their fields to be scarce for new graduates. So, they wait, and wait, passing up jobs they believe to be beneath them. They ought to take the lesser job and work their way up, like many of us have done. Nearly everyone I know has had to work at an "entry level" job. The point is that we need to *"carpe diem!"* Seize the opportunities that come your way! Don't let them pass you by.

But *"carpe diem"* also has a negative sense. As used originally in poetic literature, in about 1817, the expression meant "the enjoyment of the pleasures of the moment without concern for the future." By following this harmful advice, many intelligent, sensitive, and capable men and women have rushed recklessly to their personal ruin.

Life is too short, too precious, to be thrown away for temporary pleasures. Let us accept responsibility for our actions, being careful to act and speak in responsible ways, so that in the end we will truly be successful in our life, before men, and before Almighty God. We cannot blame the French for our inability to speak proper English!

"FILTHINESS AND SILLY TALK"

I WAS ABOUT NINE OR TEN YEARS OLD, I SUPPOSE, when I went "camping out" with my brother and a couple of his teen friends, one of whom was Roy W. We spent the night in the hay loft of a barn belonging to Roy's father. Roy was "worldly wise" for his age and before he got to high school he was already on the path to alcohol addiction and a premature death. That evening, after drinking some nasty coffee heated in a tin can over a fire of sticks, and eating a "picnic" sandwich or two on the bank of the muddy pond behind the barn where the cows were drinking and wading, we went up to the hay loft where we would sleep. I lay down to sleep, but the older boys sat around telling dirty jokes. My brother just listened; he did not participate otherwise in the joke telling. He told me many years later that he was ashamed as he thought about me, his little brother, having to listen to the filthy jokes they were telling.

I tell this to stress the seriousness of the subject. This scene occurred nearly sixty-five years ago, but it is as fresh in my memory as if it were only yesterday. Even today, I remember jokes they told. If I said they did not affect me, I would not be telling the truth. It is weird how things like that can find such permanent lodging in one's memory, and it is tragic how much damage they can do in the adolescent mind.

Our Lord Jesus obviously loved little children. On one occasion, when His disciples were "rebuking" the parents who were bringing children to Him (Mark 10:13), He set a small child on his knee, and told his disciples, "Whoever causes one of these little ones who believe in Me to stumble, it would be better for him to have a heavy millstone hung around his neck, and to be drowned in the depth of the sea" (Matthew 18:6). That night in the hay loft with my brother and his friends left scars in my childish mind that would require years to heal.

Paul wrote to the Ephesians, "There must be no filthiness and silly talk, or coarse jesting, which are not fitting, but rather giving of thanks" (Ephesians 5:4). I suppose that we all have engaged at times in some degree of "silliness," but not the kind of "silly talk" spoken of by Paul. Paul used the words "filthiness" and "silly talk" in the context of a discussion about *immorality* and *impurity* (Ephesians 5:3). The word "immorality" translates the Greek word from which we get our word *pornography*, and includes all of the sexual perversions invented by mankind. The KJV translates it "fornication." Paul's word "impurity" refers to *moral uncleanness* and specifically to the *perverted mind and heart.* Jesus said that "the mouth speaks out of that which fills the heart" (Matthew 12:34), so that a "clean" heart will not put forth immoral speech. He further said that if our spiritual "eye" is healthy, "the whole body will be full of light," but if our spiritual "eye" is bad, our "whole body will be full of darkness" (Matthew 6:22-23).

Children are like sponges. They hear everything we say and see everything we do, and they soak it all up. Unfortunately, they are not mature enough to reject the harmful things they see and hear, and the very young are not able to tell the difference between what is bad or good. We must be careful not to fill their pure minds with impure ideas which would corrupt them before they are able to defend themselves. This is why our blessed Lord Jesus warns us severely not to put "stumbling blocks" in their way. It is better not to have been born than to treat God's purest creatures in this manner.

"HOLY COW!" ETC.

PERHAPS THE MOST COMMON MEAT DISH SERVED in the United States is beef, and burger restaurants seem to be on every corner. But when Americans travel in the Orient, they soon discover that the ubiquitous hamburger often cannot be found. In fact, they may find it difficult to find meat dishes of any kind. In India, for example, most people believe that God – the "Divine" – resides in all animals, and that the killing of any animal is sinful (*Wikipedia*, "*Cattle in Religion*").

Hinduism, the dominant religion of India and several other oriental countries, does not present God as the Bible describes Him (*Wikipedia*, "*God in Hinduism*"). While the Bible speaks of God as a divine *person*, Hinduism usually presents Him more as a *concept* – "the Divine Absolute" – and the Divine, being omnipresent, resides also in animals. For several reasons, cattle have been especially revered by Hindus. Cows, in particular, are held in highest esteem, or "worshiped," and are considered to be *sacred* or *holy* because they function as *mothers* and provide both *milk* (for food) and *dung* (used for fuel).

I sometimes hear the expression, "Holy cow!" In India this expression might actually be logical, but it makes very little sense here. Quite often, however, instead of "Holy *cow*" one hears "Holy (s) *bleep!*" or "Holy (c)*bleep!*" More and more, those who use the "bleeped" words are less and less careful about when and where they use them. These expressions, in former times never heard in polite conversation, are now commonly used without apology; most people seem not to care.

The word "proper" comes to mind. What kind of conversation is "proper"? Or, has the notion of *propriety* completely disappeared with a much-regretted past era when, rightly or wrongly, there seemed to be a clearer distinction between right and wrong, between "proper" and "improper"? Could it be that "rightness" is determined *democratically*, by what the *majority of people* consider to be "right"? Although it is true that, over time, some "good" words have accrued "bad" connotations (e.g. "gay," "queer"), God's word remains a constant definition of the concept of rightness and holiness, and it can easily be shown that the majority of men have often been on the wrong side.

In connection with "rightness" or "wrongness," there is the concept of "holy" or "holiness." When asked to define the word "holy," we may quickly respond that it means "separate," and that is technically correct. However, a better definition of "holy" or "holiness" would include words like "pure," "good," or "righteous."

The word "good" reminds me of a conversation Jesus had with a wealthy young public official (Luke 18:18). This bright young man, running up to Jesus, hailed Him in this way: "Good Teacher, what shall I do to inherit eternal life?" Jesus responded, "Why do you call Me *good*? No one is *good* except God alone." Jesus was not denying that He was "good." Rather, He was saying that if the young man recognized that He was "good," he must also recognize that He was what he claimed to be, the Messiah. And Jesus was indeed "good." *Goodness, godliness* and *God* go hand in hand. In fact, the modern English word "God" derives from the Old English word for "good." For example, when we bid someone "Goodbye," we are saying, in contracted form, "God be with you." God is good! Jesus is good! We should imitate their goodness, even if we cannot attain it perfectly.

Words do matter. Right concepts of what is "holy" also matter. The Lord Jesus taught that "the mouth speaks *out of that which fills the heart*" (Matthew 12:34). He went on to say that "every careless word that people speak, they shall give an accounting for it in the day of judgment" (Matthew 12:36). What was Jesus teaching by these statements? One might conclude, but wrongly so, that it would be better never to speak again, rather than to risk misspeaking. During the Middle Ages, certain religious orders such as the Cistercians, Benedictines, and Carmelites imposed almost complete silence, permitting speech only to certain persons and in certain extreme circumstances. But Jesus was more interested in the spiritual purity of the heart than of the tongue, since it is the heart that controls the tongue.

"holy Cow!" Etc.

The apostle Paul wrote: "Let no unwholesome word proceed from your mouth, but only such a word as is good for edification according to the need of the moment, so that it will give grace to those who hear" (Ephesians 4:29). Paul's word "unwholesome" probably needs to be interpreted for every succeeding generation, since Paul gives no example of either a "wholesome" word or an "unwholesome" word. That may be left up partially, at least, to each generation. But there seems to be a consensus regarding what is acceptable or unacceptable. God lets us use our intelligence and wisdom, and most of the time we all, good or bad, agree concerning what is good or bad language. Paul went on to mention "filthiness and silly talk," and "coarse jesting," suggesting that such language is used by "immoral" and "impure" persons (Ephesians 5:4-5).

The Lord's brother James wrote that "the tongue is a fire, the very world of iniquity" (James 3:6). He wrote further that when Christians use evil and impure speech they send forth a contradictory message. With the tongue, he says, "we bless our Lord and Father, and with it we curse men," and this "ought not to be" (James 3:9-10). A fountain cannot "send out from the same opening both fresh and bitter water" (James 3:11). Why then would a Christian use his tongue for both "holy" and "unholy" speech?

Some things are not "holy." Neither animals nor inanimate objects can be "holy" in thought or conduct, although they can be "holy offerings" to God (Cf. Romans 15:16). Certainly, the bleeped words I have alluded to are not "holy." Why, then, do people call them "holy"?

Words To Live By

FAMOUS BECAUSE IT LEANS!

IN 1173, IN THE ITALIAN CITY-STATE OF PISA, WORK was begun on the church bell tower. By the time the tower was completed some two hundred years later, it rose to a height of 180 feet, seven stories high. Although many such towers can be seen in Italian cities, the Pisa tower is by far the most famous and the most visited by American tourists. The reason is simple – *this* tower *leans*!

It was not supposed to lean, but by the time the third level was completed, it had already begun to lean slightly. The problem was that the architects and engineers who designed the tower had miscalculated the stability of the soil upon which they would be building. As a result, the foundation turned out to be insufficient to support the tower's enormous weight. Work continued, however, as the engineers contrived ingenuous ways to correct the "lean." It remained for modern engineers, in the mid-1990s, to figure a way to reinforce the foundation, without which the "leaning tower of Pisa" would soon have come crashing down.

Good foundations are extremely important if a building is to endure. While it is true that the bell tower of Pisa stood over 800 years on a faulty foundation, it *leaned* during all of that time, when it should have stood *straight*.

In a spiritual sense, a solid foundation is necessary if a child of God is to endure and "stand straight." Jesus told His disciples that He would build His church upon a *rock* (Matthew 16:18). The "rock" upon which He built His church was not the apostle Simon, to whom He gave the name "Cephas" or "Peter," which both refer to a *rock*. When Jesus gave Simon the nickname "rock," He used a word meaning a "detached stone." But when He referred to the "rock" upon which the *church* would be constructed, He used a word meaning "a ledge of solid rock." The church was not built upon a *man*, whoever he might be or however holy that man might have been. Although Paul wrote that the foundations of "God's household" are in some sense "the apostles and prophets" (Ephesians 2:19-20), it is Christ Jesus who is the "corner stone, in whom the whole building, being fitted together, is growing into a holy temple in the Lord" (Ephesians 1:20-21). And it is in Jesus Christ that we also, as individuals, are "being built together into a dwelling of God in the Spirit" (Ephesians 1:21).

If the church itself is founded on the *solid ledge* of rock that is Jesus Christ, we must also consider that each element of the church, each man and each woman who claims kinship with Him, every Christian, every born-again believer, must also be firmly based upon Him. Paul wrote that we are "rooted and grounded" in the love of God which "surpasses knowledge" and which fills us completely with "the fullness of God" (Ephesians 3:17-19). In his epistle to the Colossians, written about the same time as that to the Ephesians, Paul urged Christians to "walk" in Christ with the same enthusiasm with which they had "received" Him, "having been firmly rooted and now being built up in Him and established" in their faith (Colossians 2:6-7).

We occasionally meet people who tell us that they were "raised up" in the church, whatever that means, or that their parents "used to be members of the church," but no longer go anywhere, and we wonder what happened to cause them to leave the church. Like the tower of Pisa, there very likely was a problem with their foundation. If the foundation is faulty, the walls may eventually begin to crack, the floors to sag, and the entire edifice to "lean." In Paul's analogy in 1 Corinthians 3:10, the foundation was carefully laid by a "wise master builder," but according to Paul, "each man must *be careful* how he builds on it." Each member of the congregation must assume the responsibility for his or her own spiritual life. We build upon a *solid ledge of Rock*, the Lord Jesus Christ, but if we do not exercise *care* in the way we "build" upon it, our edifice may develop spiritual "cracks," our walls may "sag," and our building may come crashing down upon us. The builders of the tower of Pisa could not blame the *soil* for the "leaning" of the tower, but rather *themselves*, since it was they who constructed the faulty foundation. Neither can we blame Christ if our own spiritual house does not endure. We must blame ourselves and how we have built upon the foundation.

Words To Live By

A well-constructed foundation is like the anchor of a ship which securely holds it during stormy weather. Priscilla J. Owens expressed it this way in her hymn:

> Will your anchor hold in the storms of life,
> When the clouds unfold their wings of strife?
> When the strong tides lift, and the cables strain,
> Will your anchor drift, or firm remain?
> We have an anchor that keeps the soul,
> Steadfast and sure while the billows roll,
> Fastened to the Rock which cannot move,
> Grounded firm and deep in the Savior's love.

"HELLO! IS ANYONE AT HOME?"

HAVE YOU EVER STOOD AT SOMEONE'S DOOR, knocking and ringing the bell, maybe peeking through the window, calling out, "Hello! Hello! Is anyone home?" You thought for sure they were home, since the lights were on and the T.V. was on full blast.

The Lord Jesus must sometimes feel the same frustration when He stands at a Christian's door and repeatedly knocks, without any response from within. We see such a picture in Revelation 3:20, where He says to the church of Laodicea, "Behold, I stand at the door and knock; if anyone hears My voice and opens the door, I will come in to him and will dine with him, and he with Me." "Open up!" the Lord calls. "Let me come in and we will have dinner together."

What would you not give to hear Jesus knocking and calling at your door? You would certainly rush to the door and throw it wide open so that the precious Savior could come in and sit with you at your table. But I suspect that most of us have heard, but ignored, the Lord's knocking at our heart's door. We were just too busy or were doing something we knew He would disapprove of, so we closed our ears. But please don't think you are the only one to do something like this. Most, if not all of us, have been guilty of turning a deaf ear to our gentle Lord's knocking.

During our Lord's ministry on earth, many religious leaders closed their eyes and stopped their ears, determined not to believe He was the Messiah, in spite of the overwhelming evidence provided by God. Some – even "many" – believed in Him but refused to "confess" Him, because they treasured their positions of honor within the religious community (John 12:42-43).

To change the analogy somewhat, let us think of ourselves as "houses," or "homes." The Bible even speaks of us in this way, affirming that our "heart" is the dwelling place (the "home") of both God and

Christ. Paul wrote that Christians "are being built together into a dwelling of God in the Spirit" (Ephesians 2:22). We are instructed to be "strengthened with power through His Spirit in the inner man, so that Christ may dwell in your hearts through faith" (Ephesians 3:16-17). In this analogy, you and I are houses in which God and His Son live.

Paul further wrote to the Corinthians, "Do you not know that you are a temple of God and that the Spirit of God dwells in you? If any man destroys the temple of God, God will destroy him, for the temple of God is holy, and that is what you are" (1 Corinthians 3:16-17). Since Paul used the plural form of the Greek verb "you," we can argue correctly that he meant that the *church* is the "temple of God." But Paul continued the analogy in chapter six, describing each Christian's physical body, saying, "Flee immorality. Every other sin that a man commits is outside the body, but the immoral man sins against his own body. Or, do you not know that your body is a temple of the Holy Spirit who is in you, whom you have from God, and that you are not your own?" (1 Corinthians 6:18-19). The Holy Spirit dwells *in my body*, and in *yours*, if we are children of God. How exciting is *that*! My fleshly body is a sanctuary of God's Holy Spirit!

You may have heard it suggested that the "Holy Ghost" is a "Holy *Guest*" in the Christian's body, but the truth is that He is the *owner* of the dwelling, not just a "guest." Guests are temporary. Paul says to the Christian, "You are not your own! For you have been bought with a price!" (1 Corinthians 6:19-20). I share my body with God, who is its true *Owner*. Jesus bought and paid for me when He shed His precious blood on the cross. If anything, I am the guest in my Lord's home, and should, therefore, conduct myself in *His* house in a manner that honors Him. When I am a "guest" in another person's home, I am all the more careful of my conduct. I don't want to do anything that will reflect upon the "Owner" of the house in which I am given temporary lodging.

As children of God, we must always be aware of what is going on around us. Because my physical body is still fleshly and weak, I must constantly be on the alert to avoid temptation. Although I am a Christian, it is still possible to be lured by Satan's trickery into situations where I might get involved in conduct that would bring reproach on Christ and upon His "house." My "conscience" has been instructed by the words of Jesus. One's "conscience" represents the sum of one's understanding of what is right or wrong. As such, it serves the Christian as a *warning bell*, an alarm which alerts him that danger is near. Years ago, returning home from Memphis, Tennessee, I drove through the small town of Moscow. Nearing a railroad crossing, I saw the flashing red lights and heard the clanging bell which warned me to stop, but I thought I could make it through. I remember with horror the sound of the gate crashing down on my car, and a moment later, the sound of the train rushing by just yards behind me!

Similar to this is the "warning bell" of the Christian conscience, like the Lord's "knocking" at the door of the church in ancient Laodicea. Those inside should have recognized His "knocking" as a danger signal, telling them to stop, to turn their lives around. The Lord's knocking on our "door" is an invitation to sit at His feet and hear His saving message. We are not told that the church at Laodicea responded to His invitation, but it was their loss if they did not open that door.

What about us? Do we listen for the Lord's knocking at our door? Are we eager to hear His voice asking us to open our door?

I BELIEVE IN ANGELS!

I BELIEVE IN ANGELS BECAUSE THE BIBLE TALKS ABOUT them in a matter-of-fact way. I don't know what angels look like in their natural state, but from time to time, according to the Bible, angels have appeared in human form to certain men and women. In most of these appearances, the angels looked like humans, and some were not at first recognized to be angels. At other times, in visions, angels have taken fantastic shapes or forms.

When Abraham showed hospitality to three angels, he thought at first that they were just travelers passing by (Hebrews 13:2; Genesis 18:1-8). And during the time of the Judges, when Gideon was visited by an angel, he had to have proof that this being was indeed an angel from God (Judges 6:1-22).

During Judah's exile in Babylon, Daniel was visited successively by two angels. The first one, Gabriel, appeared to Daniel while he was praying (Daniel 9:20-23), revealing to Daniel the time when the Messiah would come (Daniel 9:24-27). This same angel would, more than 400 years later, also appear to young Mary with the news that she would give birth to the Messiah, the Savior (Luke 1:26-38). Gabriel obviously appeared in human form to both Daniel and Mary. A second angel, Michael, also appeared to Daniel (Daniel 10:1-21). Michael's appearance, however, was very different from that of a human and Daniel was very frightened at what he saw. "No strength was left in me," he wrote, "for my natural color turned to a deathly pallor" (Daniel 10:8). As soon as Daniel heard the angel speak, he "fell into a deep sleep" with his "face to the ground." Gabriel and Michael are the only angels to whom names are given, and Michael is the only angel identified as an "archangel" (Jude 1:9). Daniel referred to Michael as "a great prince" (Daniel 12:1), and as "one of the chief princes," implying that there were other such "chief princes" (Daniel 10:13). The fact that there is an "archangel" strongly implies that there exists some kind of ranking among the angels.

I Believe In Angels!

The Bible also speaks of "cherubim" and "seraphim," which seem to be a lower order of heavenly beings. The *"im"* at the end of these two words corresponds to the *"s"* in English, marking a plural noun. The Hebrew word "cherub*im*" is equivalent to the English "cherub*s*." The words *cherub* and *seraph* seem to be used interchangeably in the Bible. In Isaiah's vision of the throne of Yahweh (Isaiah 6:1-7), the creatures flying around God's throne are called *"seraphim."* In a similar vision of God's throne in *Ezekiel*, these creatures are called *"cherubim"* (Ezekie1 10:1-22). In John's vision of God's throne in the *Apocalypse*, obviously based on that of *Isaiah*, similar beings are simply called "living creatures" (Revelation 4:5-8).

How many angels are there? The Bible doesn't say, but it is certain that there are many. Hebrews 12:22 speaks of "an innumerable company of angels." Jesus reminded the apostles, who would have attempted to save Him from the Romans, "Do you think that I cannot appeal to My Father, and He will at once put at My disposal more than twelve legions of angels?" (Matthew 26:53).

The more important question might be, "What is the *work* of angels?" The writer of *Hebrews* observed, "Are they not all *ministering spirits*, sent out to render service for the sake of those who will inherit salvation?" (Hebrews 1:14). The Old Testament records that God's angels often fought with Israel against their enemies. One memorable instance was when the king of Aram (Syria) was trying to capture and kill the prophet Elisha (2 Kings 6:13-23), and the servant of Elisha was terrified to see the Syrian army encamped around their village. The prophet chided his servant, saying "Do not fear, for those who are with *us* are more than those who are with *them*." The Lord then opened the servant's eyes and he saw that the mountain was "full of horses and chariots of fire all around Elisha." God's angels were there to *protect* the servants of God. The words of Christ regarding God's concern for defenseless children are also significant: "See that you do not despise one of these little ones, for I say to you that their angels in heaven continually see the face of My Father who is in heaven" (Matthew 18:10).

Angels also ministered to Christ at certain times. When Jesus had been tempted by Satan during forty days (Matthew 4:1-11), angels came and "began to minister to Him." Mark also wrote, "And He was in the wilderness forty days being tempted by Satan; and He was with the wild beasts, and the angels were ministering to Him" (Mark 1:13). Luke recorded that angels ministered to Jesus during His almost unbearable suffering in Gethsemane (Luke 22:43), and angels were present at the tomb early on Sunday morning when Jesus arose from the dead (Matthew 28:2-7; Mark 16:5-7; Luke 24:4; John 30:12-13).

We have no reason to doubt that God's angels may be working on our behalf as well. Surely, God cares for His people under His Son's new covenant, as much as He cared for those under the old covenant instituted through Moses. Although we cannot see angels and cannot know what kind of work they are performing, we can and should believe, that God's will is being done in heaven in our favor. We humans are not alone in this universe. There are some very evil forces at work that we cannot see, under the guidance of the Devil, Satan. Paul warns us about these evil forces: "For our struggle is not against flesh and blood, but against the rulers, against the powers, against the world forces of this darkness, against the spiritual forces of wickedness in the heavenly places" (Ephesians 6:12). We may suppose that much of the work of God's angels on our behalf might involve confrontations with such evil forces of which Paul spoke. Daniel may be speaking of such confrontations in Daniel 10:12-21.

God is doing *His* work on our behalf in the *unseen* realm, and *we* must be about doing what *we* are supposed to be doing in our *own* realm of influence. We are, after all, "God's fellow workers" (1 Corinthians 3:9). He does His part and we do our part, and together we triumph over evil, so that God's will might indeed "be done on earth, as it is in heaven" (Matthew 6:10).

"I DIDN'T MEAN TO!"

MY OLDER BROTHER HAD WAITED FOR WEEKS for this day. He had ordered the boxing gloves from the Sears and Roebuck Catalog, and had eagerly met James, the rural mail rider, at the mail box every day. But my brother had not been just sitting around. He had been busily preparing (with my help) a boxing ring out in our spacious yard. He had set four corner posts in the ground and tied three levels of bailing wire from post to post. Everything was prepared for the big day. Finally, James delivered the two pairs of brand new reddish-brown boxing gloves, and we headed immediately to the waiting boxing ring. We donned the gloves and stepped to the center of the ring. I lifted my hands in the correct defensive position. My brother assumed his position and with one single blow to the jaw, he laid me on the ground!

"Richard!" screamed my mother who was watching from the kitchen window. "I didn't mean to!" my brother probably called back. That was what we always said when caught red-handed doing something we knew very well we should not have done. "I didn't mean to!"

Sure! My brother really did mean to cream me; he had been preparing for that very moment. What happened in that well-built boxing ring was no accident. Over the years, Richard and I have enjoyed many laughs as we remembered those days. He didn't "mean" to hurt me, and I was not really hurt, but he did indeed "mean" to lay me on the ground!

Personal responsibility! You and I must learn that we are responsible for what we do, say, and become in life. Most of us, if not all, have encountered setbacks or accidents that have affected our lives for good or ill. We cannot control everything that happens around us, but in the final analysis we are responsible for how we respond to these things. It is all about "character."

Words To Live By

The apostle Paul wrote: "We also exult in our tribulations, knowing that tribulation brings about perseverance; and perseverance, proven character; and proven character, hope" (Romans 5:3-4). We can't control the troubles and problems that may come our way, but we can control how we confront or deal with them, so that they do not destroy us. Paul says that such things make us strong. As we work our way through them, we learn to deal with even greater problems and become stronger. This "inner strength" is what Paul calls "proven character." People who have "proven character" rarely do or say things they will later regret. One is not *born* with "proven character," but must slowly develop it over the long run. Character is often created in a "crucible" of pain, "tested by fire." But the result is "praise and glory" (1 Peter 1:7). When we need help, we want someone with experience, someone who has endured similar trouble, someone we can trust.

On the other hand, people who have not developed "proven character" often do and say things which they shouldn't, and they say, "I didn't mean to do it." Jesus was talking about "character" when He said, "The *good man* brings out of his good treasure what is good; and the *evil man* brings out of his evil treasure what is evil" (Matthew 12:35). This, of course, is a generalization, and as always there are exceptions to the rule. Sometimes a "good man" may do or say something that is "out of character," but that is not his "lifestyle."

Sometimes, adult children blame their parents for their problems, and it is true that the home environment we provide for our young children does greatly impact their life decisions as they become adults. But they must sooner or later understand that they are largely responsible for how they direct their lives. They must no longer say, as children do, "I didn't mean it," and begin to say, "I *do mean* to do what I do!" We must all learn to live our lives with *purpose*, determining with understanding the course we wish to follow.

As we look to the future, a good question to propose is, "What do I *mean* to accomplish during the coming year?" What will be my goals? Is there some good work that I would like to achieve during this year? Is there a "ministry" which I can perform for someone on God's behalf? Paul listed some of these ministries" – "prophecy" (speaking on God's behalf), service, teaching, encouragement, giving, showing mercy, loving, opposing evil and supporting good, showing brotherly kindness, giving honor to others, serving God, praying, helping the needy saints, and practicing hospitality. Paul called these things "gifts" (Romans 12:6-13). These are not things one does "by accident"; one "means" to do them! One does them "on purpose."

The truth is that most of our actions and words, good or bad, are not accidental, but are done "on purpose." We have prepared to do or say these things. But God wants us to *live* "on purpose," to be dedicated to what is good, to be goal-oriented. When we someday stand before God, we don't want to say, "I didn't mean it."

Words To Live By

IN THE PRESENCE OF ROYALTY

GUIDO ANDRIES AND HIS WIFE WERE WAITING for us at the entrance gate of the Royal Palace in Brussels, Belgium. We had never met Monsieur Andries, but he recognized us immediately, no doubt because of the large number of university students with us. I had spoken with him a few days earlier, when he had called to invite our group to visit the palace. He would personally act as our guide as we toured this magnificent structure.

Many years earlier, Monsieur Andries had come to America to study in one of our universities, and while there he befriended a student who would eventually become the father of one of our students. When he learned that his friend's daughter would be in Belgium for a semester, he was delighted and wanted to do something special for her and our group. We learned he was not only a Major General in the Belgian army, but also a personal *Aide to the King*, one of only two men who alternated every two weeks, working 24/7 in the service of the Belgian King Albert. We felt privileged to be guided through the Royal Palace that day by such a distinguished gentleman. He knew the Palace from A to Z. He told us in detail about every painting and every room in the immense building. Then, after the tour, he and his wife treated us to ice cream and dessert, and delightful conversation. The students, however, had quickly separated themselves from the tour, eager to do their own thing. Several days later, Monsieur Andries called to invite his friend's daughter and her boyfriend to come to their home in Brussels for dinner, but she declined the invitation!

Monsieur Andries was constantly in the presence of royalty. He spent countless personal hours with the king. What an honor to sit at the king's table in his palace! No, we did not sit down with the king, but we enjoyed special time with someone who did. But many are just not interested in such as this, and when they receive the invitation, they reject it, having more interesting things to do.

In The Presence Of Royalty

Jesus told a story about just such a circumstance. A king was preparing a wedding feast for his son, and invited many people to the festivities. When the time came, he sent his servants out to tell everyone that all was ready. Come to the supper! But those who had been invited were "unwilling to come" (Matthew 22:3). I think about the young college student who could have enjoyed a meal with Monsieur Andries and his wife at their home, but she preferred to do something else. In the Lord's parable, it was the king himself whose invitation was spurned. The good king even made a second effort to persuade people to come, but "they paid no attention and went their way, one to his own farm, another to his business" (Matthew 22:5). The story that Jesus told was directed toward those who were rejecting the long-anticipated Messiah, refusing His call to come to the spiritual feast that the God of Heaven had prepared for them. They were too busy, too occupied with their personal affairs, and they would not come.

In the same way, Yahweh (or Jehovah), has called you and me to come to Him. He has prepared great things for us, wondrous things that we could not possibly describe, but the choice is ours, to accept or to reject the invitation. The time will come when those who accept the invitation will enter into God's heavenly palace and "recline at the table with Abraham, Isaac, and Jacob in the kingdom of heaven" (Matthew 8:11). Righteous Job proclaimed that even after the death of the body, "I shall see God, whom I myself shall behold, and whom my eyes will see and not those of another" (Job 19:27). The Lord Jesus promised that "the pure in heart" would "see God" (Matthew 5:8), and the beloved apostle John wrote that when Christ "appears, we will be like Him, because we will see Him just as He is" (1 John 3:2). John also wrote in the *Revelation* that "the Lamb in the center of the throne will be their shepherd, and will guide them to springs of the water of life; and God will wipe every tear from their eyes" (Revelation 7:17). The psalmist Korah wrote: "How lovely are Your dwelling places, O LORD of hosts! My soul longed and even yearned for the courts of the LORD; My heart and my flesh sing for joy to the living God! .... How blessed are those who dwell in Your house! They are ever praising You." (Psalm 84:1-4).

Jesus Christ, the Son of God, is lauded as the "King of Kings and Lord of Lords" (Revelation 19:16). He *rules* even now over God's spiritual kingdom, the church (1 Corinthians 15:23-25), and every Christian is a citizen of Christ's kingdom. When God "rescued us from the domain of darkness," He "transferred us to the kingdom of His beloved Son" (Colossians 1:13), and every time we come together to worship God (Matthew 18:20), we enter into the presence of our great king. Although unbelievers cannot appreciate this fact, those who have benefitted from His great sacrifice surely should. The Roman governor, Pontius Pilate, did not understand that the despised Jew who stood before him covered with blood and wearing a crown of thorns could really be the "king of the Jews" He perhaps thought he was being humorous when he derisively said, "Behold, your king!" (John 19:1-14). But when we praise His name in the congregation of God's people, we know *who* He is and *what* He is! And we know that we stand in the presence of true royalty!

KUMBAYA

I FIRST HEARD THE WORD "KUMBAYA" OR "KUM-bayah" at a lectureship over fifty years ago. According to the story told by the speaker, a missionary team in West Africa was going from village to village announcing the good news about Christ. One afternoon, while they were speaking, some Africans from a village unknown to the team approached them. "Kumbaya," they pleaded, "Kumbaya!" There are different ideas about the origin of this story, and even about the meaning of the word "Kumbaya," but scholars believe that it is an African *pidgin* phrase meaning, "Come by here." There are many *"pidgin"* languages, which, like Hatian Creole, imitate modern literary languages. So, "kumbaya" means "come by here." Christian youth groups often sing the song,

> Kumbaya my Lord, Kumbaya, Kumbaya my Lord, Kumbaya!
> Come by here my Lord, come by here;
> come by here my Lord, come by here!
> Someone's hurting, Lord, Kumbaya,
> Someone's crying, Lord, Kumbaya!
> Someone's dying, Lord, Kumbaya,
> O Lord, kumbaya!

Like the West African villagers, who were pleading with the missionaries to come to their village with the gospel, we plead earnestly that Christ will not pass us by.

During His three-year ministry, Jesus was often approached by people who, on their knees, sought His help. He did not make a difference between Jews and Gentiles, but went willingly into their homes. Whether it was a Roman centurion's beloved servant who lay dying (Luke 7:1-10) or the blind beggar Bartimaeus who called out to Jesus as He entered Jericho (Luke 18:35-38), the Lord stopped what He was doing and went to their aid. Whether it was a sinful woman accused of fornication (John 8:3-10) or a group of ostracized lepers who called to Him from a distance, saying, "Jesus,

Master, have mercy on us" (Luke 17:11-18), God's Son immediately stopped to help.

I remember from my youth Fanny J. Crosby's plaintive hymn, "Pass Me Not."

> Pass me not, O gentle Savior, Hear my humble cry;
> While on others Thou art calling, Do not pass me by.
> Help me at the throne of mercy find a sweet relief;
> Kneeling there in deep contrition, Help my unbelief.
> Thou the Spring of all my comfort, More than life to me,
> Whom have I on earth beside Thee? Whom in heav'n but Thee!
> Savior, Savior, Hear my humble cry;
> While on others Thou are calling,
> Do not pass me by.

Jesus never just walked on by when called upon for help. His heart was often moved with compassion as He looked out over the crowds who were "like sheep without a shepherd" (Mark 6:33-34). As He stood teaching the multitudes who were listening intently to every word which He spoke, the disciples reminded Him that it was late, the people would need to have food, and there was no place for them to buy it (Mark 6:35-37). Jesus told his disciples to get food for them. "You give them something to eat," the Lord replied. "Easy for You to say, Lord," the disciples may have thought, "but where will we buy enough food for so many?" But by the time Jesus got through feeding this huge multitude, they gathered up twelve full baskets of bread and fish!

When Jesus told the disciples to feed the people, he was in essence telling them that after His departure, *they* would be His hands and His feet. In His description of the judgment day, the Lord taught that, at least in part, our salvation will depend on how *we* treat the hungry, the thirsty, the "naked" and the sick (Matthew 25:35-40). He said that we will be judged by how we treat these people. He said that when we do the right thing for needy people, it is the same as doing it to the Lord, Himself. We become the Lord's hands as we feed the hungry. When we visit the sick, we visit the Lord.

When we hear lost people crying, "Kumbaya, Lord," *we are supposed to go in His stead.* When Paul and Luke heard the man in Macedonia saying, "Come over and help us," they immediately made plans to go. The reason missionaries go to distant lands and stay for years is that lost people are calling, "Kumbaya, Lord!" Come by here!

Words To Live By

SCARECROWS IN A CUCUMBER FIELD

WHEN WE WERE KIDS ON THE FARM, WE HAD big problems with crows. Crows could do a lot of damage to a ripening harvest. Because they were a protected species, we were not able to shoot them, and there were too many anyway. Since we could not be in the field all day to shoo them away, my dad improvised a creature that looked like a man flapping his arms. A scarecrow! It was the first one I had ever seen, except for the "Scarecrow" in the *Wizard of Oz*. When crows flew down over our field, the scarecrow's arms would flap in the wind and the crows would fly away.

Like the Scarecrow in the *Wizard of Oz*, our scarecrow had no brain. You might talk to *him*, but he could neither hear, understand, nor answer. Our scarecrow was like those mentioned by Jeremiah: "They cannot speak; they must be carried, because they cannot walk!" Like those of Jeremiah, ours was just "a scarecrow in a cucumber field" (Jeremiah 10:5).

Jeremiah was really talking about the "idols" that many of God's people were worshiping instead of the true God. Yes, God's people had been lured into the worship of the gods of the Canaanites. Since there were no stores in those days where one might buy a "god," people would cut down a small tree and carve a little "god" with a knife, and then "decorate it with silver and with gold." If it was large and heavy, one might have to "fasten it with nails and with hammers" so it would not "totter" and fall.

But one would have to be "stupid and foolish" to then bow down and worship the wooden "god" he had just created. (Jeremiah 10:8). Yet we see people even today doing just that. Buddhists speak to images of Buddha, a mystic philosopher who himself was an atheist. Multiplied millions of sincere people bow before altars to their long dead ancestors whom they revere as "gods." Most do this because *they do not know* the "true God," the "living God," "who made the earth by His power" and "established the world by His wisdom" (Jeremiah 10:10-12).

Unfortunately, many who wear the name "Christian" have also erected "idols" in their *hearts*, and serve these "gods" with more ardor than they serve the God of Heaven. One of the more prominent of these "gods" is the one named *"Mamona"* (Hebrew) or *Mammon* as Jesus personified "wealth" (Matthew 6:24). Instead of *mamona*, Jesus could have used the common word for "wealth" (*ploutos*), but He wanted to emphasize how men enthrone and worship material wealth instead of God. Paul referred to "greed" as "idolatry" (Colossians 3:5), and many otherwise good men and women have sacrificed family and friends, and even their own lives, on the altar of that ultimately powerless "scarecrow," only to discover too late that worldly wealth cannot bring happiness or fulfillment.

But "Mammon" is not the only "scarecrow" in the "cucumber patch." In the same verse where Paul spoke of "greed" as *idolatry*, he also listed *immorality, impurity, passion,* and *evil desire* (Colossians 3:5). Who hasn't heard of prominent politicians who have rushed headlong into *immoral activity*, apparently without even considering what they might lose of prestige or reputation, not to mention their families! And many ordinary people privately tune in to porn on the internet, in the so-called "adult" stores that one sees advertised along the highways, or in self-styled "gentlemen's" magazines. And they *do not know* "it will cost" them their lives (Proverbs 7:23).

Many continue to barter their souls at the altar of Bacchus, the "god" of wine and revelry, only to discover in the end that this "god" who promises good times and prestige at the table of the rich and famous can only deliver sadness, unhappiness, and loss. "Wine is a mocker, strong drink a brawler, and whoever is intoxicated by it is not wise" (Proverbs 20:1). "Who has woe? Who has sorrow? Who has contentions? Who has complaining? Who has wounds without cause? Who has redness of eyes? Those who linger long over wine" (Proverbs 23:29-30).

These "gods" are powerless to deliver what they promise. They are nothing more than "scarecrows in a cucumber patch." We must turn our backs on such "gods" and turn our faces toward Yahweh, the true God, and to the Son of God, who "has given us understanding, so that we may know Him who is true; and we are in Him who is true, in His son Jesus Christ. This is the true God and eternal life. Little children, guard yourselves from idols" (1 John 5:20-21).

IF I HAD ONLY ONE DAY LEFT TO LIVE!

THE PSALMIST COMPARED ONE'S LIFESPAN TO A *sigh*, saying that it is "soon gone and we fly away" (Psalm 90:9-10). The older we become, the more we understand the truth of Job's words, "My days are swifter than a weaver's shuttle" (Job 7:6). Years ago, I visited the cotton mill in Opelika, Alabama, where my mother-in-law worked for many years, and I saw firsthand the swiftness of the "weaver's shuttles" as they zipped back and forth faster than the eye could follow.

The Lord's brother James cautioned his readers against making extravagant plans for the future *without including God* in those plans, since one does not know what tomorrow might bring. "You are just a vapor that appears for a little while and then vanishes away," James wrote (James 4:14-16). This, however, does not mean that we should *not* plan for the future. The best insurance for failure and ruin is a lack of planning and preparation. Not to plan for success is really to plan for failure. James's emphasis is that one must include God in his plans.

But what if you knew for certain that you only had one more day to live? This is a question which youth cannot ask, because death is not a condition that youth can readily grasp. Nor should the young, in my opinion, be overly occupied with thoughts of death. We who are older, however, naturally think about the shortness of life, and about the reality of the ending of life. The question of "one more day" is a question which we can grasp and which we should consider.

My friend and colleague, Richard England, passed from this life with no warning that he was about to meet his Maker. In fact, he had just concluded a sermon in Maury City, Tennessee, and three people had responded to the invitation. As Richard sat talking quietly with the second of these three, to discover their wishes, he was suddenly struck with a cerebral aneurism and fell to the floor. He died at the hospital without ever recovering consciousness. His sermon that evening was titled *"If I had only one day more to live."*

Many people give death only a passing thought and make no plans at all for the future, either for good or ill. But the thoughtful Christian knows that without preparation there can be no fulfillment and no reward. Jesus taught three parables in which success depends upon proper planning and fruitful activity: (1) the *Parable of Ten Virgins* (Matthew 25:1-13), where the wise "Virgins" were prepared with oil for the coming of the bridegroom; (2) the *Parable of the Talents* (Matthew 25:14-30), in which the rich man's stewards were instructed to make a profit with their master's money; and (3) the *Parable of the Judgment* (Matthew 25:31-46), in which eternal life is given only to those who actively accomplished something good.

The Lord Jesus was aware that His lifespan would be cut short early. He told His disciples, "I must work the works of Him who sent Me as long as it is day; night is coming when no one can work. While I am in the world, I am the Light of the world" (John 9:4-5). Jesus knew what the Father wanted Him to do, and knew that He had to do it before "night" came. As children of God, we should apply these words to ourselves, and "work the works" of God in and through our lives. Just as death would cut short the Savior's time for work, so death will cut short our opportunities. The trick for us is not to allow opportunities to pass us by. *Carpe deum!* "Seize the day!" Opportunities are all around us, but all too often we either do not see them or we claim not to be capable or equipped to take them on.

I have before me a book entitled *"From Riches to Poverty to Glory,"* a study of the life of Christ, by H.B. Frank. I met my friend "H.B." in Germany in the early 1960's. Having preached for congregations in Texas, he served as a missionary in Orleans, France, for several years, then in England. He was a much appreciated "missionary in residence" at Freed-Hardeman University for a year, after which he preached for congregations in Georgia. This was an active servant of God. But early in life, H.B. had contracted polio and needed extensive leg and body braces and crutches in order just to walk. I heard H.B. speak at a youth gathering in Kaiserslautern, Germany, and his only need was to be helped up to the rostrum. Otherwise, he never requested help from anyone. H.B. and his wife Lavern, who had also suffered from polio and needed a wheelchair, drove themselves where they needed to go; his car was equipped so that he needed only his hands to drive. If ever anyone had valid excuses for not doing things, these two people certainly would have qualified. But they never allowed physical handicaps to get in their way or to prevent them from doing the Lord's work in their lives.

What about you and me? What if we had only one more day to live? How would that change our lives? Would it not be better to do those life changes *today*, since we cannot know for sure how much longer we might have to live?

"SUMMING UP!"

"IN CONCLUSION" OR "SUMMING UP" ARE TERminal expressions that signal to listeners that a speech is nearing its end. And it is usually a good thing for a speaker to "sum up" what he or she has been saying.

A casual reader of Peter's first epistle may miss the thread of thought, but a careful reader will observe that the apostle's words are well organized. When Peter arrived at the appropriate place, he wrote, "To sum up...." (1 Peter 3:8). His "summary" goes from verse 8 through 16.

It is important to understand that Peter addressed his first epistle to *new Christians*, to *recent converts to Christianity*, who were "scattered" throughout the eastern region of what we now know as the nation of Turkey. Of course, we do not know for sure how much of "holy Scripture" these new converts may have possessed, but it is probable that they possessed none or only a few of the New Testament letters we take for granted. They desperately needed the information presented to them in this great letter.

Peter began his letter with a reference to the "sanctifying work of the Spirit" which had led to their obedience to Christ and to His cleansing blood (1 Peter 1:2). Peter spoke to them about the "imperishable and undefiled" inheritance that was even then "reserved in heaven" for them, how they would be "protected by the power of God through faith" (1 Peter 1:3-4), and how God had revealed to them things "into which angels long to look" (1 Peter 1:12). He then urged them to prepare their "minds for action" and to "keep sober in spirit," so as "not to be conformed to the former lusts" which had for years characterized their behavior (1 Peter 1:13-15). He reminded these new believers that having "been born again" through the "living and enduring word of God" (1 Peter 1:23), they should "put aside" malice, deceit, hypocrisy, envy, and slander, and grow up to

"Summing Up!"

maturity (1 Peter 2:1-2). New Christians, like newborn babies, need the "milk" of the word of God, but they must not stop growing.

The latter part of chapter two of Peter's epistle constitutes an impassioned appeal to "abstain from fleshly lusts which wage war against the soul" and to keep one's "behavior excellent among the Gentiles" (1 Peter 2:11-12). There would be many attempts to destroy the influence of these new converts and they would have to be strong. In spite of the fact that the law of the land often contradicted Christian principles, these new Christians were instructed by Peter to submit themselves "to every human institution" as much as possible (1 Peter 2:13-17), even to "honor the king." By so doing they would "silence the ignorance of foolish men" who would use every opportunity to persecute the church. Since the practice of human slavery was intricately woven into the fabric of Roman society, slaves who became Christians were encouraged to submit to their human masters, even to "those who are unreasonable" (1 Peter 2:18). Although they were "free men" in Christ, they were encouraged, in their suffering, to look to Jesus Christ as an example of one who had suffered for them, leaving them an example to follow (1 Peter 2:21-25). And Christian marriages, as different from pagan unions, were to be characterized by "submission," "chaste and respectful behavior," and "understanding" (1 Peter 3:7).

Peter's "summing up" of what he had written up to this point seems to be under three headings. The **first point** of his summary concerns the *appropriate character* of the Christian. Peter uses five words to describe how a Christian should interact with other people. These words are as follows: (1) harmonious, (2) sympathetic, (3) brotherly, (4) kindhearted, and (5) humble in spirit (1 Peter 3:8). To be "harmonious" is to be "of one mind," "concordant." For example, in a "barber shop quartet" every singer will "harmonize" with the others. If one singer cannot harmonize, the whole quartet fails, and when, in a congregation, there is a contrary individual who just cannot get along with anyone, there is controversy, hard feelings, and problems. To be "sympathetic" is to feel the pain of others, to be able to "walk in their shoes." To be "brotherly" is to treat people like family, to love another person as one would love a brother. To be "kindhearted" is to be compassionate, tenderhearted, able "to rejoice with those who rejoice, and weep with those who weep" (Romans 12:15). To be

Words To Live By

"humble in spirit" is to have a humble opinion of oneself, as opposed to the individual who must always have his own way.

Peter's **second point** in his "summing up" concerns the Christian's readiness "to make a defense to everyone who asks you to give an account for the hope that is in you" (1 Peter 3:15). Peter had earlier said that the newborn Christian must "grow in respect to salvation" (1 Peter 2:2). He must not remain a "baby" in understanding or in conduct. This "growth" would certainly include one's ability to describe to another person what Christ has meant to him. And it would certainly include his ability to "defend" his hope when questioned about it. This does not mean that everybody needs to have a degree in theology, but it does mean that every mature child of God ought to be able to tell an unbeliever what it means to be a Christian.

The **third point** of Peter's summation is that the Christian needs to maintain "a good conscience" (1 Peter 3:16). In the early days of the Christian era, Christians constituted only a very small minority of the general population, and were, therefore, often "slandered." The Christian who continued to act as though he were still *of the world* would, therefore, have *no defense* when unbelievers chided or mocked him for his actions. In modern times, Christian principles have so permeated society that even *unbelievers* have been affected by these principles. It may even be that persons who profess no religion at all may maintain a more virtuous conduct that do some who profess to be Christians. Christians today may *rarely* be "slandered" as they were in the first century. However, it still happens that unbelievers may challenge Christians who, because they have not matured, are *unable to give a proper answer.*

Therefore, we ought to consider seriously what Peter wrote to those early saints. Peter believed that new Christians *needed this information*, and it is still true, not only for new converts to Christ, but for those who have been Christians for many years. To sum up, consider the following:

- "Be harmonious, sympathetic, brotherly, kindhearted, and humble in spirit" (1 Peter 3:8).

- Grow in your faith, so as to be "ready to make a defense" of the hope that is within you (3:15).

"Summing Up!"

- "Keep a good conscience" so that those who might slander you will be put to shame by your good behavior.